Taylor's Guides to Gardening

Barbara J. Barton

Frances Tenenbaum, Series Editor

HOUGHTON MIFFLIN COMPANY
Boston · New York 1993

Taylor's Guide to Specialty Nurseries

Copyright © 1993 by Barbara Barton
All rights reserved

For information about permission to reproduce selections from
this book, write to Permissions, Houghton Mifflin Company,
215 Park Avenue South, New York, New York 10003.

Library of Congress Cataloging-in-Publication Data
Barton, Barbara J.
    Taylor's guide to specialty nurseries / Barbara J. Barton.
        p.   cm. — (Taylor's guides to gardening)
    Includes index.
    ISBN 0-395-60836-8
    1. Nurseries (Horticulture) — United States — Directories.
2. Ornamental plant industry — United States — Directories.   3. Mail-
order business — United States — Directories.   I. Title.
II. Series.
SB118.486.B37   1993   92-30802
635.9′029′473 — dc20   CIP

Printed in Japan

DNP 10 9 8 7 6 5 4 3 2 1

Cover photograph by Michael H. Dodge of White Flower Farm

Title-page drawing by Steven Buchanan

In happy memory of Marshall Olbrich,
a generous and witty plantsman;
his praise was greatly treasured.

BIO-QUEST INTERNATIONAL
Artist: Shari Smith

Contents

Taylor's Guide to
Specialty Nurseries

NICHE GARDENS   *Artist: Dot Wilbur*

NICHE GARDENS *Artist: Dot Wilbur*

Introduction

When I first published *Gardening by Mail: A Source Book,* a friend with a reputation as a terrific gardener complained that it had taken him years to find all his sources, which he kept deeply secret, and now I was going to give them all away. He wasn't joking! But the nurseries he bought from probably wanted to attract more interested plant buyers. And my friend would have been the first to complain if they'd gone out of business or stopped offering rarities for lack of customers.

In the course of writing and twice revising that book, I've come to know about some wonderful specialty nurseries and the very interesting people who run them. You'll notice as we go along that the nurserypeople seem to fall into three categories: the relative few who were born into the business and wanted to stay in it, those who knew early what they wanted to do and studied horticulture, and those who started out doing something else but were inexorably drawn to growing the plants they loved.

Some were hobbyists who found that they had plants left over when they dug and divided what they'd grown; others wanted special plants and couldn't find them in other nurseries, so they learned how to propagate them. Still others wanted to preserve native plants from extinction or try their hand at hybridizing. In the course of reading thousands of plant catalogs, I've known the delight of picking up a fine booklet or a few crudely typed pages to find my heart racing at some discovery or another — something from my ever-growing wantlist!

I want to share these nurserypeople and their plants with you, to take you on a trip through the world of ornamental garden plants and their sources. This is a world that never stands still. As I started writing this book, a friend and neighbor, Marshall Olbrich of Western Hills Nursery, died suddenly of a heart attack. Marshall was not only a great plantsman, but a kind mentor and generous friend to many just starting out in the world of plants. The great sadness of losing him and his lifetime of knowledge is tempered by knowing that there are always others coming along with a good eye and the passionate desire to know about plants; if we're lucky, some will also have his wicked sense of humor! I'd like this book to be a salute to Marshall and all the other American plantsmen who run nurseries; they deserve our praise and a pat on the back.

One thing that struck and delighted me was the fact that many of the nurserypeople I talked to told me that they learned to love plants as children, usually from helping parents or relatives in their gardens or playing in natural areas. One got his own special peony for his eighth birthday; another snuck into a bamboo grove to play with his friends; another went to flower shows with his parents; still another got his first real job weeding at the age of eight. In my childhood, we rode our horses through wildflower meadows and hills covered with blue ceanothus and manzanita, weeded vegetables and picked and canned fruit, and slept out all summer under the crab apple trees. It's obviously no waste of time to encourage children to love plants.

As you get into the world of rare and special plants, you'll find that there's a plant underground, a network of plant people who are on the cutting edge of what's new and who burn up the phone lines passing on plant discoveries and good gossip. It's amazing how quickly good new plants become available, but what goes on behind the scenes is just as much fun.

Let's say you've received some very rare seed from a seed exchange or found a plant on your wanderings that was just a bit different. You grow seedlings or cuttings and watch them very closely. When they finally bloom or take off, you realize that you have something very special. Other plantsmen in your circle of friends will be hanging on your report, eager to have some samples to try. You might then pass on seedlings or cuttings to a friend, who might trade you for something rare from his collection.

Plants move around the network, are propagated, passed on again, and end up on the lists of specialty nurseries. Sometimes the selection is named for the person who found it, or that person is given the privilege of naming it. It's fun to read catalogs, like those of Montrose Nursery and Holbrook Farm, that tell you the provenance of their new plants. Some plants move on into the big-time nursery trade, but some never do because they're too hard to propagate, tricky to grow, or not likely to appeal to unsophisticated gardeners.

Frequently, when you see something new and rare in a nursery or catalog, the nurseryman will tell you that so-and-so found it along the Big Horn River, or someone else found it in China and brought back seed. Old-rose lovers spend days combing old cemeteries and homestead sites for roses planted a hundred years ago and now neglected, their names forgotten.

This network is full of wonderful characters; some are breathtakingly generous with the treasures they rightly look on as their jewels. I recently visited two old-rose collectors who live on top of a mountain, without electricity, hot water, or a bathtub; in a very simple one-room cabin. From this peaceful spot, they correspond with rose collectors all over the world, read voraciously about plants, grow every type of plant they can, either outdoors or in a homemade greenhouse, and live as happily as is possible without either a cat or a dog. They gave me a tour of their garden and sent me home with pots and pots of cuttings. I came home and looked upon my snug little house as the world center of luxurious living, and as I unloaded the plants I marveled at the generosity of these collectors to a virtual stranger. What made us friends immediately was our mutual love of plants; I was only sorry that I had much less interesting treasures to offer them.

All experienced gardeners will point out plants that have been given to them; these plants are precious because they represent friendships. As an inexperienced gardener who moved out to the countryside and needed a lot of advice and lots of plants, I've come in for more than my share of both from old and new friends, for which I am very grateful.

This active trading of plants, along with the knowledge and gossip that goes on between gardeners and plant collectors, is only part of the way plants make their way to nurseries. Some are the products of active breeding or selection programs by keen amateurs, nurseries, and universities. Others come into the trade from botanical gardens (which have their own world-wide network of plants and gossip). What's lovely about the whole process is the people in all their variety. The mutual interest happens to be plants; the charm is the friendships that the plants create.

The nurseries mentioned in this book provide a very broad selection of plants for gardens in every region of the United States. It's been great fun talking to nurserypeople all over the country, and I thank them all for their cooperation. I'd also like to thank Frances Tenenbaum for her encouragement, and my friends, family, and my garden for their patience.

About the Nurseries

There are two types of directories useful for the plant lover: the plant directory and the nursery directory. A plant directory lists individual plants and gives you the names of specific nurseries that sell them; it's compiled from nursery catalogs. The advantage to plant directories is that you can find a specific plant quickly; the drawback is that it is time-consuming (actually sheer hell) to compile, and goes out of date fairly quickly, as many catalogs change every year. Some excellent plant directories are the *Anderson Horticultural Library's Source List of Plants and Seeds* published by the Minnesota Landscape Arboretum and the *Garden Seed Inventory* (vegetables) and the *Fruit, Berry and Nut Inventory* published by the Seed Savers Exchange.

A nursery directory will give you a good idea of what types of plants each nursery specializes in; this gives you a choice of nurseries that very likely will have the plant you want. A nursery directory goes out of date a bit more slowly than a plant directory (as nurseries are started or go out of business); it does not depend on the contents of catalogs of a specific year. *Taylor's Guide to Specialty Nurseries* is a directory of selected nurseries, focused only on ornamental garden plants.

Are these "the best" nurseries in America? I hate to use that term for a variety of reasons; certainly among those mentioned are the very best of their kind. Let's just say that the nurseries described supply a staggering variety of plants and that they're run by people devoted to their plants. Some of the nursery owners are renowned for their own hybridizing or selection of plants; others have studied at botanical gardens or at the side of great plantsmen. Many are people who were just swept away by a passion for a particular type of plant and found themselves in the nursery business before they knew it. If it's always been your dream to start a nursery, you'll find many nurseries in this book which have been started by people just like you; there are many paths into the nursery business.

I agonized over the problem of how to list the nurseries without favoritism and settled on what I hope is a useful way. Stand facing a map of the United States and grandly wave your right hand, starting in New England, swooping down the Atlantic coast to the South, then rising majestically up the east side of the Mississippi River into the Midwest. Sweep across to the west side of the Mississippi and plunge down into the Southwest, including everything east of the Rockies. Then finish with a flourish through the desert Southwest to the Pacific coast, and soar northward with the eagles to the Pacific Northwest. So — the nurseries in each category are grouped roughly by location; you can keep track of which ones are nearest to you. There is also a geographical index in the back of the book for nursery trotters and plant voyagers.

I've tried to list nurseries so that there is some geographical spread; many of you will be able to visit them. Unfortunately, it's not possible to list every last source, so I've had to make the choices for you, usually based on the thrill-content of the catalog. My chagrin when I find an intriguing new nursery too late to investigate is extreme; obviously I don't know about *every* good nursery in the United States, though I make every effort to learn about as many as I can.

A few of the nurseries I discuss in this book are large enterprises with many workers, but many of them are run by one or two people who got started because of their love of plants and who may work at it nights and weekends, or struggle alone with the effort of keeping it all going with little or no help. Some of these small nurseries will ask that you telephone early in the morning or after dark; the rest of the time they're working outside away from the phone.

Therefore, I'd like to suggest some ground rules for plant buyers so that you and your business will be welcome, and the nurseryfolk won't be tempted to do me in when they hear from me again.

Two things are in short supply for many of these nurseries: time and money. Please don't drop in without calling first if the proprietors ask that you do so; if you do just drop in, they're well within their rights if they tell you they haven't time for you, since they may have to dash to the dentist or attend a school play, or just need the time to struggle with their usual work load. While it may be great fun for you to stop by and chat endlessly about plants, you're using time that could be spent caring for plants or doing personal business, so please don't take a lot of time unless you're also willing to buy plants.

There's one basic conflict to keep in mind when visiting; while you may love your children and plants almost equally (with perhaps a slight edge toward the kids), the nursery owner loves his plants much more than he likes your children, and you must be careful to keep your children under watch. Little hands picking flowers and little feet racing through the nursery rows can be nerve-racking to the anxious nurseryperson. Encourage your kids to love plants in *your own garden.*

When you visit these small nurseries, you should not expect that they will have large, manicured display gardens. Some of them are shoehorned into suburban back yards, and there's usually very little time for keeping things perfect. Some do have lovely display gardens to show the plants in the ground and in landscape situations; many don't, but just being able to see the plants blooming in cans or field rows might be all you want. A very few are not set up to welcome visitors and sell by mail order only.

It's important that you send the amount asked for when you request a catalog. Printing and postage are expensive and always increasing, and many of the people who request mail order catalogs don't later order merchandise. Nurseries have to recover their costs if they are small; one terrific nursery told me that they didn't want to be mentioned in this book because *Gardening by Mail* readers "never" sent the money asked for the catalog with their request. Another told me that he always ignored the request if he didn't receive the money asked for the catalog, so don't write to me and complain if you didn't comply with the nurseries' terms.

All of the nurseries mentioned in this book will ship plants. I feel that it's only fair to tell gardeners where they can get the plants they want without having to travel to the far ends of our large country. In Britain, one can go almost anywhere to pick up plants over a two- or three-day weekend — here we can't. But when a nursery sells special plants by mail, the whole country is its market; when it sells only locally, the market is very much diminished. Selling by mail has made it possible for plantsmen to establish nurseries in wonderfully remote areas where land is reasonably priced, without having to take into account the location of their customers. And don't forget, what is a mail order nursery to most people is a terrific local nursery if you happen to live nearby.

To my delight and surprise, many people bought and used *Gardening by Mail* to order plants from overseas. As a general rule, if you live outside the United States you should send requests for catalogs with U.S. bank notes or a check drawn on a U.S. bank to pay for the catalog and postage (Canadians are able to write checks in U.S. dollars). You should add at least $1 to the price of the catalog for the extra postage and expect that the catalog will be sent to you by surface mail. If the nursery asks for a long self-addressed stamped envelope

(SASE), send a self-addressed long envelope and $1 note.

Many of the nurseries will ship overseas and to Canada (though shipping to Canada seems to be getting difficult, and fewer nurseries are willing to do it), but it is customary that their minimum order for a foreign customer is higher than it is for domestic customers. There may also be extra charges for necessary customs and agricultural inspection certificates. It's a good idea to check with your national agricultural authorities to see what certificates are necessary before you place your order. Shipping is usually by air mail or air freight and is also much more expensive.

There are obviously many wonderful nurseries that are known and loved for their wonderful selection of plants, but which don't ship. Some, like my neighbor Western Hills Nursery, are worth traveling a long way to visit, even if you do have to carry the plants home on your lap in the airplane. You'll learn about them as your interest grows and you get to know other gardeners who share your taste in plants. You'll also find their displays at plant and garden shows, their proprietors featured in gardening magazines or the garden section of your newspaper, and their advertisements in local horticultural and plant society magazines and newsletters or even listed in the yellow pages.

Easterners may think that I mention too many nurseries along the West Coast while the potential gardening population is greater in the East, but there are good reasons for this. The West Coast is an area of very intense gardening interest, containing some of the most interesting nurseries in the country. However, because of the strict agricultural regulations of Washington, Oregon, and California, and several other western states, many out-of-state nurseries will not or cannot ship to us. Listing western nurseries gives us westerners a way to find plants and gives easterners a much broader choice, too.

You'll notice that I frequently mention that a nursery grows many more cultivars or varieties of a plant than it lists in its catalog. The plants grown but not listed may include older varieties no longer in great demand, popular varieties withdrawn for propagation and increase, new varieties being increased for future catalogs, or seedlings of new crosses being evaluated for introduction. If you have a want-list of plants that have been difficult to find, you might send it to some of these nurseries to see if they have any of the plants you yearn for.

Many of these nurseries *want* to remain small and don't want publicity except to the sort of people who will appreciate what they grow. Some rarely advertise except in small plant society publications, in order to reach only those in the know. Unfortunately, some fanatic gardeners thoughtlessly collect catalogs without discrimination, as if it were a competitive sport, and brag about having hundreds! Please request only those catalogs that offer plants you really want, and from nurseries that will ship to your state.

Look at it this way: we're very lucky that there are people willing to give up comfortable lives to take on the risk and effort of starting nurseries. These people can remain in business only if we give them our support when they deserve it, tell interested friends about them, buy their plants instead of always trying to locate a cheaper source, and don't waste their precious time and resources without buying what they have to sell.

Finally, you'll become acquainted with the Barton Animal Index, a very personal rating system that gives extra points to nurseries with appealing pets. On a scale of 0 to 10, only We-Du Nurseries in North Carolina scores a perfect 10, but I've visited many which rate quite highly. As the loving owner of dogs and cats, I can't imagine living or working outside without their company. In fact, I'm living what I consider the perfect life: country cottage and garden, lots of pets, and I get to wear old clothes and putter around — at least almost as much as I'd like to.

The pleasure I get from my pets makes me feel an instant kinship with others who love plants and animals, too. Recently a plant collector called to ask me something, and while we were talking my dogs began to bark. My caller immediately said, "That must be Alice!" He could only have known that from reading *Gardening by Mail* with close attention to detail. I now have two dogs, Alice and Sandy, and two cats, Trout and Phoebe. You really aren't expected to remember their names!

FLOWERPLACE PLANT FARM
Artist: P. R. Henson

How to Read a Catalog and Order Plants

It may seem ridiculous to give basic training in how to read a catalog and place an order, but a few pointers now may keep you out of trouble later and will be useful for the rest of your gardening life. It's not the same as ordering clothes from Lands' End.

Look the catalog over carefully when you get it; it can be a slick booklet with color pictures or a typewritten list full of typos — either is good if it gives you the basic information you need to know before you even look at the plant listings.

Does it tell you the name of the proprietor? Is there a full address and phone number?

Does it explain all terms and conditions of sale?
  Are plants guaranteed to be true to name?
  How and when do you order and how do you pay?
  How does the nursery charge for shipping?
  Does it confirm orders when received?
  How and when will it ship plants?
  What is the replacement and/or refund policy?
  What is the substitutions policy?
  How long do you have to complain after receiving
    the plants?

When you're satisfied that you understand and agree to the stated methods of doing business, then you can turn to the plant listings.

Are plants listed by botanical name?
Are plant size and/or container size given?

Are plants adequately described for your needs?

If you can visit the nursery, does it tell you when and how to get there?

Can you buy plants when you arrive at the nursery or do you have to order ahead for pickup?

I may be too picky, but my idea of a good catalog is a listing of plants in alphabetical order by the full botanical name. There are a few exceptions to this; many nurseries list similar plants such as ornamental grasses and ferns as a group, then alphabetically by botanical name. Some large plant groups, such as rhododendrons, iris, or daylilies are listed only by type and cultivar name, usually with information on plant size at maturity, bloom color, parentage, and hybridizer. Herbs are often listed by "popular name," but the botanical name should immediately follow. Either way, the catalog should include a cross index.

Sometimes you'll find catalogs that list plants by family or by plant habit or form; this is a little bit like a telephone directory that lists people by country of origin or by eye and hair color. It's sometimes hard to remember whether someone is Norwegian or Danish, with dark blond hair or light brown; it's easier to remember a name and look someone up that way. I've been known to call and plead with a nurseryperson to change the list to alphabetized botanical names. A list in any other order is just not logical to the avid plantsman and catalog reader, and it's too hard to remember where you saw a plant listed and how to find it again. When you find a plant list confusing or frustrating to read, tell the nurseryperson; the result will be better plant lists.

Does the plant list use correct "botanical nomenclature"? Most of us are not qualified to judge, but you should avoid ordering from catalogs that habitually finesse the question of exactly which plant is being discussed. The worst example is a list that uses only "common names" since these are far too imprecise; the most dastardly offenders make up names with no relationship to the botanical name. I recently saw a lemon-scented geranium called something like "JUST DISCOVERED! THE AMAZING NEW MOSQUITO PLANT!!!" Another example is a list that gives botanical names like "*Viburnum sp.*" The only time such vagueness is acceptable is when a very new discovery is offered, and then the list will explain why the species name is not yet established or confirmed. Some lists mangle and misspell plant names, which is really careless but not fatal if you get the feeling that the lister knows the plants but not how to spell.

You'll notice that some of the nurseries publish both a "descriptive" catalog, which contains detailed plant and growing information, and a separate price list. They do this so that they can write about their plants in the sort of detail they think necessary and still charge enough for the catalog to recover their printing and mailing costs; the price list is usually free or nearly so. Some catalogs give a lot of detail, others are very brief, and with the cost of postage, good catalogs may eventually shrink to telegrams in order to stay at the same price.

Catalogs frequently recommend additional reading for those interested in their plants. This is a very good sign; it shows an interest in fine plants and a desire to help you educate yourself. These books frequently will have good pictures of the mature plants, too, and give information on the eventual size, habit, and hardiness of the plant. They might also provide cultural information, including bad habits and susceptibility to damage, pests, and disease.

Reading about the plants in advance might help you better understand such catalog descriptions as:

Tends to reseed	Lax habit
Vigorous grower	Vibrant color
Needs shelter from wind	Confine roots
Susceptible to mildew	Needs support
Prune severely to retain desired shape/height	

As with all good nurseries, a good plant list changes from year to year as new plants are introduced and others are dropped; this is also an advantage, and you should read all catalogs carefully to pick up on the new offerings. I like it when they tell you who introduced the new plant or who shared it with them; sometimes good friends or customers will discover something new and exciting going on in their gardens and share the plants with favorite nurserymen.

Does the catalog make clear what size plant you will receive? A good list tells you, and some offer plants in assorted sizes. Some specify container size rather than plant size, but all plants should be well developed for the size of their shipping container. It stands to reason that it's difficult and expensive to ship big plants. If you get a tiny plant without a good root system in a gallon container, call for an explanation. Why pay to ship potting mix when what you expected was a well-developed plant?

Some plants, such as Japanese maples and dwarf conifers, even several years old, will be quite small but rather expensive; such plants are usually very slow growing, hard to propagate, or have to be kept around and grown on for a year or two to be sure that the graft or cutting "took." They represent a greater expense to the nursery. If you want a larger plant you'll have to buy it from a nearby nursery, since it can't be grown on and shipped at a reasonable cost.

Because many of these nurseries are small and some of their plants quite rare, stock is often very limited; sometimes they limit the number of plants per customer. They may ask you if you want a substitution or a refund if they are out of stock, or sometimes they'll ask if you want to wait for the plant until they have available stock. It must be a nightmare to estimate a small demand for a particular plant, only to find it's been featured in a national magazine and that you could have sold hundreds more than you have. Of course, the opposite sometimes happens.

A good nursery will pack and ship plants early in the week so that they will arrive before the weekend. Most nurseries actually use United Parcel Service, not parcel post, and if you're far away, some will insist on UPS 2nd Day Air or U.S. Priority Mail so that plants won't have to sit over the weekend at the sorting facility. Some nurseries will give you the option of selecting the most convenient shipping date for your climate; good nurseries won't ship during seasons of extreme heat or cold.

No nursery can guarantee that you will give the plants proper care after you receive and plant them, but they should guarantee that they ship healthy plants. Plants arriving within a few days in moderate weather should be in good planting condition. Packages should have proper state inspection labels if there is a problem with shipping to your state because of agricultural inspections.

It's a good idea to check with your state agriculture department before you order to see if there are special plant quarantine or inspection requirements, particularly if you live in the West. Packages without the required labels may be subjected to plant-killing delays or may even be confiscated by the inspectors.

If you have friends who have ordered plants from various nurseries, ask them what their experiences have been with the nurseries you've chosen, or ask them which nursery they feel offers the best and healthiest plants and ships them well. Always make a copy of your order and the face of your check. If a nursery doesn't confirm orders and you want a confirmation, enclose a stamped self-addressed postcard and write, "We received your order and check for $XX.xx on _____; your order will be shipped on about _____." Be sure to put the name and address of the nursery at the bottom of the message so you know which one is confirming.

If a nursery's terms of doing business are vague, or if you have specific concerns, call and discuss them before placing an order. I always suggest placing a small order the first time so that you can see if you like the plants and packing methods. If you pay by credit card, it's easier to handle disputes later.

When the package arrives, open it right away and check the plants off on your copy of the order. Remove any plastic wrap from the plants, see that the soil is not too loose in the containers, and be sure the soil is damp. Put them in shade for a few days. Some nurseries send detailed instructions with their plants, but if they don't, use your common sense.

What do you do when plants arrive in bad shape? First, check the package to see when the plants were shipped; if they have been wandering around too long in transit, you should complain to the carrier. If they've been placed out of the sun, and you didn't notice them for several days, that's the carrier's fault for not notifying you, or yours for not checking around when you expect an order.

If they were shipped only a few days before, quickly reread the conditions of sale and replacement policy, then contact the nursery immediately and describe the exact condition of the plants. If you are sure that they are not the plants you ordered, or the quantity is wrong, do the same.

A few of the nurseries mentioned in this book asked that their phone numbers not be included. Some of these nurseries do put the number in their catalog so that customers can call them. Others have various reasons for not wanting to give their numbers. When you do call a nursery during the day, be sure and let the phone ring many times; one reason some people don't want to give their phone numbers is that it's hard to get to the phone before the caller hangs up. Most nurseries will not, and should not have to, accept collect telephone calls. If you are not satisfied with the other information about the nursery given in a catalog or list and don't like being unable to phone, don't place an order.

Before you pick up the phone and start yelling, imagine yourself at the other end of the line. No one wants to answer the phone and be called a cheater! State your complaint and, based on the terms of doing business, what you expect the nursery to do about it. If you are treated rudely, or if the nursery does not want to honor its own terms of business, be sure to get the name of the person you are talking to. Write a detailed letter to the head of the nursery or company and be sure to keep a copy. If the matter is not cleared up fairly, you should send a copy to the local Better Business Bureau and Chamber of Commerce, too, since they keep track of customer complaints. If you do not get any response at all, send a copy of your order, canceled check, and correspondence to the postal inspector in the town where the nursery is located.

Of course, I expect that you won't encounter any problems

with the nurseries described in this book; I just want to be sure you know how to go about dealing with them in case you've never ordered plants by mail before. I should tell you frankly that I haven't ordered from very many of these nurseries, but only for pecuniary reasons; I'll see the UPS truck every day when I win the lottery. I've made every effort to choose nurseries with good reputations, those that I think will deal with you fairly and that I believe to be in business for the foreseeable future.

I'd be delighted if nurserypeople reading this book would take another look at their catalogs and plant lists to be sure that they are clearly communicating all of the necessary information to their customers. In working on *Gardening by Mail*, which lists about a thousand nurseries and seed companies, I've long wished that I could award the really special catalogs a "Tuskie" — something like an "Oscar" for plant selection, frankness of description and opinion, and growing information above the ordinary, and named for my excellent ginger tomcat Tusker. Many of the nurseries included here deserve the coveted "Tuskie." In the course of writing this book I've visited a number of them, and talked to all of them.

The following abbreviations are used in the catalog information line:

d	Price of the catalog is deductible from your first order
cn	Plants listed by common name
cn/bn	Plants listed by common name, with botanical name given
bn	Plants listed by botanical name
bn/cn	Plants listed by botanical name, with common name given
SASE	Long self-addressed stamped envelope
FCS	First-class stamp
CAN	Nursery will ship plants to Canada
OV	Nursery will ship plants overseas

Aquatic Plants

TILLEY'S NURSERY/THE WATERWORKS
Artist: Virginia Barz

After years of yearning, I still have only one aquatic plant, a water lily 'St. Louis', which blooms in a big iron soap-making pot from my parents' ranch. This year I'm going to have to divide the root, which is getting huge, and start a second pond of some sort — something lovely that won't invite wallowing by my dog Alice, who's part shepherd and part hippo. How I envy people who have soggy areas in their gardens, or stream banks flat enough for planting, and especially those who have dainty dogs who hate mud.

To most of us, the ultimate aquatic plant is a water lily or a lotus, both of which are spectacular, but even a diamond needs its setting. It's the other, plainer plants in and around the edges of a pond which provide the setting and keep the water in proper balance.

Why is there such a concentration of aquatic nurseries in Maryland, Pennsylvania, and New Jersey? If you don't live in that region, you tend to forget how many people do. These days water gardens have shrunk from lakes on estate grounds to containers as small as a barrel sawed in half, so nearly everyone can have one. The new flexible "plastic" pond liners (usually made of synthetic rubber) also make it possible to install a pond in a day without pouring cement and to be creative about the shape, making it fit in just about anywhere.

■ **Waterford Gardens** in Saddle River, New Jersey, is located at the long-time site of another water nursery, which means that it has well-developed display gardens and ponds; the nursery is even mentioned in guidebooks to New Jersey as a worthwhile visit.

John Meeks, the owner, is a landscape architect who has designed and built many ponds, starting with one that he built with his father when he was a child. Waterford Gardens has a broad selection of water lilies and lotus and other aquatic plants, many of which are shown in color in the catalog. They also sell everything for the water garden "except the hole."

Visitors are welcome Monday through Saturday, and Sunday from mid-April through June; plants are in bloom from mid-May through August. Waterford Gardens is located three miles north of Paramus and about twenty-four miles west of the Hudson River in northeast New Jersey.

> **Waterford Gardens**
> 74 E. Allendale Road
> Saddle River, NJ 07458
> James A. Lawrie, Mgr.
> (201) 327-0721 or 0337
> Catalog: $5.50, cn/bn

■ Tom and Rick Tilley started as landscapers soon after leaving college in 1976, where they had both studied horticulture. In the early eighties they opened Tilley's Nursery in Coopersburg, Pennsylvania, and as part of their display garden, they installed a pond. Customers began to ask for aquatic plants, and Tom says that they've been dropping other plants to make more room for aquatics and fish. Now their nursery is called **Tilley's Nursery/The WaterWorks**, and their parents also come in to help out at their retail nursery. They offer water lilies, lotus, and other aquatic plants, as well as water-gardening supplies and fish in the catalog.

Visitors are welcome daily from March through Christmas, though blooming season for the aquatic plants is usually June to first frost. The nursery is located about forty-five miles north of Philadelphia, a few miles south of Allentown.

> **Tilley's Nursery/The WaterWorks**
> 111 E. Fairmount Street
> Coopersburg, PA 18036
> Tom and Rick Tilley
> (215) 282-4784
> Catalog: $3, cn/bn

■ For Richard Schuck of **Maryland Aquatic Nurseries,** having a nursery for aquatic plants was a lifelong dream; his whole family have been gardeners, and as a boy he gardened and had ponds. He runs the business with his niece, Kelly Billing, who also grew up gardening and who's come to love the aquatic plants, too. In 1986, when she heard that her uncle had started a nursery, she got her mother to drive her there to see if he could use some help.

Schuck offers water lilies, lotus, aquatic plants, and moisture-loving perennials and grasses in his catalog, as well as water-gardening supplies and ornaments that he and Kelly have designed. Visitors are welcome at the nursery, display ponds, and gardens. They're located in Jarrettsville, Maryland, which is halfway between Baltimore and the Pennsylvania state line, about half an hour from central Baltimore.

Maryland Aquatic Nurseries
3427 N. Furnace Road
Jarrettsville, MD 21084
Richard J. Schuck
(301) 557-7615
Catalog: $2, CAN, bn

WICKLEIN'S AQUATIC FARM & NURSERY
Artist: Judith A. Bates

■ **Wicklein's Aquatic Farm & Nursery** in Baltimore, Maryland, was started in 1954 by Walter Wicklein's father, Walter, whose father (Walter) had grown and loved water lilies. After a career as an air force officer, Walter III retired to run the nursery and is now assisted by his oldest son, Eric, who studied horticulture at Penn State. They offer hardy and tropical water lilies, lotus, many bog plants (including some tropicals that have to winter inside), and other aquatic plants. They also sell water-gardening books and supplies and give various seminars on water gardening at the nursery.

The nursery has nice display gardens and lily ponds and is open Monday through Saturday all year, except the last week of December and Sunday afternoon in the summer. The nursery is located near Exit 29A on the Baltimore Beltway, northeast of the city center.

Wicklein's Aquatic Farm & Nursery, Inc.
1820 Cromwell Bridge Road
Baltimore, MD 21234
Mr. and Mrs. Walter Wicklein
(301) 823-1335
Catalog: $1, CAN, bn/cn

■ Those of you going to look for the town of Lilypons, Maryland, are going to be puzzled; Lilypons is not even a wide place in the road but just an old stone farmhouse and a nursery. Charles Thomas of **Lilypons Water Gardens** told us that his grandfather, in a burst of marketing genius, persuaded the post office to let him use that town name on his mail, and persuaded Lily Pons, the French diva, to come and be honored by the naming of the town. What a difference a *d* makes!

Charles Thomas is the third generation of his family in the water-garden business, and his wife, brother, nephew, four daughters, and two sons-in-law all work for the nursery. The day we visited he was expecting the birth of a fifth grandchild, so there is no end to gardening Thomases in sight. Lilypons has grown to two nurseries, in Maryland and Texas and new growing and shipping facilities in Thermal, California. But the focus is still the same: many water and bog plants and everything needed for making a water garden.

Those who live near the Maryland farm (located near Buckeystown) or the nursery in Brookshire, Texas, can visit and see the display ponds; the Thomases also give demonstrations on how to set up a pond. Charles travels extensively to lecture on water gardens and is the author of *Water Gardens for Plants and Fish* (T.F.H. Publications).

Lilypons Water Gardens
6800 Lilypons Road
P.O. Box 10
Buckeystown, MD 21717-0010
Charles B. Thomas
(301) 874-5133
Catalog: Free, bn

839 FM 1489
P.O. Box 188
Brookshire, TX 77423
(713) 391-0076

■ **William Tricker, Inc.** calls itself "America's Oldest Water Garden Specialists since 1895." No longer run by the Trickers, the nursery was purchased in 1986 by William Lee, a college biology professor with an interest in water plants.

William Tricker was a hybridizer who introduced a number of water lilies, many still offered in the color catalog. He is commemorated by the name *Victoria trickeri*. The catalog offers a large selection of water plants and seems to list lots of pygmy water lilies, which are perfect for smaller urban ponds and tub gardens. Bill Lee says he sells a lot of those to New Yorkers with balconies. He also sells a full line of water-garden supplies and fish. Visitors are welcome; the nursery is open Monday through Saturday and Sunday afternoon. The best months for bloom are May through August. There are display ponds and gardens at the nursery, and five greenhouses, which extend the blooming season for tropical plants. Independence is eight miles south of Cleveland.

William Tricker, Inc.
7125 Tanglewood Drive
Independence, OH 44131
William Lee
(216) 524-3491
Catalog: $2d, CAN/OV, cn/bn

■ It's obvious that water gardening must be in the genes, because the Uber family at **Van Ness Water Gardens** in Upland, California, is in its third generation, too, and involves Bill Uber and his wife, Carol, his father, Ted, his brother and sister and his children. The nursery was started in 1922 by the Ubers' cousins, Edith and Robert Van Ness, who read an article called "There Is Gold in Goldfish" on raising and selling fish, but who found out that their customers wanted water lilies more than they did fish.

Bill Uber now consults on water gardens all over the world, and the color catalog reflects his interest in using water in the landscape. Offered is a broad selection of plants and supplies, and the catalog gives detailed plant descriptions and instructions on how to build water gardens and how to establish fish and keep the water balanced. Bill wrote *Water Gardening Basics* (Dragonfly Press), all that its name implies.

Sadly, when I was in the neighborhood to go to my college reunion, Van Ness Water Gardens was closed, so I had to peek longingly through the fence. When I totter off to the next reunion I'll plan ahead. Visitors are welcome Tuesday through Saturday; the best time to visit is spring and summer. Upland is thirty miles east of Los Angeles, four and a half miles north of Interstate 10, up one of the all-time classic boulevards, Upland's Euclid Avenue.

Van Ness Water Gardens
2460 N. Euclid Avenue
Upland, CA 91786
William C. Uber
(714) 982-2425
Catalog: $2, OV, cn/bn

There is a difference between ornamental ponds and a few water lilies on a pond and plantings to attract wildlife, but both use aquatic plants. You don't have to hunt waterfowl and other animals; you could just as easily create plantings to attract and feed them for your own pleasure. All of the following nurseries said that these days most of their sales are for wildlife habitat preservation and ornamental plantings.

■ Founded in 1896 as Terrell's Aquatic Farms and Nurseries, **Wildlife Nurseries** in Oshkosh, Wisconsin, has been providing plants for feeding wildlife for nearly a hundred years. Current owner John Lemberger was a hunter and outdoorsman with an interest in wildlife habitat; the nursery is now run by his son Jim. Among the plants offered are wild rice, native water lilies and lotus, and all sorts of aquatic and seed plants for wildlife food, with good information on where and how to establish the plants. Mail order only.

Wildlife Nurseries
P.O. Box 2724
Oshkosh, WI 54903-2724
John J. Lemberger
(414) 231-3780
Catalog: Free, cn/bn

■ **Kester's Wild Game Food Nurseries** in Omro, Wisconsin, was also started around the turn of the century and was bought by David and Patricia Kester in 1970; David had been growing plants for wildlife for years before that. The focus here is also attracting wildfowl and game, and the Kesters' customers include both government wildlife refuges and people who want to create natural habitats in their yards or on their farms so that they can watch the birds and animals. The catalog is full of information on creating habitats and offers most plants and seeds in quantity. Visitors are welcome Monday through Saturday all year, but summer is the best time to see the display area.

Kester's Wild Game Food Nurseries
P.O. Box 516
Omro, WI 54963
David and Patricia Kester
(414) 685-2929
Catalog: $2, CAN, cn/bn

COUNTRY WETLANDS NURSERY
Artist: Steve Sandlin

■ Also in Wisconsin, Jo Ann Gillespie's **Country Wetlands Nursery** in Muskego focuses on preserving wetlands and their native plants. The emphasis here is on preservation, not specifically attracting and feeding wildlife. A research chemist, Jo Ann went back to college to study wetland ecology and now consults on restoring native wetland habitats, both public and private. She's lyrical in her description of the beauty and usefulness of her wetland plants, which are being used more and more for their low maintenance and water-cleaning properties.

Country Wetlands offers 26 sedges and many other native wetland plants for bogs and wet meadows, sedge meadows, and some fen species for wet alkaline soils. They also offer the 2 native American water lilies, 1 white and 1 yellow. There's a display garden at the nursery which is at its best from June to September; visitors are welcome by appointment only. Muskego is just south of Milwaukee.

Country Wetlands Nursery
S75 W20755 Field Drive
Muskego, WI 53150
Jo Ann Gillespie
(414) 679-1268
Catalog: $3, bn/cn

■ *Another source of aquatic plants is:*

Kurt Bluemel, Baldwin, MD

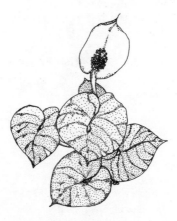

COUNTRY WETLANDS NURSERY
Artist: Steve Sandlin

Bamboos

■ **Steve Ray's Bamboo Gardens** in Birmingham, Alabama, offers about thirty-five varieties of bamboo, many of which are hardy to zero degrees Fahrenheit, and all of which are very well described in an informative catalog. Steve is a captain in the local fire department. As a child, he snuck into and played in a landscaped grove of Japanese timber bamboo in his neighborhood; he never did know who owned or planted it. He's been collecting, growing, and studying bamboo for thirty years and has also been an active member of the American Bamboo Society, helping to organize local chapters.

Steve has a collection of more than 100 varieties, so he may have something rare you've been looking for. Both his mother and his son help out with the nursery; visitors are welcome at the bamboo groves in any season, but definitely should call for an appointment. He has a display garden in Birmingham and a big country grove in New London, about forty miles from Birmingham; larger plants are available at the country nursery.

> **Steve Ray's Bamboo Gardens**
> 909 Seventy-ninth Place South
> Birmingham, AL 35206
> Steve Ray
> (205) 833-3052
> Catalog: $2, bn/cn

■ I hope you don't grow tired of hearing about plant sources that just happen to be in my own neighborhood. I think that I live in a horticultural heaven, with so many wonderful plant people nearby. We recently started our own little horticultural society and figure we can go on for years just by asking local people to talk at our meetings.

On the side of a steep hill west of Sebastopol is **Bamboo Sourcery**, a truly amazing bamboo collection and nursery. Gerald Bol is a former college art teacher who fell in love with bamboo and started collecting; he's traveled all over Central and South America searching for new forms.

At the nursery he grows 280 varieties and forms, and he offers about 100 of these on his list. If you live close by you can buy quite large and tall clumps — naturally quite expensive. In his spare time Gerald collects and grows all sorts of plants and is president of the American Bamboo Society. Visitors are welcome at any season but must make prior arrangements to visit. Sebastopol is about ten miles west of Santa Rosa, about an hour and a half north of San Francisco.

> **Bamboo Sourcery**
> 666 Wagnon Road
> Sebastopol, CA 95472
> Gerald Bol
> (707) 823-5866
> Catalog: $2, bn

■ *Other sources of bamboo are:*

Kurt Bluemel, Baldwin, MD
Louisiana Nursery, Opelousas, LA
Neon Palm Nursery, Santa Rosa, CA
Stallings Exotic Nursery, Encinitas, CA
Tripple Brook Farm, Southampton, MA
Woodlanders, Inc., Aiken, SC

Bulbs

If you're like me, you sit down in the summer when your garden is really looking its best and study the bulb catalogs as if winter is upon you and all is bleak and drear; only spring bulbs are able to lift the imaginary gloom. It's the gardener's greatest fault: what's happening at this very moment is never quite as wonderful as that just past or still to come. Of course, there are bulbs that bloom at different times of year, but the gardening season seems always to start with the first early spring bloomer.

I've been trying a few new kinds every year, and the delight they provide is all out of proportion to their size or expense, especially when you forget where you've put them and they pop up unexpectedly.

There is a type of expert gardener-writer who especially loves to write about these "little bulbs" and who grandly refers to the seasons by Church of England holidays. I'm always a bit flummoxed to read that "to my amazement, the first of the dear little mouse crocuses was peeking out of the grass by Birchmass, and by Oakmass, all of the dainty fairy lilies had dropped their gaudy raiment!" I never seem to have thoughts like that when I walk gingerly around my garden in early spring looking for the first bulbs, skidding around in the mud and plunging through into gopher runs. But I yield to no one in my excitement when I see the first bulbs begin to bloom.

Of course, not all bulbs are spring bloomers or very hardy. Included here you'll find some native bulbs from California and South Africa, and summer bloomers like gladiolus and tuberous begonias which put on a great show but need winter storage out of the cold.

■ Jeffrey Rice is a bank auditor (as a former bank librarian, I can relate to this) who started a bulb business to prepare for his retirement; as his catalog grows, retirement probably is approaching faster and faster. His **Mad River Imports** in Moretown, Vermont, issues two catalogs a year. The spring catalog offers about 75 summer-blooming bulbs and some bare-root perennials. The fall catalog offers about 200 kinds of spring-blooming bulbs: daffodils, tulips, crocus, muscari and other hyacinths, and various types of lilies. Moretown is in north central Vermont. Visitors must have an appointment, and the best seasons are spring and summer.

Mad River Imports
P.O. Box 1685
Moretown, VT 05660
Jeffrey M. Rice
(802) 496-3004
Catalog: Free, cn/bn

VAN ENGELEN, INC.
Artist: Bobbi Angell

■ For those who want to buy bulbs in larger quantities, **Van Engelen** in Litchfield, Connecticut, has been importing most of the popular spring bulbs since the 1940s and offers them by the hundred at very competitive prices. They also offer mixed collections and color mixtures so that you get a sampling of many. Offered are tulips, daffodils and narcissus, crocus, alliums, anemones, freesias, lilies, and other "little bulbs." Van Engelen was at one time one of the huge Dutch bulb companies. Their American branch was founded in 1930 and eventually sold to Jan Ohms, a Dutchman who's been in the bulb business in this country for many years. Mail order only.

Van Engelen, Inc.
313 Maple Street
Litchfield, CT 06759
Jan S. Ohms
(203) 567-5662 or 8734
Catalog: Free, cn/bn

■ Started by an uncle of Jan Ohms, the proprietor of Van Engelen, **John Scheepers** of Bantam, Connecticut, is an eighty-year-old company importing spring- and summer-blooming bulbs: tulips, daffodils, alliums, fritillaria, and many of the lovely little bulbs for spring, as well as lilies, tuberous begonias, bulbous iris, and dahlias, even some perennials. The company has recently become part of Van Engelen, keeping it in the original family. For many years, the address was Wall Street in New York City, giving a nice horticultural lift to the grim canyons of finance. Jan says his uncle used to visit his customers on the grand estates of Long Island in a chauffeured Cadillac and wanted a Wall Street address to impress them. Scheepers sells top-quality bulbs in retail quantities. Mail order only.

> **John Scheepers, Inc.**
> P.O. Box 700
> Bantam, CT 06750
> Jan S. Ohms
> (203) 567-0838 FAX 567-5323
> Catalog: Free, bn

■ **Bundles of Bulbs** in Owings Mills, Maryland, offers narcissus and daffodils, tulips and other spring-flowering bulbs. Kitty Washburne was a teacher who started growing bulbs so that she'd have armloads of flowers to take to the children. She got a big return for a couple of weekends' work in the fall. Washburne started her small bulb business in 1984; now her daughter-in-law helps her. They sell bulbs by mail order only. Visitors may wander around the display beds on Saturday and Sunday from mid-March to early May but must call ahead to be sure someone will be there and to get directions. Owings Mills, known to fans of public television's "Wall Street Week," with its investment wisdom and terrible puns, is a half hour northwest of Baltimore.

> **Bundles of Bulbs**
> 112 Green Springs Valley Road
> Owings Mills, MD 21117
> Kitty Washburne
> (301) 363-1371
> Catalog: $2d, bn

■ Alice Hosford started showing the flowers she grew from bulbs about ten years ago; when she began to win a lot of prizes, her friends encouraged her to start raising and selling bulbs. **The Bulb Crate** in Riverwoods, Illinois, offers a nice selection of Asiatic, trumpet, Aurelian, and Oriental lilies, and a mixed collection for lily bloom from June through September. She also offers selected tall and dwarf bearded iris, Japanese and Siberian iris, peonies, and tulips. Mail order only.

The Bulb Crate
2560 Deerfield Road
Riverwoods, IL 60015
Alice Hosford
(708) 317-1414
Catalog: $1d, CAN/OV

MCCLURE & ZIMMERMAN

■ A source of many daffodils and other specialty bulbs is **McClure & Zimmerman** in Friesland, Wisconsin. Founded by Kenneth McClure and Mark Zimmerman in 1982 in Chicago, the firm quickly earned a reputation as a source of unusual bulbs; it's now part of the Jung Seed Company, but the founders are still involved in the business. The catalog is a good evening's browse, so set it aside until you can sit down with it and a book with good colored pictures of bulbs. Here are a lot of collector's bulbs, many of the special little species bulbs that expert gardeners are always going on about. McClure & Zimmerman offers good selections of alliums, hybrid and species tulips, daffodils, crocus, fritillaria, and bulbous iris, among others.

McClure & Zimmerman
P.O. Box 386
Friesland, WI 53935
J. W. Jung Seed Company
(414) 326-4220
Catalog: Free, bn

Years ago I went to a luncheon given by a friend who had married an Englishman. She told us that he loved to garden, and finally took us into the back yard, an expanse of cement with gladiolus standing at attention around the perimeter like guardsmen. I swallowed hard and said, "Wow! He really loves glads!" Don't let anyone tell you that garden taste is an inherent national trait or is absorbed by walking through Kew Gardens!

Unsurpassed as dramatic cut flowers, glads are definitely not graceful garden plants and really only look good massed in a cutting garden. Glads seem like a great money-making crop for kids to grow and sell around the neighborhood and to decorate local churches. The smaller species *Gladiolus byzantinus* and others sold as "hardy gladiolus" really look very pretty in a border, as can the drooping white Abyssinian gladiolus (*Acidanthera murielae*), which are deliciously fragrant.

■ **Skolaski's Glads & Field Flowers** in Waunakee, Wisconsin, is a good source of regular, species, and Abyssinian glads. Stan Skolaski started working for a grower called Flad's Glads when he was ten years old; when he was a high school senior he bought the little company and ran it as a sideline for twenty-six years while working for a huge cut-flower grower. Recently the family moved to the country and bought the business of Nancy Skolaski's father, a garden center and large orchid greenhouses called Orchids by the Acres.

Now they sell cut glads and other flowers all summer, and the corms of a broad selection of large- and medium-flowered glads and pixiolas, which are smaller-flowered and lower-growing. Also listed are a few Asiatic lilies and some other summer-flowering bulbs. Waunakee is about three miles northwest of Madison. Visitors are welcome to come and see the fields of glads and the orchid range.

> **Skolaski's Glads & Field Flowers**
> 4821 County Trunk Highway Q
> Waunakee, WI 53597
> Stan and Nancy Skolaski
> (608) 836-4822
> Catalog: Free, CAN/OV

■ Started by George and Robert Melk's grandparents in 1924, **The Waushara Gardens** in Plainfield, Wisconsin, have been offering a huge selection of gladiolus corms to both cut-flower growers and home gardeners ever since. They offer about 130 cultivars of glads and pixiolas, as well as Asiatic lilies and a few other summer-flowering bulbs.

George Melk says Waushara moves its growing fields every year, so he suggests that visitors stop at the Amoco gas station at the intersection of U.S. Highway 51 and Wisconsin Highway 73 and pick up a map that will show the location of the office and the current growing fields. Plainfield is in central Wisconsin, about ninety miles north of Madison. The best month to visit is August.

The Waushara Gardens
Route 2, Box 570
Plainfield, WI 54966
George and Robert Melk
(715) 335-4462 or 4281
Catalog: $1, CAN/OV

BIO-QUEST INTERNATIONAL
Artist: Shari Smith

■ Richard Doutt at **Bio-Quest International** is both a retired professor of entomology at the University of California at Berkeley and a retired attorney. He moved to Santa Barbara, California, and now devotes himself to his true love, growing the tender bulbs of the Cape Province of South Africa. His wife, Betty, whose great love is theatrical costumes, has helped him create a wonderfully informative catalog, which is beautifully illustrated.

Bio-Quest is a very small business, really an extensive private collection, and supplies are usually very limited, but if you are looking for some of these lovely plants, you can't do better than to contact Dr. Doutt. His bulbs are best grown in a Mediterranean climate, such as southern and central California. Doutt sells both bulbs and seeds so serious hobbyists can try them. He has recently written the book *Cape Bulbs: Their Collection, Cultivation and Conservation,* to be published by Timber Press.

> **Bio-Quest International**
> P.O. Box 5752
> Santa Barbara, CA 93150-5752
> Dr. Richard Doutt
> (805) 969-4072
> Catalog: $2, CAN, bn

■ Herbert Kelly, Jr., is a man obsessed: he is growing and hybridizing cannas, lycoris, and crinum, and at present is evaluating hundreds of crosses. His **Kelly's Plant World** canna list offers more than 100 varieties; he indicates which ones are being held back for increase, but he lists them so that you'll know what will be available before long. Some of these are introductions from the last century, ideal for those restoring old gardens with heirloom plants; the oldest variety seems to be from 1863.

Herb is also growing more than 160 clones of lycoris and about 100 crinums, both species and hybrids (he's even hybridized a yellow crinum), though I have not seen those lists yet. Visitors may come and walk through the fields; the best months are April to September. Call for an appointment and directions to the nursery, which is in Sanger, California, about ten miles east of Fresno.

> **Kelly's Plant World**
> 10266 East Princeton
> Sanger, CA 93657
> Herbert Kelly, Jr.
> (209) 294-7676
> Catalog: $1d, bn

■ The **Antonelli Brothers** of Santa Cruz started selling begonia tubers in 1935; since then begonias have been getting more and more spectacular and are a terrific bang for the buck. Even in the north they can be started indoors and put out in planters when the weather warms up. Antonelli's offers many colors and forms of tuberous begonia, some mixed collections, and some other summer bulbs, as well as a fall list of fuchsias. The nursery is now run by the second generation, Skip Antonelli and his cousin Dennis Bobbitt; they both have children working with them. Visitors are welcome daily except for

Thanksgiving, Christmas, and New Year's Day. Santa Cruz is about thirty miles south of San Jose on the coast.

> **Antonelli Brothers, Inc.**
> 2545 Capitola Road
> Santa Cruz, CA 95062
> Skip Antonelli
> (408) 475-5222
> Catalog: $1

■ Anthony J. Skittone has been fooling with plants since the third grade, when he was introduced to the accomplishments of Luther Burbank by growing radish seeds. He became the family vegetable gardener in his San Francisco back yard, and when he got out of the army in the seventies, his interest turned to bulbs. He began collecting rare bulbs and sold the extras to other collectors to help cover his costs. Since he was spending so much time giving growing advice on the telephone, the next step was a catalog; now he's got a thriving wholesale bulb business, but he still sells unusual bulbs to collectors.

Tony has recently changed the name of his San Francisco business from his own name to **GreenLady Gardens** and offers a very good selection of species bulbs: alliums, crocus, iris, muscari, scilla, fritillaria, lachenalias, arisaemas, colchicums, and many South African bulbs, as well as many spring-blooming bulbs such as tulips, anemones, daffodils, and hyacinths. Mail order only.

> **GreenLady Gardens**
> 1415 Eucalyptus Drive
> San Francisco, CA 94132
> Anthony Skittone
> (415) 753-3332
> Catalog: $3, CAN/OV, bn

■ In order to be perfectly honest and aboveboard, I have to tell you right off that the proprietors of **Robinett Bulb Farm** in Sebastopol, California, are my good pals: Georgie March helped me with two revisions of *Gardening by Mail* (she's a much better speller and proofreader than I am), and her husband, Jim Robinett, grows tubs of bulbs in my back field. In the spring I have big tubs of calochortus, triteleia, and other lovely native bulbs flowering in back of my house — heaven when I want to be very horticultural and amaze guests.

Jim and Georgie first started growing ordinary garden bulbs in a suburban garden, then got interested in growing California native bulbs. They moved to Sebastopol to have more room for plants and now have covered their entire property, literally edge to edge, with pans and boxes of bulbs; one is sometimes hard put to find a place to set down a foot. Jim spends most weekdays as a computer whiz, and Georgie is a social worker, but they spend most weekends in the spring searching for and noting the location of blooming bulbous plants, then going back later at the peak of summer's heat to collect a few (never all) of the seeds.

One of their mentors is the legendary Wayne Roderick, who seems to know the plants on every inch of California soil and is always called upon to escort distinguished horticulturists around California. Wayne loves to call out the plants to be seen around the next corner, a constant source of amazement to his guests.

Each August the Robinetts publish a list of what will be available; within a month or two they're usually sold out. Many of their customers are in Europe and consider growing California native bulbs a real challenge. Mail order only, as Jim and Georgie aren't set up to welcome visitors (nowhere to put your feet).

> **Robinett Bulb Farm**
> P.O. Box 1306
> Sebastopol, CA 95473-1306
> James Robinett
> Catalog: Long SASE, bn/cn

■ For years, one of the best-known hybridizers of begonias and lilies was Leslie Woodriff of **Fairyland Begonia Garden** in McKinleyville, California. One of his hybrid lilies is 'Star Gazer', the top-selling lily cultivar in the world, and he won a number of awards for others. Now retired from active hybridizing, he consults with his daughter Winkey, who is carrying on his work; they are still introducing new hybrids.

The Woodriffs offer a nice selection of lilies, mostly their own Oriental and Aurelian hybrids; also offered are some *Amaryllis belladonna*, nerines, a yellow calla lily with a purple heart (throat, actually), and yearling lily bulbs of their breeding which will flower the second year. The best time to visit the nursery is June through August. Call for directions. McKinleyville is just north of Eureka.

> **Fairyland Begonia Garden**
> 1100 Griffith Road
> McKinleyville, CA 95521

Winkey Woodriff
(707) 839-3034
Catalog: $.50, CAN/OV

■ **Dr. Joseph C. Halinar** in Scotts Mills, Oregon, has a Ph.D. in plant breeding and genetics. A hybridizer of lilies and daylilies, he sells seeds of his crosses to gardeners, collectors, and other hybridizers; he says that growing both flowers from seed is very easy. For the information of those who want to use his plants for hybridizing, Dr. Halinar describes crosses both for flower and for breeding potential. He offers species and crosses of Asiatic, Martagon, Caucasian, trumpet, and native American lilies. He also offers seeds of alliums and sisyrinchums. Visitors must write for an appointment. Scotts Mills is northeast of Salem.

Dr. Joseph C. Halinar
2333 Crooked Finger Road
Scotts Mills, OR 97375
(503) 873-2218
Catalog: 1 FCS, bn

■ **B & D Lilies** is located in Port Townsend on the Olympic Peninsula of Washington, one of the most beautiful places on earth — so it's fitting that B & D grows and sells lilies, which are so near to perfection themselves. I know they're tougher than they look, but they always seem so fragile, and such a luxury! I'm determined to grow some lilies next year to honor my new grandniece, Lily Strelich. B & D offers a large selection of lilies of all types in a color catalog and has added alstroemerias and some evergreen daylilies, which do well in the Northwest.

Bob and Dianna Gibson started growing lilies as a hobby; Bob worked in a paper mill and Dianna was a housewife. One thing led to another, they began to sell their surplus bulbs, and ended up as a major lily nursery. They have a three-acre display garden outside Port Townsend. Visitors may request an appointment and a "Field Pass" either by mail (send a self-addressed stamped envelope) or in person. The garden is open Thursday through Saturday from late June to early August.

B & D Lilies
330 P Street
Port Townsend, WA 98368

Bob and Dianna Gibson
(206) 385-1738
Catalog: $3d, CAN/OV, bn

■ *Other sources of lilies are:*

Ambergate Gardens, Waconia, MN
Borbeleta Gardens, Faribault, MN

■ *Another source of pleiones is:*

Red's Rhodies, Sherwood, OR

■ *Another source of spring-blooming bulbs is:*

The Daffodil Mart, Gloucester, VA

BIO-QUEST INTERNATIONAL
Artist: Shari Smith

Cactus: Hardy

Luckily for cactus lovers, there are several genera that are very hardy and can be grown in climates in which temperatures fall to zero Fahrenheit, some even lower. Most winter-hardy cactus thrive where winters are consistently cold but dry; winter wet is more threatening than cold.

■ **Midwest Cactus** in New Melle, Missouri, was started by Chris Smith in 1984; he decided to grow cold-hardy cactus when he realized how much it cost to heat and cool greenhouses in his climate. When he was twelve, his grandfather gave him a fascinating collection of little cactus plants for Christmas; on a later trip to the Grand Canyon he saw photos of cactus covered with winter snow and realized that he could grow them at home in Missouri. He offers thirty-six species and cultivars of opuntia and several hardy sedums and yuccas.

Chris is a structural dynamics engineer for McDonnell Douglas in St. Louis, and the nursery is a part-time effort. Visitors can come and see the cactus by appointment, on weekends and evenings, but can't buy at the nursery, which sells by mail order only because of zoning laws. New Melle is thirty miles west of St. Louis near Interstate 70.

> **Midwest Cactus**
> P.O. Box 163
> New Melle, MO 63365
> Chris M. Smith
> (314) 828- 5389
> Catalog: $1, CAN, bn

■ John Cipra, Jr., was a farmer and greenhouse grower in love with flowering plants. His nursery, **The Cactus Patch** in Radium, Kansas, offers many species and cultivars of opuntia, some coryphanthas, echinocereus, and escobarias, all of which have beautiful blooms, mostly with red, yellow, pink, or white flowers. All the plants are seed- or cutting-grown outside in the Kansas winter — they're tough! There is no display garden as such, but visitors can come to see the cactus; bloom time is mid-May to mid-June. Please call before visiting to be sure someone will be there. Radium is in central Kansas, about sixteen miles southwest of Great Bend.

The Cactus Patch
RR 2, Box 159
Radium, KS 67550-9111
John Cipra, Jr.
(316) 982-4670
Catalog: 1 FCS, bn

■ Robert Johnson of Kaysville, Utah, is an accountant in love with cactus and their beautiful blossoms; he's cleverly arranged his life so that he works from November through the tax season, then spends the best months outside with his cactus. His **Intermountain Cactus** offers many cultivars of opuntia, echinocereus, and coryphanthas chosen for lovely bloom, including 8 to 10 of the special varieties with unusual flower colors originally sold by hardy-cactus pioneer Claude Barr of South Dakota.

Johnson grows about 150 cactus and lists about 45. All of his plants are grown outside at five thousand feet, covered with snow most of the winter. Visitors are welcome from May to October; bloom time is May and early June. Please be sure to call ahead. Kaysville is halfway between Salt Lake City and Ogden.

Intermountain Cactus
2344 S. Redwood Road
Salt Lake City, UT 84119
Robert A. Johnson
(801) 972-5149
Catalog: Long SASE, bn/cn

■ Shirley Nyerges of **Desert Nursery** in Deming, New Mexico, also offers winter-hardy cactus: echinocereus, opuntia, some mammillarias, coryphanthas, and escobarias. She and her husband went to New Mexico when he got a job there in construction, fell in love with the high desert, and never left.

They started in cactus with a few little pots from the grocery store. Friends gave them more, and now they raise both garden and greenhouse cactus. They're at 4,500 feet and have winter cold down to zero at times. The nursery is open Monday to Saturday from March to mid-September or by appointment.

Deming is about 105 miles west of El Paso, Texas, on Interstate 10.

> **Desert Nursery**
> 1301 S. Copper Street
> Deming, NM 88030
> Shirley J. Nyerges
> (505) 546-6264
> Catalog: Long SASE, bn

■ **Mesa Garden** in Belen, New Mexico, is known for its huge seed list. It sells cactus seed to collectors all over the world, but it also sells a broad selection of seed-grown plants, many of them garden-hardy in winters either cold or southern. Read Mesa Garden's list with a good cactus book at hand.

Steve and Linda Brack started growing cactus in Eau Claire, Wisconsin, but realized that they needed a better cactus-growing climate to be really successful. Steve found a job in New Mexico and off they went; now they spend their whole lives with cactus. Visitors are welcome by appointment but should understand that the Bracks are very busy; Linda says they have cactus in flower most of the year, either outdoors or in. Belen is forty miles south of Albuquerque on Interstate 25.

> **Mesa Garden**
> P.O. Box 72
> Belen, NM 87002
> Steve and Linda Brack
> (505) 864-3131
> Catalog: 2 FCS, bn

■ *Other sources of hardy cactus are:*

Colvos Creek Nursery, Vashon Island, WA
Desert Moon Nursery, Veguita, NM
Neon Palm Nursery, Santa Rosa, CA

Camellias

When I came to live in the country (I call my vast estate "Lafa-lot"), there were four camellias, overgrown but giving me great pleasure during the first rainy winter in my new home. Since then I have added nearly a dozen more, including several small-flowered species camellias, and I'm torn between the dainty and sometimes fragrant flowers of the species and the spectacular flowers of the hybrids. I think that the little flowers look better on the plant and the big flowers look better in the house. I grew up in warm southern California where it seemed as if camellias were part of everyone's garden, almost urban native plants, but I've discovered that they really are hardier, more drought resistant, and easier to grow than most people imagine. After it fell to twelve degrees Fahrenheit here last year, they bloomed later than usual but went on blooming until it turned hot in May.

■ Camellias are very much grown in the South, and **Camellia Forest Nursery** in Chapel Hill, North Carolina, is a good source of many types of camellias: *C. sasanqua* selections and hybrids, *C. japonica* selections and hybrids, some japonicas hardy to USDA Zone 6a, older *C. japonica* cultivars, and some camellia species, as well as a list of the nursery's own new camellia selections, which are still only numbered, not named. Camellia Forest also offers camellia seeds.

Camellia Forest Nursery is run by Kai-Mei Parks, whose husband, Clifford, is a botanist at the University of North Carolina. They've made several collecting trips in recent years to China and Japan and offer a number of unusual Far Eastern woody plants, many grown from seed collected on their trips. Among these are callicarpas, linderas, pterostyrax, hollies, prunus, magnolias, and many dwarf conifers; some are very rare and mouth-watering in their appeal. Visitors are welcome by appointment only; the best times are fall for the *Camellia sasanqua* varieties and spring for the *C. japonica* varieties and other blooming trees and shrubs.

Camellia Forest Nursery
P.O. Box 291
Chapel Hill, NC 27516

Kei-Mei Parks
(919) 967-5529
Catalog: $2, CAN/OV, bn

■ No nursery is more closely identified with camellias than
Nuccio's Nurseries in Altadena, California. It was started in
1935 by Joseph and Julius Nuccio as a regular nursery, but
they soon decided to specialize in the plants they loved the
best, camellias and azaleas. They have introduced hundreds
of camellia and azalea varieties; some, like the perfect white
camellia 'Nuccio's Gem', are classics. They have a yellow cultivar on the way which they say is quite wonderful.

I was lucky enough to visit in winter, when a walk through
the shade houses was at its very best, and to chat with Tom
Nuccio, whose enthusiasm and love of his plants is catching.
Tom, his brother Jim, and cousin Julius are the second generation to be running this busy nursery.

The nursery is not far from Descanso Gardens in Glendale,
a mecca for camellia lovers in the winter with its many
hundreds of varieties planted under a forest of native live oaks.
The nearby Huntington Botanical Gardens in San Marino also
has good camellia plantings. Take a pad and pencil; you'll find
many of your favorites in the Nuccio catalog, which offers a
very broad selection of *Camellia japonica, C. sasanqua,* and
C. reticulata cultivars, many hybrids, species, Higo and Rus-
ticana camellias, and camellias with remarkable foliage. Information on flower color and form and bloom season is
included. The nursery is open Friday through Tuesday (closed
Sunday from June through December); there's no display garden, but there are lots of camellias and azaleas blooming in
winter and spring.

Nuccio's Nurseries
3555 Chaney Trail
P.O. Box 6160
Altadena, CA 91003
Julius, Tom, and Jim Nuccio
(818) 794-3383
Catalog: Free, bn

■ *Other sources of camellias are:*

The Bovees Nursery, Portland, OR
Greer Gardens, Eugene, OR
Louisiana Nursery, Opelousas, LA
Roslyn Nursery, Dix Hills, NY
Transplant Nursery, Lavonia, GA
Whitney Gardens, Brinnon, WA

Chrysanthemums

Many chrysanthemums are excellent garden plants, not just color spots for fall, and come in such a dizzying variety of colors, shapes, sizes, and forms that there are certainly choices for every sort of gardener. Even if you don't want to train cascades or bonsai, grow "football" mums in your school colors, or mass them for autumnal effect, many are great in a mixed border, extending bloom and providing good foliage when other plants are dying down.

■ **Mums by Paschke** is a wholesaler of chrysanthemums in North East, Pennsylvania, which offers 43 varieties to retail customers by mail order. Jack Paschke's father started the nursery in 1932 and died only a few years ago at 101. Jack's the only one of six children who stayed on the farm to grow mums. Customers get a wholesale list, with a retail order list and form.

Visitors are welcome the last week of September and all of October; the fields are well marked so that you can note the varieties you like. North East is in the northwest corner of Pennsylvania, eighteen miles east of Erie and three-quarters of a mile from the New York state line. Jack says you can see the fields in bloom from Interstate 90 (take Exit 12) and from Route 20.

> **Mums by Paschke**
> 12286 East Main Road
> North East, PA 16428
> Jack Paschke
> (814) 725-9860
> Catalog: Free

■ **Dooley Gardens** in Hutchinson, Minnesota, grows about 200 varieties and lists about 60 varieties of garden mums, including many of the chrysanthemum introductions of the University of Minnesota. Vincent Dooley was a 3M employee for many years but got hooked when he bought a dozen mums for his own garden, learned to propagate them, and began to feel like the Sorcerer's Apprentice. In 1958, when his garden was full of mums and all his neighbors had more than enough, he started to sell them. He's now retired from 3M after both working and running the nursery for many years, and his son helps him part-time; they do not ship to California. Blooming plants are on display from late September to mid-October; call ahead at other times. Hutchinson is about fifty miles west of Minneapolis and St. Paul.

> **Dooley Gardens**
> Route 1
> Hutchinson, MN 55350
> Vincent Dooley
> (612) 587-3050
> Catalog: Free

■ **Huff's Garden Mums** in Burlington, Kansas, was founded in 1955 by Charles Huff, a former Boy Scout executive. His son Harry is also in the business, and they run other wholesale nurseries and a retail nursery as well. In 1990 they took over another mum grower, Thon's Mums in Illinois, increasing their offerings to about 700 cultivars. Huff's offers many types of chrysanthemums and a number of collections by type for those who want to grow a variety of colors or types.

Visitors are welcome at the nursery Monday through Saturday in late September and October to see the plants blooming in stock beds. Burlington is in southeast Kansas, about sixty miles south of Topeka.

> **Huff's Garden Mums**
> P.O. Box 187
> Burlington, KS 66839-0187
> Charles A. Huff
> (800) 279-4675
> Catalog: Free, OV

■ **Sunnyslope Gardens** in San Gabriel, California, was started in 1933 by Phil Ishizu's father and uncle. After studying ornamental horticulture at Cal Poly Pomona, Phil did research for four years in plant physiology at Cal Tech; when research grants began to dry up, he joined his father at the nursery. Sunnyslope offers a very broad selection of chrysanthemums in a color catalog. In addition to the usual garden mum varieties, they offer a number of varieties popular for flower arranging and show: spider and threadlike varieties, bonsai mums, cascades, spoons, even some shaped like tassels. They also offer about a dozen cultivars of "everblooming carna-tions," the florist varieties grown for cut flowers. Blooming chrysanthemums are on display at the nursery in October and November; the nursery is about two miles west of the Los Angeles State and County Arboretum and Botanic Garden.

Sunnyslope Gardens
8638 Huntington Drive
San Gabriel, CA 91775
Phil Ishizu
(818) 287-4071
Catalog: Free

■ **King's Mums** in Clements, California, is another source of chrysanthemums of all types, including their own and other American hybrids and introductions from England, Japan, New Zealand, and Australia. King's specializes in varieties for people who love to collect and show chrysanthemums, so many of their plants are the latest introductions. They offer about 250 cultivars in the catalog and another 150 on the limited stock list (send a self-addressed stamped envelope for that list); the limited stock list includes older varieties and newer vari-eties and recent introductions.

A hobby grower since 1947, Ted King formerly ran a pest control business; now the nursery is his full-time occupation, in partnership with his daughter Lanna. Clements is horse country, and Lanna and her mother also like to train and show Morgan horses. Visitors are welcome daily during October and November; peak bloom is around Halloween. Clements is about twenty-four miles east of Stockton on Highway 88, halfway to Jackson.

King's Mums
P.O. Box 368
Clements, CA 95227
Ted and Lanna King
(209) 759-3571
Catalog: $2

Daffodils

I'm going to use the word *daffodil* for everything we casually call "daffodils," even though some are really narcissus, and the daffodil folk break them down in many finely detailed categories. You'll see that I use both the terms *daffodil* and *novelty daffodil*. Novelty daffodils are generally new in trade, available in limited quantities, and, because of their higher prices and rarity, very much in demand for the show bench. Just plain daffodils are the tried-and-true older varieties, propagated by the hundreds of acres and inexpensive enough to plant in dramatic drifts and swaths.

■ Brent and Becky Heath of **The Daffodil Mart** are Virginians so charming and full of enthusiasm for daffodils that it's hard to imagine them doing anything else. Their business was started by Brent's grandfather in 1900 and has made a major contribution to the village of Gloucester, Virginia, which has a daffodil festival in the first week of April every year. They have been responsible for mass plantings of daffodils in several botanical gardens, and they travel and lecture extensively.

Their list of daffodils is very extensive (more than 350 varieties), but they also sell a very broad variety of other spring-flowering bulbs as well. They issue two catalogs; the main catalog lists hundreds of daffodils and lots of other popular bulbs such as tulips, crocus, and alliums; these are sold in small quantities at retail and in larger quantities at wholesale prices. A second catalog offers "specialty bulbs," such as novelty daffodils, colchicums and autumn crocus, rarer alliums, fritillaria, species tulips, and many of the other charming and harder-to-find little bulbs sought after by plantsmen. Altogether, the Heaths list more than 1,000 different bulbs in their two catalogs. Call for the exact date of the Daffodil Festival in Gloucester; during the festival they have bus tours of their growing fields. No visitors at other times. Gloucester is on Highway 17, about twenty-five miles north of Newport News.

The Daffodil Mart
Route 3, Box 794
Gloucester, VA 23061

Brent and Becky Heath
(804) 693-3966
Catalog: Free, cn/bn

■ **Cascade Daffodils** in West St. Paul, Minnesota, offers mostly
novelty daffodils for show, collectors, and amateur hybridizers, but it also offers the popular garden and naturalizing
varieties in its list. Here are more than 500 daffodil cultivars
from all of the famous hybridizers in this country and from
Australia and New Zealand, including some new and special
varieties priced like the jewels they are. Older cultivars are
quite reasonably priced and are the sort of special daffodils
which would be wonderful beside a path or where you could
watch them with special attention.

Cascade's David Karnstedt grew up imprinted by daffodils;
he began to notice the early arrival of spring in Minnesota if
the daffodils bloomed before his birthday at the end of April.
He and his wife, Linda, grow 2,300 cultivars in three states;
the Karnstedts' young son is more interested in baseball at
present, but perhaps he's also imprinting on daffodils, relating
bloom to the first weeks of the baseball season.

David, a much-traveled management consultant, says he
may eventually follow the bulbs he's sent to Oregon for propagation and increase; that state obviously has a wonderful
daffodil-growing climate. Visitors to Cascade must call ahead
to arrange a visit to the displays in April and May.

Cascade Daffodils
1790 Richard Circle
West St. Paul, MN 55118-3821
David and Linda Karnstedt
(612) 455-6177
Catalog: $1

CASCADE DAFFODILS *Artist: Rod Barwick*

■ **Nancy Wilson Species & Miniature Narcissus** is owned by a home health care nurse who collects and grows miniature and species narcissus. Over the years she's brought a number of them to meetings of the California Horticultural Society, where they never fail to draw a crowd. Some are so tiny she grows them in little pots because they would get lost in grass or leaves; most grow to only a few inches.

Nancy is very concerned with saving and preserving rare species and cultivars. She's recently moved up near Garberville, California, where she has more room to grow her bulbs from seed; an avid collector, she is always looking for species narcissus that she can increase and add to her list for other collectors.

Visitors must call ahead for an appointment; the best months to visit are January, February, and March. Nancy actually lives in the little town of Briceland, six miles west of Redway; she's probably three to three and a half hours north of San Francisco.

> **Nancy Wilson Species & Miniature Narcissus**
> 6525 Briceland-Thorn Road
> Garberville, CA 95440
> Nancy Wilson
> (707) 923-2407
> Catalog: $1, bn

■ **Bonnie Brae Gardens** in Corbett, Oregon, specializes in classic daffodils from miniatures to standards; dependable, steady performers both in the garden and on the show bench. Jeanie McKillop Driver says her selection is not large, about 50 varieties; some are in very limited supply. Visitors should call ahead to be sure someone will be there; bloom season varies from late March to early May, depending on winter cold. Corbett is about twenty miles east of Portland.

> **Bonnie Brae Gardens**
> 1105 S.E. Christensen Road
> Corbett, OR 97019
> Jeanie McKillop Driver
> (503) 695-5190
> Catalog: 1 FCS

■ Diane Tribe of **Oregon Trail Daffodils** in Corbett, Oregon, is the niece of the esteemed daffodil hybridizer Murray Evans, and she and her husband, Bill, have taken over the business her uncle started with his grandfather and uncles. Murray's mentor in hybridizing was Grant Mitsch, so there is a wonderful interconnectedness in the high daffodil world. The Tribes offer many Evans hybrids and are introducing some new ones that he was working on at the end of his life (he died in 1988); they're also working on hybrids of their own and are just beginning to introduce them.

They also offer the hybrids of Bill Pannill, a talented amateur hybridizer from Virginia who makes annual spring trips to Oregon to check on his crosses and make new ones. Pannill's interest is primarily in showing daffodils, and his introductions are selected for the qualities that make excellent show flowers. Visitors should call ahead; March and April are usually bloom time. Corbett is about twenty miles east of Portland in the beautiful Columbia River Gorge.

Oregon Trail Daffodils
3207 S.E. Mannthey Road
Corbett, OR 97019
Bill and Diane Tribe
(503) 695-5513
Catalog: Free, CAN/OV

OREGON TRAIL DAFFODILS *Artist: Estella Evans*

■ Probably the best-known name in American daffodils is Grant Mitsch of Hubbard, Oregon, who hybridized many stunning daffodils and was still doing so until a few years before his death in 1989. He won many awards from the American Daffodil Society and the Royal Horticultural Society in the sixty-two years he worked on daffodils; he was responsible for many new forms and colors in the American

Daffodil Society's Division 8 and up. His daughter Elise and her husband, Dick Havens, have continued his business. They are doing their own hybridizing and are still introducing Mitsch's later hybrids. As a birdwatcher, I am delighted that so many of his hybrids were named for birds, so that names like Bittern, Bobwhite, Canary, Catbird, Cedarbird, Chaffinch, and Chukar are sprinkled in with the more ordinary; Elise told me that her father loved birds all his life and at one time thought of being an ornithologist.

The **Grant Mitsch Novelty Daffodils** catalog contains many color photographs, the work of Elise, and includes introductions of the Havens, as well as those of Roberta Watrous and Eileen Frey (Elise Haven's sister), who are both known for their miniatures. They offer about 300 cultivars, many of unusual color, including older cultivars of other hybridizers. Dick Havens retired from teaching, Elise from computer program analysis, to run the daffodil farm; they love living in the country and growing bulbs, and their children come home to help out during school vacations. The nursery is open at bloom time (mid-March to mid-April) so that you can see the varieties and place orders for fall delivery if you like; you should call ahead to see if someone will be there and to ask if the daffodils are in bloom. Hubbard is about twenty miles south of Portland.

Grant Mitsch Novelty Daffodils
P.O. Box 218
Hubbard, OR 97032
Dick and Elise Havens
(503) 651-2742 (evenings)
Catalog: $3d, CAN/OV

■ *Other sources of daffodils are:*

Bundles of Bulbs, Owings Mills, MD
GreenLady Gardens, San Francisco, CA
Mad River Imports, Moretown, VT
McClure & Zimmerman, Friesland, WI
John Scheepers, Inc., Bantam, CT
Van Engelen, Inc., Litchfield, CT

Dahlias

■ If Kalispell, Montana, sounds a bit frigid for a dahlia nursery, it should also encourage northerners to grow dahlias. Bill and Lois McClaren started **Alpen Gardens** in 1979; Bill is a part-time mathematics professor and former dean of students at Flathead Valley Community College; he also works "more than full-time" with dahlias and race-walks in his "spare time."

The McClarens have been active for years in showing dahlias in Montana and eastern Washington, and two of their children are also growing and showing. Bill has hybridized and introduced more than 40 cultivars, including several prizewinners both here and abroad. They also introduce new varieties for other American and foreign hybridizers, so both "show folk" and regular gardeners will find dahlias for their interests. Alpen Gardens grows 750 varieties and offers 370 for sale. Bill and Lois cut and store 45,000 tubers every year!

Visitors are welcome all summer, but bloom time is August through first frost and you can walk through the field then and compare blooms. Bill says there are several sensational gardens to visit in the area, and he'll direct you to them. Kalispell is halfway between Spokane, Washington, and Great Falls on Highway 2.

> **Alpen Gardens**
> 173 Lawrence Lane
> Kalispell, MT 59901
> Bill and Lois McClaren
> (406) 257-2540
> Catalog: Free

■ **Garden Valley Dahlias** in Roseburg, Oregon, is a nursery you can see from way down the road. Bright stripes of color cover a whole field, and you can hardly wait to get out of the car and walk out among the flowers.

Leon Olson is a former government worker who started growing dahlias — well, you know the rest of the story. Some years ago he moved out into the country near Roseburg to have room to grow in quantity and to try his hand at hybridizing in a very competitive field.

I was amazed to hear how many of his hybrids he roots out and throws away because they are too similar to other hybrids, not the right color or size, or he just doesn't like them. He says that he's still looking for a big winner, but he does offer nearly 300 varieties in every size and color. The exceptions are anemones, collarettes, orchids, and singles, which he says are too promiscuous and cause havoc with his selection and breeding efforts. He also grows raspberries and filberts, so the days are pretty full.

Garden Valley Dahlias
406 Lower Garden Valley Road
Roseburg, OR 97470
Leon V. Olson
(503) 673-8521
Catalog: 1 FCS

■ I went to visit **Swan Island Dahlias** in Canby, Oregon, with several busloads of garden writers; you could hear the "ohhhhs!" from the front of the bus before we arrived, and from our high perch, the fields looked like bright bedspreads or rag rugs. We piled off the buses and set off on the path that ran through the fields, notebooks and pencils at the ready.

I put my notebook away pretty quickly. The choice was just overwhelming, and it begins to be difficult for a non–dahlia expert to tell the difference between similar cultivars. They're all here, from huge to tiny, from white to nearly black, in almost every color and within each color, from pale to dark, from shy to brazen, from neat to casual. Many are the varieties hybridized by Ted Gitts, who bought the nursery with his wife, Margaret, in 1944. He's won national and international awards for some of his dahlias. The nursery is now run by Nicholas and Ted Gitts, their sons, but Ted Sr. is still hybridizing. Visitors are welcome from August through first frost; the Gittses have open house and a dahlia show on Labor Day weekend and the following weekend. Canby is twenty miles south of Portland.

Swan Island Dahlias
P.O. Box 700
Canby, OR 97013
Nicholas, Ted, and Margaret Gitts
(503) 266-7711
Catalog: $3d, CAN

■ **Connell's Dahlias** in Tacoma, Washington, offers the introductions of Les Connell and Phil Traaf and other northwestern hybridizers, as well as varieties and new introductions from New Zealand, Australia, Japan, England, and Holland. They grow about 1,000 varieties and list about 450. Les, a former teacher, has won twenty national awards for his hybrids and leads dahlia-oriented garden tours abroad.

Les started the nursery in 1972; he now has three of his sons as partners. They have an annual open house from Wednesday to Monday over Labor Day weekend, but visitors are welcome from mid-August through first frost.

> **Connell's Dahlias**
> 10216 40th Avenue East
> Tacoma, WA 98446
> Les Connell
> (206) 531-0292
> Catalog: $1d, CAN/OV

■ Louis Eckhoff was an electronics technician at Boeing, which may explain why his nursery in Seattle is called **Sea-Tac Gardens,** like the airport. He and his wife, Patti, started as hobbyists and put out their first list in 1979. They specialize in dahlias for gardeners who grow for the the show bench and cut-flower sizes, offering more than 300 blue-ribbon varieties, including about 15 of their own hybrids. Their single-page list gives information in very concise tables, so collectors have to know something about dahlias to make their choices. Visitors are welcome from August through the first frost. The Eckhoffs sell cut flowers at the nursery.

> **Sea-Tac Gardens**
> 20020 Des Moines Memorial Drive
> Seattle, WA 98198
> Louis and Patti Eckhoff
> (206) 824-3846
> Catalog: Long SASE

Daylilies

Daylilies are one of the most popular garden plants, something I didn't really appreciate until I had a large derelict garden to fill and hideous problems with gophers. My friend Jack Romine, formerly the president of the California Horticultural Society (more of him later), gave me about twenty daylilies when he dug and divided his, and from this start about five years ago I now have fine clumps of color throughout the summer, almost without care. I'm not claiming that daylilies are gopher-proof, only that mine survive pretty cheerfully here in the world capital of gopherdom. Snails seem to have a chummy relationship with them but don't seem to do them too much harm; the snails mostly live and hide in the clumps of foliage, which makes them easy to pick off.

Daylilies are in the high-fashion world of garden plants; with so many people working on hybridizing it's natural that certain styles come in, sweep the field, and are elbowed aside by newer innovations. Daylilies come in sizes from large to mini, in a variety of shapes, forms, colors from off-white to dark red or purple, and multicolors. I like them best planted in drifts or groups of harmonious colors, not individually spotted about. The tiny ones are wonderful in pots where you can see them up close. I think they could be used much more in the sort of "grass garden" now so popular, especially the lilies with smaller flowers and narrow leaves.

Because they multiply rapidly, many hobby growers get started in the nursery business by selling their surplus, and nurseries that specialize in daylilies are numerous. I've mentioned nurseries scattered around the country because it's such a pleasure to go and see them growing in the field and to choose them in person. I love the pale yellow ones, but when I go and look I'm always seduced by others that I would have passed over in a catalog.

There may be more intense hybridizing going on in daylilies than with any other plant except iris — the number of new names that have to be thought up each year is staggering! Many of the lists include information of interest to hybridizers; many of the growers grow many hundreds more plants than they list in their catalogs. If you're looking for a daylily cultivar that no one seems to list, it's worth writing to various nurseries to ask if they grow it and will sell it to you.

Daylily nurseries, like iris nurseries, are usually generous with "extras," adding a few treats to your order, usually plants in good supply or those that are no longer in their catalog, and usually their choice.

■ Ron and Cindy Valente of **Valente Gardens** in East Lebanon, Maine, offer about 300 daylilies in their catalog, but also sell Japanese and Siberian iris at the nursery, as well as field-grown perennials. Visitors to the nursery will also see between 1,000 and 2,000 seedling crosses from Ron's hybridizing program. Visitors are welcome on weekends, and the best months are mid-July to mid-August. The nursery is about an hour northwest of Portsmouth, New Hampshire, or forty-five minutes inland from Wells, Maine (which is on coastal Highway 1).

> **Valente Gardens**
> RFD 2, Box 234
> East Lebanon, ME 04027
> Ron and Cindy Valente
> (207) 457-2076
> Catalog: $.50

■ After twenty years as a computer systems programmer, Bob Seawright had to make a choice between computers and daylilies. He said he could do daylilies without computers, but couldn't even imagine doing computers without daylilies, so **Seawright Gardens** came into being. He got interested in daylilies as a twelve-year-old in Mississippi and saved his lawn-mowing money to buy fifty-cent plants.

For the last twelve years it's been just daylilies; he's been hybridizing and leans toward tetraploids that are eyed or have blotched patterns. He also introduced the hybrids of the late Don C. Stevens, including the highly regarded 'Jerusalem'. He offers the hybrids of many other hybridizers, mostly newer varieties; he grows about 700 and lists about 300. In recent years, he's also gotten interested in hostas and is now listing about 200.

Visitors are welcome in July and early August. There's a display garden at 134 Indian Hill and another display at the "selling garden" at 201 Bedford Road. Carlisle is twenty miles west of Boston on the northwestern edge of Concord.

> **Seawright Gardens**
> 134 Indian Hill
> Carlisle, MA 01741

Bob Seawright
(508) 369-2172
Catalog: $1

■ **Tranquil Lake Nursery** in Rehoboth, Massachusetts, grows
more than 4,000 varieties of daylilies and lists about 400. It
also lists about 85 Siberian iris and 30 Japanese iris, but the
owners grow many more at the nursery, as well as some perennials, which they sell only at the nursery. They offer new
introductions by Eleanor and Bill Lachman, Don Marvin, and
other New England hybridizers. There are some restrictions
on shipping overseas, depending on your country's regulations.

Partners Philip Boucher and Warren Leach purchased the
nursery in 1986; they're both trained horticulturists. The display garden looks very attractive, and since Boucher and Leach
are also landscapers, it will give you good ideas on using plants.
Visitors are welcome from May to October. Rehoboth is ten
miles east of Providence, Rhode Island, just off Route 195.

Tranquil Lake Nursery
45 River Street
Rehoboth, MA 02769-1395
Philip Boucher and Warren Leach
(508) 252-4002 or 252-4310
Catalog: $1, CAN/OV

■ Stanley Saxton retired after forty years as a professor of
music at Skidmore College; years ago he started growing daylilies in his cold northern Adirondack garden and admired
their persistence under harsh conditions. He started his **Saxton
Gardens** in Saratoga Springs, New York, in 1940, and now
his son Peter gives him some help in the busy season. He offers
his own hybrids, which he calls the "Adirondack Strain" of
superhardy daylilies; he has registered more than 250 named
cultivars. He grows about 1,000 cultivars at the nursery, and
offers several hundred of his own hybrids and other hardy
cultivars in the catalog, as well as mixed collections for landscaping (no shipments to Texas). Stanley is an active composer
who continues to write and publish music. Saratoga Springs
is about halfway between Albany and Glen Falls. Visitors are
welcome by appointment only.

Saxton Gardens
1 First Street
Saratoga Springs, NY 12866
Stanley Saxton
Catalog: $.50

■ Lee Bristol of **Bloomingfields Farm** in Gaylordsville, Connecticut, was formerly a professor of botany and a plant explorer in tropic regions; in 1969 he became a landscape designer and began searching for long-lived, carefree, and colorful perennials for his designs. He and his wife, Diana, are assisted by their children; they offer about 100 varieties in their catalog but grow several hundred at the nursery. The catalog lists plants by flower color, then by season of bloom, making it easy to choose plants for special effect and long season of bloom. The nursery is open to visitors Wednesday through Sunday from June through August. Gaylordsville is near Danbury and the New York state line.

> **Bloomingfields Farm**
> Route 55
> Gaylordsville, CT 06755-0005
> Lee Bristol
> (203) 354-6951
> Catalog: Free

■ Clayton Burkey of **Hickory Hill Gardens** in Loretto, Pennsylvania, grows about 1,000 cultivars of daylily and lists between 400 and 600 from many hybridizers in his catalog at any one time. He also offers hostas; peonies; and tall bearded, Siberian, and spuria iris at the nursery.

Clayton and his wife are both music teachers and raise canaries and budgies for the pet market, so visitors are welcome at the nursery by appointment only. The best season is mid-July to mid-August; Loretto is about 90 miles southeast of Pittsburgh between Altoona and Johnstown.

> **Hickory Hill Gardens**
> RD 1, Box 11
> Loretto, PA 15940
> Clayton Burkey
> (814) 886-2823
> Catalog: $2.50, CAN

■ **Jernigan Gardens in** Dunn, North Carolina, offers hundreds of old and new varieties of daylilies and about 200 hostas. Bettie Jernigan has lived all her life in the same house; the property came into her family generations ago by land grant. By the time she was four or five she was collecting flowering plants and weeds for her own little garden. She loves having visitors; her catalog says "you-all come!" You can come every day; she's closed from noon to three, and opens at three on

Sunday. No daylily sales on Sunday, but you can buy hostas in pots. The best bloom time is mid-April to early July. Dunn is about thirty-five miles south of Raleigh, near Interstates 40 and 95.

> **Jernigan Gardens**
> Route 6, Box 593
> Dunn, NC 28334
> Bettie Jernigan
> (919) 567-2135
> Catalog: $1

■ Bill Munson, an architect, started **Wimberlyway Gardens** in Gainesville, Florida, and has become one of the best-known daylily hybridizers in the country. Bill is the author of *Hemerocallis: The Daylily* (Timber Press, 1989). The offerings are mostly his own introductions and those of his sister Betty Hudson Salter, who hybridizes doubles, and her daughter Elizabeth Salter; at any one time they're growing 40,000 seedlings to evaluate. The garden looks lovely. Visitors are asked to call before coming. The best months to visit are May through July.

> **Wimberlyway Gardens**
> 7024 N.W. Eighteenth Avenue
> Gainesville, FL 32605-3237
> R. W. Munson, Jr.
> (904) 331-4922
> Catalog: $3

■ David Kirchhoff and Morton Morss of **Daylily World** in Sanford, Florida, have registered and introduced more than 150 cultivars, many of which have been winners of major awards. They are working on many others, testing between 2,000 and 3,000 seedlings a year to select a few to develop further. Kirchhoff has introduced a number of double varieties, and Morss specializes in eyed varieties.

David Kirchhoff is a fourth-generation horticulturist; he was a musician before coming back to Florida to join his father in growing daylilies. They offer hundreds of cultivars in their catalog and welcome visitors to their display area. The best season is May to mid-June. The nursery is about twenty miles north of Orlando.

> **Daylily World**
> P.O. Box 1612
> Sanford, FL 32772-1612

David Kirchhoff
(407) 322-4034
Catalog: $2, CAN/OV

■ Pat and Grace Stamile have recently moved their **Floyd Cove Nursery** from New York State to Sanford, Florida, which seems to be a very active state for daylily growers; Pat also likes to fish, which is possible all year in Florida. The Stamiles offer newer varieties of daylilies, including their own and those of George Rasmussen of New York, and other hybridizers; as with others, the newest introductions are quite expensive, but eager daylily breeders are always looking for new stock (the catalog indicates which ones are good for crosses).

Many of Pat's hybrids seem to have prominent eyes, which I think is very attractive; he says that most hybridizers are aiming toward an ideal daylily which reblooms, has lots of branches and buds, and will go on blooming for ten weeks! Visitors are welcome from April to June if they call ahead; Sanford is about forty-five minutes north of Orlando, and Floyd Cove is fairly close to Daylily World if you want to visit both on the same day.

Floyd Cove Nursery
725 Longwood-Markham Road
Sanford, FL 32771
Patrick M. Stamile
(407) 324-9229
Catalog: $3d

■ **Oakes Daylilies** in Corryton, Tennessee, offers about 500 daylily cultivars in its catalog — of the 3,000 named cultivars grown at the nursery. The Oakeses grow a complete collection of the award-winning daylilies of the American Hemerocallis Society, have an extensive collection of spider variant–type daylilies, and also grow a historic collection of older hybrids and the species daylilies from which modern hybrids come.

Started in 1978 by William Oakes and his son Stewart, the nursery is now run by Stewart and his son Ken. The Oakeses have a farm background; the daylilies were originally a hobby that "got out of hand." Stewart says they try to offer the best of all types; plants are available in all price ranges. Oakes Daylilies has an official American Hemerocallis Society display garden and welcomes visitors on Friday and Saturday from mid-June to mid-July or by appointment. Corryton is near Knoxville in eastern Tennessee.

Oakes Daylilies
8204 Monday Road
Corryton, TN 37721
Stewart Oakes
(615) 689-3036 or 687-1268
Catalog: $2

■ **Sunnyridge Gardens,** about four miles east of Knoxville, Tennessee, grows more than 3,000 daylilies and offers more than 1,000 cultivars in its catalog, including spider variants and older varieties. They also grow more than 1,500 iris, and offer about 200 iris, including bearded of all sizes, species iris and species hybrids, Japanese and Siberian iris. It all started when John Couturier offered to help his wife with her hobby in 1984 . . .

This is a good source of older, less expensive cultivars of both daylilies and iris. Sunnyridge is an official display garden for both the American Hemerocallis Society and the Historical Iris Preservation Society. Visitors to the garden will also enjoy the old garden roses, which are not for sale. Call ahead for directions. The best months are May for iris and the last two weeks of June for daylilies.

Sunnyridge Gardens
1724 Drinnen Road
Knoxville, TN 37914
John B. Couturier
(615) 933-0723
Catalog: $1

■ **Pinecliffe Daylily Gardens** in Floyds Knob, Indiana, is run by Don and Kathy Smith. Don is an international consultant, teaching people how to prepare for computer disasters. But he and Kathy are also active hybridizers who've introduced a number of daylilies and won prizes; Don's trying for a blue daylily. They also introduce the hybrids of Wallace Gould of Ojai, California, who's working on reblooming tetraploids with lots of branching and bloom.

In addition to the 1,500 cultivars the Smiths grow, they have about 30,000 seedlings being grown for evaluation and possible introduction; all this started when Kathy wanted a few daylilies to plant around a pool. Most of their offerings are recent hybrids, reflected in the price. They also sell hostas (nearly 300 cultivars) at the nursery. Visitors are welcome by appointment; the best months are late June to mid-August. Floyds Knob is a suburb of Louisville, Kentucky, about six miles north of the Ohio River.

Pinecliffe Daylily Gardens
6604 Scottsville Road
Floyds Knob, IN 47119
Donald and Kathy Smith
(812) 923-8113
Catalog: $1

■ Philipp Brockington is a law professor at Valparaiso University, the perfect job for him because it leaves his summers free for working at his daylily nursery, **Coburg Planting Fields.** He and his partner, Howard Reeve, grow about 700 cultivars at the nursery and offer about 500, specializing in spider forms and pink colors. They have a lovely garden, and visitors are welcome to drop by in July; please call ahead at other times. Valparaiso is in northwestern Indiana, about an hour from Chicago.

Coburg Planting Fields
573 East 600 North
Valparaiso, IN 46383
Philipp Brockington and Howard Reeve, Jr.
(219) 462-4288
Catalog: Free, CAN

■ Mary Herrema and her husband, Ken, run **Englerth Gardens** in Hopkins, Michigan, which Mary's parents, Larry and Winifred Englerth, started in 1931; now the Herremas' two children and three grandchildren are also involved in the business. They grow about 2,000 varieties of daylily, offering several hundred in their catalog; most are older varieties, which sell at very reasonable prices, and the nursery has a bargain corner for plants to fill up borders. They also grow about 500 varieties of hosta and offer several hundred cultivars in the catalog.

The Herremas have a display garden and welcome visitors Monday through midafternoon on Saturday; the best months are June through August. The nursery is closed from September through March. Hopkins is halfway between Grand Rapids and Kalamazoo in southwestern Michigan, an easy drive from Chicago.

Englerth Gardens
2461 Twenty-second Street
Hopkins, MI 49328
Mary Englerth Herrema
(616) 793-7196
Catalog: $.50

■ **Gilbert H. Wild & Son** in Sarcoxie, Missouri, was founded in 1885 and has been famous for daylilies, peonies, and iris. In 1991 Greg Jones and John Huitsing bought the nursery from the grandchildren of the founder; Greg had been doing propagation and production for other nurseries for years. Gene Wild is still hybridizing daylilies for the nursery, and Greg is starting to hybridize peonies under the tutelage of Jim Wild.

Wild's offers a very large selection of daylilies in a color catalog, with many herbaceous peonies as well. By 1994, the nursery hopes to offer iris again, after selling its iris collection some years ago. Visitors are welcome to come to the display gardens Monday through Saturday; the best months are April to mid-July. Sarcoxie is 140 miles south of Kansas City and 20 miles east of Joplin.

> **Gilbert H. Wild & Son, Inc.**
> P.O. Box 338
> Sarcoxie, MO 64862-0338
> Greg Jones and John Huitsing
> (417) 848-3514
> Catalog: $2d

■ **Cordon Bleu Farms** in San Marcos, California, specializes in the newest and best varieties of daylilies from many hybridizers, which means that its prices reflect the relative scarcity of the plants; most of the cultivars seem to have been introduced in the last five or six years. This is not the place to look for older varieties to fill broad sweeps but for new cultivars to show or a special specimen to feature in a border.

Run by Bob Brooks, Ray Chesnik, and Steve Brigham, Cordon Bleu also offers new varieties of spuria and Louisiana iris. Janice Chesnick and Bob Brooks have won awards for their daylily hybrids, which are offered in the catalog. Visitors are welcome to visit their retail nursery, called Buena Creek Nursery, open Wednesday through Saturday; there they offer perennials, drought-tolerant plants, unusual subtropicals, and of course, daylilies. San Marcos is between Vista and Escondido, northeast of San Diego.

> **Cordon Bleu Farms**
> P.O. Box 2033
> San Marcos, CA 92079-2033
> Bob Brooks, Ray Chesnik, and Steve Brigham
> Catalog: $1, CAN/OV

■ Linda Moore of **Ramona Gardens** in Ramona, California, has two horticultural passions and one madness: daylilies, iris, and black Arabian horses. She raises 300 daylily cultivars of all types, 200 cultivars of tall bearded iris, and has 19 horses. Visitors are welcome during bloom time, May for the iris and mid-June for the daylilies, but should always call ahead for directions and to be sure someone will be there. Ramona is in San Diego County, east of Escondido on Highway 78.

> **Ramona Gardens**
> 2178 El Paso Street
> Ramona, CA 92065
> Linda Moore
> (619) 789-6099
> Catalog: $1

■ **Greenwood Daylily Gardens** is a recent mover, from Santa Barbara to Whittier and then to Long Beach in southern California. John Schoustra is a landscape architect who found that daylilies were great landscape plants in southern California and bought Jane and Ken Taylor's daylily nursery in Santa Barbara and moved all the plants; at present Schoustra is growing about 1,500 cultivars at the growing grounds and lists about 700 varieties in his catalog.

Greenwood has a display garden at the Pacific View Nursery at 698 Studebaker Road in East Long Beach and holds daylily open houses there on the first and third Saturday of the month except in December and January. It has occasional open houses at the growing grounds in Riverside, which is the California test site for the All-American Daylily Selection Council; call for dates and directions.

> **Greenwood Daylily Gardens**
> 5595 East Seventh Street, No. 490
> Long Beach, CA 90804
> John Schoustra
> (310) 494-8944
> FAX 494-0486
> Catalog: $5d, CAN/OV

■ Now back to Jack Romine of **The Pollen Bank** in Walnut Creek, California, who gave me my first daylilies. These have been divided, and I've bought more since, but thanks to Jack I now see the great value of a plant I'd only thought of as a space filler. Jack is mainly a hybridizer of tetraploid daylilies and small-flowered and miniature varieties. He offers dozens of tetraploid conversions, especially for the use of other hybridizers; his list often gives information for their use in hybridizing. He also offers about 100 currently popular and new daylily cultivars.

Jack has also hybridized dianthus, tulips, daffodils, and iris, written more than a dozen college English textbooks, and since retiring from teaching has written two novels and a collection of short stories. Visitors are welcome but should call ahead for directions and to be sure someone will be there. Walnut Creek is about forty-five minutes east of San Francisco.

> **The Pollen Bank**
> 2065 Walnut Boulevard
> Walnut Creek, CA 94596
> Jack S. Romine
> (510) 939-7744
> Catalog: Long SASE

■ My neighborhood daylily grower is **Alpine Valley Gardens** in the mountains behind Santa Rosa. Wilbur Sloat is a minister, a psychologist, and a soil scientist, who, with his wife, Dorothy, grows about 500 daylilies on their ranch, a wonderful sight in early summer when the fields are in bloom. It's a dangerous but exhilarating thing to follow Dorothy with her digging fork through the field — I'm easily seduced by a pretty bloom. Most of these are offered in the catalog and cover a range of rareness and prices. The Sloats also offer several collections by color range and one of small-flowered varieties. Visitors are welcome daily during bloom time, which is June and July; the garden is an official AHS Display Garden. The nursery is on the road from Santa Rosa to Calistoga; it's about an hour and a half from the San Francisco Bay area.

> **Alpine Valley Gardens**
> 2627 Calistoga Road
> Santa Rosa, CA 95404
> Wilbur and Dorothy Sloat
> (707) 539-1749
> Catalog: Long SASE, CAN

■ *Other sources of daylilies are:*

A & D Peony and Perennial Farm, Snohomish, WA
Adamgrove, California, MO
Busse Gardens, Cokato, MN

Caprice Farm, Sherwood, OR
Garden Perennials, Wayne, NE
Dr. Joseph C. Halinar, Scotts Mills, OR
Klehm Nursery, South Barrington, IL
Louisiana Nursery, Opelousas, LA
Mary's Plant Farm, Hamilton, OH
Nicholls Gardens, Gainesville, VA
Powell's Gardens, Princeton, NC
Savory's Gardens, Inc., Edina, MN
Thomasville Nurseries, Thomasville, GA
Andre Viette Farm & Nursery, Fishersville, VA

Ferns

Ferns should be part of every garden! There, the oracle has spoken! But surely, there's hardly a garden in America, except perhaps in the desert Southwest, which wouldn't be improved by a fern, and some woodland or shady patio gardens couldn't exist without them. Ferns are able to convey a sense of lushness and greenness beyond the capability of many plants; a few ferns in pots can transform a room or a deck into a tranquil retreat. Ferns offer such a variety of foliage types that there are plants for every effect.

■ **Varga's Nursery** in Warrington, Pennsylvania, is a big wholesaler of hardy and tropical ferns, which also sells many plants to gardeners. Barbara Varga is a former electrical engineer who got interested in plants through college botany courses; she's been growing ferns for twenty years and is propagating unusual ferns through tissue culture. She offers more than 250 varieties, both hardy and tender, and provides a list of fern references to help you decide. Visitors must call for an appointment. The nursery is about twenty miles north of Philadelphia.

> **Varga's Nursery**
> 2631 Pickertown Road
> Warrington, PA 18976
> Barbara L. Varga
> (215) 343-0646
> Catalog: $1, CAN/OV, bn

■ For tropical and subtropical climates, **Skula's Nursery** in Miami, Florida, offers ferns that need temperatures above fifty degrees Fahrenheit to thrive; of course, they'll do well in a greenhouse, too.

Frank and Dorothy Skula are not commercial growers but collectors who propagate from their collection of about 150 species and varieties, and supplies are usually fairly limited. Among those offered are aglaomorpha, davallia, drynaria, humata, microsorium, polypodiums, pyrrosia, and scyphularia.

These come from tropical zones all over the world: Malaya, Australia, India, the Philippines, Sumatra, New Guinea, and Polynesia. (Looking at the list is like thumbing through a stack of old *National Geographics*!) The Skulas also offer other tropicals, including a good selection of platyceriums, some aroids, and anthruiums. Visitors must call for an appointment and directions.

Skula's Nursery
130 N.W. 192 Street
Miami, FL 33169
Frank and Dorothy Skula
(305) 652-3955
Catalog: Long SASE, bn

■ Judith Jones of **Fancy Fronds** got into ferns when she needed to create a garden around her restored craftsman bungalow in Seattle, Washington; with a major in children's theater and interests in antiques, baroque music, and eighteenth- and nineteenth-century literature, Judith would seem an unlikely nurseryperson, but people come to gardening from every direction. She says that she grew up in Yuma, Arizona, the absolute opposite of green and rainy Washington, and that her mother grew many kinds of desert plants.

Judith first got interested in Victorian hardy ferns for her own garden, then began to collect others and got into propagation from spores and vegetative division. She offers Victorian-named forms, Japanese species ferns, and a few Xeric (dry-land) species from Arizona, Mexico, South America, and South Africa, which, like alpine plants, cannot stand winter wet.

Known as a lively speaker at plant symposia and for her infectious laugh, Judith is planning a book on landscaping with ferns. There are display gardens at the nursery (called Barfod's Hardy Ferns), which is in Bothell, northeast of Seattle. Visitors should call for directions and hours.

Fancy Fronds
1911 Fourth Avenue West
Seattle, WA 98119
Judith I. Jones
(206) 284-5332
Catalog: $1d, CAN, bn/cn

■ Sue Olsen of **Foliage Gardens** in Bellevue is another Washingtonian who wanted to grow ferns in her woods and around her rhododendrons. When she could find only wild collected

Eastern species in catalogs, she tried her luck with spore and got 300 progeny on her first try. Sue says her recently retired husband has been a great help, having just built a shade structure out of surplus materials from a Boeing 737. She says it's not certified for flight!

In her color catalog, Sue offers about 100 species, varieties, and cultivars of ferns, including some silvery ones for sunny spots and a number of Japanese evergreen ferns that are quite cold hardy; all are grown from spore. The nursery is east of Seattle, and visitors should call for an appointment.

> **Foliage Gardens**
> 2003 128th Avenue S.E.
> Bellevue, WA 98005
> Sue Olsen
> (206) 747-2998
> Catalog: $2, bn

■ *Other sources of ferns are:*

Kurt Bluemel, Inc., Baldwin, MD
Carroll Gardens, Westminster, MD
Coastal Gardens & Nursery, Myrtle Beach, SC
Forestfarm, Williams, OR
Limerock Ornamental Grasses, Port Matilda, PA
Mary's Plant Farm, Hamilton, OH
Orchid Gardens, Andover, MN
Roslyn Nursery, Dix Hills, NY
Squaw Mountain Gardens, Estacada, OR
Sunlight Gardens, Andersonville, TN
Wildginger Woodlands, Webster, NY
Woodlanders, Inc., Aiken, SC

Geraniums:
Tender

Hardy they certainly aren't, but garden-worthy, yes! They almost define the summer planter, tub, or window box, and many people buy them year after year like annuals, instead of taking them indoors for the winter. Plant breeders are always working on new hybrids that will grow from seed; hobbyists are working on them, and the choices are almost overwhelming. These geraniums come in many sizes, flower and leaf patterns, colors, flower types, and, of course, scents. Please note that many of the nurseries in the "Herbs" section also sell scented geraniums.

Lest there be any confusion, let me hasten to add that these plants are called "geraniums" by most of us, but they are actually pelargoniums. Plantsmen usually refer to true geraniums as "hardy geraniums" or "species geraniums." Some of these nurseries also list species geraniums; you will find good selections of species or hardy geraniums from nurseries in the "Perennials and Vines" and "Rock Garden and Alpine Plants" sections.

■ Barbara Wilson and Marilyn Davidson of **Davidson-Wilson Greenhouses** in Crawfordsville, Indiana, offer about 300 varieties of geraniums of all types in their catalog of exotic houseplants; there are some restrictions on shipments to California.

Barbara's family has been in the greenhouse business since 1919, and though she's a former music teacher, she says she has greenhouse in her blood. Marilyn was a physical education teacher who went to work for Wilson Brothers; the women formed their own business in 1980. Bully for them, their business has been growing steadily, and all of the employees are women.

Visitors are welcome Monday to Saturday all year at the nursery, and Sunday afternoons in April through June. Davidson-Wilson also sells perennials, bedding plants, herbs, and houseplants at the nursery. Crawfordsville is forty miles west of Indianapolis, south of Lafayette, near Highway 231.

Davidson-Wilson Greenhouses
RR 2, Box 168
Crawfordsville, IN 47933-9423
Barbara Wilson and Marilyn Davidson
(317) 364-0556
Catalog: $2

■ **Shady Hill Gardens** in Batavia, Illinois, grows and lists a huge selection of geraniums, more than 1,100 varieties of every type; Chuck Heidgen says that he and his two sons work eight days a week, twenty-six hours a day, and it must almost be true. They offer every type of geranium, all of which are included in their color catalog. In his "spare time" (the ninth day of the week?), Chuck's hobby is growing fruit and nut trees, and trying his hand at training espaliers. Visitors can come to the one-and-a-half-acre greenhouse and buy plants; the best months are April and May. Batavia is thirty-five miles west of Chicago, just north of Aurora.

Shady Hill Gardens
821 Walnut Street
Batavia, IL 60510-2999
Chuck and Mary Ellen Heidgen
Catalog: $2d, CAN, bn

■ I don't quite know where to slip in **Color Farm** in Auburndale, Florida. Vern Ogren specializes in old-fashioned coleus, tender plants usually treated as annuals. He was introduced to them by his mother and remembers being fascinated by their fantastic colors when he was a child. Like geraniums, these plants are popular for bedding out and for planting in mixed planters, and they can be grown from cuttings and taken indoors during the winter. Vern has done some hybridizing and introduced a number of cultivars, but he also searches for and offers heirloom varieties to keep them from disappearing. These plants are great for historical garden restorations, especially in warmer climates. Mail order only.

Color Farm
2701 Thornhill Road
Auburndale, FL 33823

Vern Ogren
(813) 967-9895
Catalog: $.50

■ *Another source of geraniums is:*

Rabbit Shadow Farm, Loveland, CO

Grasses: Ornamental

Grasses have been riding high over the last few years, proclaimed as the backbone of the "new American garden" and an important component of "natural" gardens and prairie restorations. I feel that there's no one answer for all garden situations or one magic plant that everyone must use, but there are many beautiful grasses that gardeners should use more, and that look terrific mixed with other plants.

■ Norm Hooven of **Limerock Ornamental Grasses** in Port Matilda, Pennsylvania, got interested in grasses when he did work for an advanced degree using wheat and wild rye grasses as germ plasm in a hybridizing program, then worked to improve native grasses for strip mine reclamation in Wyoming and the intermountain West. He started his nursery in 1980, and now his parents, wife Phyllis, and children all help him. He offers more than 100 varieties for sale, as well as fall-blooming perennials as companion plants and some hardy ferns and bamboos. Visitors are welcome Monday through Saturday; call ahead if possible. Port Matilda is nine miles west of State College in central Pennsylvania.

> **Limerock Ornamental Grasses**
> RD 1, Box 111C
> Port Matilda, PA 16870
> Norman Hooven III
> (814) 692-2272
> Catalog: $2.50, CAN/OV, bn/cn

■ One of the first nurseries to specialize in grasses was **Kurt Bluemel, Inc.** in Baldwin, Maryland, which offers a huge selection: hundreds of grasses, sedges, and rushes, including many German cultivars (the Germans have been using grasses in gardens for much longer than we have). Kurt Bluemel also offers a good selection of perennials, such as Japanese anenomes, astilbes, daylilies, hostas, Siberian iris, monardas, Oriental poppies from the collection of the Countess von Zeppelin in Germany, phlox, sedums, and verbascums, as well as some bamboos, aquatic plants, and hardy ferns.

The nursery is thirteen miles north of the Baltimore Beltway, has extensive display gardens, and will give group tours. If you don't have a group to visit with, call and ask if you can join another group scheduled for a tour. Plants are sold by mail order only; there are restrictions on orders to California, Oregon, and Washington.

Kurt Bluemel, Inc.
2740 Greene Lane
Baldwin, MD 21013-9523
Kurt Bluemel
(301) 557-7229
Catalog: $2, CAN/OV, bn/cn

■ John Greenlee of Pomona, California, has been trumpeting the virtues of ornamental grasses up and down the "Left Coast" for years. Begun on a shoestring, John's nursery has apparently taken over most of the back yards in his neighborhood.

The **Greenlee Nursery**'s descriptive list is impressive and gives the performance of about 150 varieties under western growing conditions, with lists of suggested plants for various uses. John is the author of the *Encyclopedia of Ornamental Grasses* (Rodale Press). He can't ship plants to Hawaii.

Visitors must call ahead for an appointment (Monday to Friday only); John is a busy landscaper, and it's hard to find him at the nursery unless he expects you. There's a half-acre display garden. Pomona is about twenty miles east of central Los Angeles.

Greenlee Nursery
301 E. Franklin Avenue
Pomona, CA 91766
John Greenlee
(714) 629-9045
Catalog: $5, CAN, bn
Price list free.

■ *Other sources of ornamental grasses are:*

Carroll Gardens, Westminster, MD
Crownsville Nursery, Crownsville, MD

Donaroma's Nursery, Edgartown, MA
Forestfarm, Williams, OR
Garden Place, Mentor, OH
Heronswood Nursery, Kingston, WA
Louisiana Nursery, Opelousas, LA
Milaeger's Gardens, Racine, WI
Robyn's Nest Nursery, Vancouver, WA
Woodlanders, Inc., Aiken, SC

Ground Covers

Many of the nurseries in this book sell plants that can be used as ground covers (hostas and daylilies, for instance), and yet they are not specialists in ground covers. The nurseries lumped together here specialize in plants *used* for ground cover — but hark! These are not just rugs to cover an ugly floor. They're attractive plants in their own right and should be chosen as carefully as any other plant.

■ **Rock Spray Nursery** in Truro, Massachusetts, specializes in heaths and heathers, cultivars that are hardy to USDA Zone 5 + and that do well on sandy Cape Cod and any other regions that offer them good drainage and a soil on the acidic side. They offer more than 50 *Calluna vulgaris* cultivars and about 25 species and cultivars of erica.

Betsy Erickson and Kate Herrick started the nursery in 1980 and have a display garden at the nursery on Depot Road. Visitors are welcome daily from March to October; the plants are at their best in spring and summer. Truro is on Cape Cod, about two hours southeast of Boston. For stress reduction, Betsy and Kate jump on their horses and ride on the beach.

Rock Spray Nursery
P.O. Box 693
Truro, MA 02666
Betsy Erickson and Kate Herrick
(508) 349-6769
Catalog: Free, bn

■ **Peekskill Nurseries** in Shrub Oak, New York, offers green and variegated pachysandra, both *Vinca minor* 'Bowles' variety and alba, euonymus, Baltic ivy, and 'Bar Harbor' and 'Blue Rug' juniper; all are available in quantity. These are essentially cast-iron plants that can be used anywhere in the country except the Deep South. Proprietor Gary Lundquist's father started the nursery in 1937 in Peekskill and decided to keep the name when they moved. Plants are not sold at the nursery, but you can order your plants ahead and pick them up there. Shrub Oak is fifteen miles southeast of West Point in the Hudson River valley and forty miles north of New York City.

> **Peekskill Nurseries**
> Shrub Oak, NY 10588
> Gary Lundquist
> (914) 245-5595
> Catalog: Free

■ **Prentiss Court Ground Covers** in Greenville, South Carolina, offers a number of traditional ground cover plants: ivies, liriope, euonymus, hostas, pachysandra, daylilies, and vinca — a good variety in quantities from 50 plants up.

Gene Dickson decided that home gardeners ought to be able to buy ground covers in smaller containers than one-gallon cans, which can get very expensive. Gene and his wife, Lesesne, say they wish they had a more engaging story to tell: "Ours is a real family business, small and joyfully uncomplicated." What could be more engaging?

Gene was formerly head of an advertising agency and still does consulting; he's always loved plants and grows Japanese maples as a hobby. At one time he tried growing trees in a stony field in the mountains of North Carolina "in partnership with God." He quit when he decided that he was doing most of the work and God wasn't holding up his end of the bargain. For fun, the Dicksons travel, hike, fish, make wine, read, cook, and ride bikes, or work at their "kitchen table office." Mail order only.

> **Prentiss Court Ground Covers**
> P.O. Box 8662
> Greenville, SC 29604
> Lesesne and Gene Dickson
> (803) 277-4037
> Catalog: $.25, bn

■ **Ivies of the World** of Weirsdale, Florida, is a nursery that has changed owners, names, and locations several times since it was called the Alestake and was located in Virginia. Tim and Judy Rankin are busy wholesale-fern growers for the florist trade. They bought the ivy business in 1986 and now offer more than 200 varieties of ivies, including English, Japanese, Persian, Nepalese, and Algerian ivy cultivars. Their catalog gives good information on each variety, and if they don't have what you want in stock, they propagate to order. Of course, not all of these are suitable for ground cover or even outdoor growing, but many are ideal. They sell by mail order only.

Ivies of the World
P.O. Box 408
Weirsdale, FL 32195
Tim and Judy Rankin
(904) 821-2201 or 2322
Catalog: $2, CAN/OV, bn

GILSON GARDENS *Artist: Pam Bode*

■ The Gilson family of Perry, Ohio, started their nursery in 1947 and gradually found themselves specializing in plants for ground cover. They offer ivies, pachysandra, vinca, junipers, hostas, euonymus, sedums, and many others, including some perennials, vines, and small shrubs that grow up to four feet. The **Gilson Gardens** catalog gives good descriptions and cultural information; you can buy from one plant to a zillion. Their retail nursery is open daily from March to Christmas. Perry is thirty-five miles east of Cleveland.

Gilson Gardens
P.O. Box 277
Perry, OH 44081
The Gilson Family
(216) 259-2378
Catalog: Free, bn/cn

GILSON GARDENS
Artist: Pam Bode

■ I arrived at **Heaths and Heathers** in Elma, Washington, not quite expecting to find such a big nursery. Alice Knight quit her job as sales promotion manager at a large department store when her daughter Cindy came along, then started growing heathers, first for fun and then as a sideline. One thing led to another and soon the Knights had a big wholesale heather business. In 1982 they began to sell by mail order as well, and that part of the business is their favorite. Now Bob, Alice, and Cindy Knight all work at the nursery; Cindy also has a stand at the nursery in spring, selling vegetable plants.

Heaths and Heathers offers 24 species and nearly 400 cultivars of callunas, ericas, daboecias, and a few related species like bruckenthalia and hardy tree heaths. Alice is a tireless promoter of heaths and heathers; in the office she has a file of articles about heather gardens, all wonderful.

You've probably seen photographs of the conifer and heather garden of Adrian Bloom at Bressingham Gardens in England. It gives an idea of the variety of color in both flower and foliage which makes heaths and heathers fun to use in a garden. I, of course, succumbed to their charm and bought a few plants to give my garden some winter interest; I'm not extravagant — I just spend my discretionary income on plants instead of clothes or entertainment.

Visitors are welcome at the nursery by appointment; there's a small display garden and many plants in pots. Elma is thirty miles west of Olympia.

Heaths and Heathers
P.O. Box 850
Elma, WA 98541
Bob, Alice, and Cindy Knight
(206) 482-3258
Catalog: Long SASE, CAN, bn

■ *Other sources of plants used for ground cover are:*

The Cummins Garden, Marlboro, NJ
Garden Place, Mentor, OH
Hartmann's Plantation, Grand Junction, MI
Joyce's Garden, Bend, OR
Roslyn Nursery, Dix Hills, NY
Squaw Mountain Gardens, Estacada, OR
Tripple Brook Farm, Southampton, MA
Whitney Gardens, Brinnon, WA

■ *Other sources of ivy are:*

Mary's Plant Farm, Hamilton, OH
Merry Gardens, Camden, ME
Squaw Mountain Gardens, Estacada, OR
Sunnybrook Farms Nursery, Chesterland, OH

■ *Other sources of heaths and heathers are:*

The Cummins Garden, Marlboro, NJ
Roslyn Nursery, Dix Hills, NY
Squaw Mountain Gardens, Estacada, OR

Herbs

Herbs are one of the most popular plant groups in the whole world, it seems, yet one of the slipperiest also. Some people see herbs only as culinary plants, others as medicinal plants, others as plants to be grown only in special gardens full of history and lore and sometimes a little too precious for words. I think most gardeners use herbs as ornamental garden plants, and like all plants, some are better than others; just having a quaint historical name doesn't make a good plant!

In choosing specialist herb nurseries, I decided to leave out the nurseries that emphasize herb products as much as they do herb plants; there are many of these, and many offer decent selections of plants, but this book is a plant book. Of course, many of the plants listed by the perennial nurseries are called herbs by some gardeners and perennials by others.

■ **Merry Gardens** in Camden, Maine, lists more than 200 herbs and 125 ivies and also issues an extensive list of greenhouse and house plants. Ervin and Mary Ellen Ross have been in the herb business more than forty-five years; they are the founders of Merryspring Nature Park in Camden. Mary Ellen also writes a garden column and has been a 4-H leader. There is a large display garden at the nursery which is open Monday to Saturday all year. Camden is on the "midcoast" of Maine, about two hours north of Portland.

> **Merry Gardens**
> P.O. Box 595
> Camden, ME 04843
> Mary Ellen Ross
> (207) 236-9064
> Catalog: $1, CAN, bn/cn

■ **Tinmouth Channel Farm** in Tinmouth, Vermont, offers certified organically grown herbs and scented geraniums, which means, I suppose, that many of the herbs are grown for cooking, but of course, these are also good ornamental garden plants. The nursery offers about 100 varieties, with good selections of basils, thymes, and scented geraniums.

Tinmouth Channel is not a coastal inlet but an extended bog and stream known for its rare plants, which are protected by the state. Carolyn Fuhrer and Kathleen Duhnoski both grew up on Long Island farms but sought an area with more space and fewer people. Visitors are welcome at the nursery and display garden on Friday and Saturday, May through October. The nursery is about fifteen miles south of Rutland.

Tinmouth Channel Farm
RR 1, Box 428B
Tinmouth, VT 05773
Carolyn Fuhrer and Kathleen Duhnoski
(802) 446-2812
Catalog: $2, cn/bn

■ For years I thought that Well-Sweep Herb Farm was called Well-Swept Herb Farm and that it was a traditional name based on herb gardens tended by fanatical colonial housewives — who else would sweep their gardens? Dyslexics of the world, untie! I finally realized my error when I studied the picture of the old-fashioned water-drawing mechanism on the catalog cover.

Cyrus Hyde's **Well-Sweep Herb Farm** in Port Murray, New Jersey, has a traditional herb garden, beautifully laid out with brick paths (and they look well swept) and a huge selection of herb plants; in fact, the word *fanatic* might apply to Cyrus's passion for plant collecting. Among the larger selections are alliums, artemisias, basils, scented geraniums, lavenders, mints, origanums, rosemaries, rues, salvias, thymes, violas, and yarrows, and many more. In his spare time, Cyrus raises Japanese Nagadori show chickens, famous for their very long tails; in Japan they're never allowed off their perches. The whole layout sounds like pure poultry in motion!

Visitors are welcome Monday through Saturday from April through December. Well-Sweep doesn't ship to California, Oregon, or Washington. The nursery is about an hour from New York near Hackettstown.

Well-Sweep Herb Farm
317 Mt. Bethel Road
Port Murray, NJ 07865
Louise and Cyrus Hyde
(908) 852-5390
Catalog: $2, cn/bn

■ Flo and John Hackimer found themselves in the nursery business after the death of their son Keyth. They knew almost nothing about herbs and had to learn a lot in a hurry, but over the years they have become real nurseryfolk with a very good selection of herbs and other garden perennials. Flo has become particularly fond of sedums because they're tough and provide a long season of bloom in adverse conditions.

Their **Wrenwood of Berkeley Springs** is located in Wrenwood, West Virginia (on Pious Ridge Road, perfect for an herb garden). They have developed a display garden to show the mature plants in the ground. Visitors are welcome from Wednesday to Sunday; spring and summer are the best seasons to visit. The nursery is located about two hours from northern Virginia, Washington, D.C., and Pittsburgh.

> **Wrenwood of Berkeley Springs**
> Route 4, Box 361
> Berkeley Springs, WV 25411
> Flora and John Hackimer
> (304) 258-3071
> Catalog: $2, bn/cn

■ **Edgewood Farm & Nursery** in Stanardsville, Virginia, is another herb nursery that grows a huge selection of herbs — more than 500 varieties, including 50 cultivars of thyme, 30 cultivars of rosemary, more than 30 oreganos, and 40 scented geraniums. Partner Norman Schwartz took his interest in gardening with him all over the world when he served in the air force; he and his wife, Eleanor, operate a bed and breakfast on the same property in the foothills of the Blue Ridge Mountains. Partner Robert Cary started as a vegetable gardener, grew a few herbs for flavoring, began collecting herbs . . .

Norman also has a collection of species iris and now grows more than 75 species. He and Robert Cary also collect and offer more than 30 cultivars of dianthus, including many historic cultivars. Not all of these plants are listed in the catalog, nor are the hundreds of perennials they sell at the nursery, but it certainly would be worth inquiring about cultivars on your want-list. Edgewood has a display garden and welcomes visitors Monday to Saturday and Sunday afternoon; the best months to visit are April through September. The nursery is located near Route 33, about twenty-five miles north of Charlottesville.

> **Edgewood Farm & Nursery**
> Route 2, Box 303
> Stanardsville, VA 22973-9405

Robert Cary and Norman Schwartz, Jr.
(804) 985-3782
Catalog: $2, bn

■ A favorite catalog of mine comes from **Sandy Mush Herb
Nursery** in Leicester, North Carolina, so it was on my must
list when I went to the area on a visit. It turns out that getting
there is half the fun; the paved road turns to gravel, then to
dirt, and as it climbs up a steep and remote canyon it turns
to ruts and boulders beside a rushing stream. We were sure
we'd somehow missed the nursery, but we kept climbing to
find a place to turn around — suddenly the road widened
slightly and we were there. We were amazed to hear that the
UPS truck comes up all the time; I'll bet the drivers fight over
that route!

We were greeted by Kate Jayne and then joined by a man
in a tattered plaid shirt and wild, curling hair who turned out
to be her husband, Fairman, a horticulturist trained at Kew
Gardens and formerly with both the Morris Arboretum and
Scott Horticultural Foundation in Pennsylvania. Both were
charming, and I enjoyed their combination of plant sophisti-
cation and simple rural style; what's the use of living in the
country if you can't work in your old clothes? The Jaynes
started their nursery in 1977, wanting to move from an urban
setting to raise their children; both children helped as they
were growing up, and now Kate's sister Ellen and her children
help out.

Until recently, the Sandy Mush catalog was written entirely
in beautiful calligraphy; unfortunately their calligrapher has
moved on to other things, so if you have that catalog, save
and treasure it. Now Sandy Mush is sending a more conventional catalog every few years, with a combined plant list and
order form sent between catalogs. Both catalog and list contain
many treasures: they are particularly strong in artemisias,
dianthus, hardy and scented geraniums, ivies, lavenders, mints
and oreganos, rosemaries, salvias (a very large selection),
thymes, willows, and yarrows. That's only a smattering; they
have so much more, including some shrubs and trees and lots
of good perennials.

The nursery is a series of homemade greenhouses added on
to one another and a casual garden behind them; there I was
thrilled to see a franklinia in bloom, with its burgundy autumn
leaves, and a beautiful *Viburnum wrightii*, which I fell in love
with.

One reads a lot about Sandy Mush, and deservedly so. It is
the source of a number of excellent plants, some hard to find
anywhere else. The Jaynes may be way off in the country, but

we found Kate unloading shredded financial reports from the local Merrill Lynch office to use for packing plants! Kate and Fairman welcome visitors Tuesday through Saturday. You should call ahead for directions; the nursery is about three-quarters of an hour north of Asheville (not so far in miles, but you can't speed on that road!).

Sandy Mush Herb Nursery
Route 2, Surrett Cove Road
Leicester, NC 28748
Fairman and Kate Jayne
(704) 683-2014
Catalog: $4d, CAN, bn/cn

■ **Sleepy Hollow Herb Farm** in Lancaster, Kentucky, was another back-yard project that blossomed. Julie and Steve Marks started growing herbs for pleasure but got totally absorbed. Julie quit her job as a printer, soon to be followed by Steve, who was a medical equipment technician. The next move was out of town so that they'd have more room. They're bucking for a nine and a half on the Barton Animal Index: they've got dogs, cats, rabbits, geese, ducks, and a pig.

The Markses list a very good selection of organically grown herbs, which includes a number of garden perennials: artemisias, hardy and scented geraniums, epimediums, lavenders, salvias, thymes, and many more. Visitors are welcome by appointment; there are display gardens at the nursery. Lancaster is forty miles south of Lexington on Highway 27.

Sleepy Hollow Herb Farm
568 Jack Black Road
Lancaster, KY 40444-9306
Steve and Julie Marks
(606) 792-6183
Catalog: $1, cn/bn

■ Another large selection of herbs is available from Peter and Susan Borchard's **Companion Plants** in Athens, Ohio. They offer more than 500 varieties, including about 40 species and cultivars of thyme, more than 40 salvias, and about 20 basils. This catalog is worthy of an evening's snug reading with a color guide to herbs at your side; some are very unusual, including some African herbs. As on all herb lists, many very ornamental plants appear, including some shrubs and trees and many attractive ground covers.

The Borchards started their business in 1982 partly because of Susan's interest in culinary herbs. Peter is a former carpenter who's always been interested in native American plants, particularly medicinal and edible plants. There are display gardens open Thursday through Sunday from March to Thanksgiving; Athens is about sixty-five miles southeast of Columbus.

Companion Plants
7247 N. Coolville Ridge Road
Athens, OH 45701
Peter and Susan Borchard
(614) 592-4643
Catalog: $2, cn/bn

SUNNYBROOK FARMS NURSERY
Artist: Tim Ruh

■ **Sunnybrook Farms Nursery** in Chesterland, Ohio, offers a very broad selection of ivies, perennials, and herbs, including about 30 thymes and many mints and rosemaries. Tim Ruh's grandfather started the nursery in 1928. Then his parents, Peter and Jean Ruh, who are well known in hosta circles, took it over. Now Tim and his partner, Martha Sickinger, stick to their herbs and perennials but offer about 140 hostas from the "Homestead Division" of Sunnybrook Farms, Peter and Jean Ruh's retirement business.

Tim grew up in the nursery business and attended Pershore College of Horticulture in England; his interest is in bringing in new varieties. Sunnybrook doesn't ship to California, Hawaii, or Alaska. Visitors are welcome daily; the best months are May through September. The nursery is located about twenty miles east of Cleveland and has several display gardens.

> **Sunnybrook Farms Nursery**
> P.O. Box 6
> Chesterland, OH 44026
> Timothy Ruh
> (216) 729-7232
> Catalog: $1d, cn/bn

■ **Goodwin Creek Gardens** is one of two interesting nurseries in tiny Williams, Oregon (also home to Forestfarm). Jim and Dotti Becker started their nursery in 1977 after working at other nurseries; their specialties are organically grown herbs, including many native American plants, everlasting flowers, and fragrant plants. Their interest in everlastings led to a book, *A Concise Guide to Growing Everlastings* (available from the nursery itself), and to a retail shop in Ashland where they sell plants, dried flower arrangements, and other garden items, even giving Sunday lectures on the herbs and flowers of Shakespeare during the annual Shakespeare festival.

Among their offerings is 'Goodwin Creek Grey' lavender and a variegated *Stachys officinalis*. Visitors may come to the nursery by appointment only; plant orders must be placed in advance for pick up. Williams is off Highway 238, between Ashland and Grants Pass in southern Oregon.

> **Goodwin Creek Gardens**
> P.O. Box 83
> Williams, OR 97544
> Jim and Dotti Becker
> (503) 846-7357 or 488-3308
> Catalog: $1, cn/bn

■ Another Oregon nursery well known for its herbs is **Nichols Garden Nursery** in Albany, started in 1950 by Nick and Edith Nichols; it's now run by Edith and her daughter and son-in-law, Rose Marie and Keane McGee. The nursery actually offers a broad range of seeds for vegetable gardeners west of the Cascades, and a very good selection of herbs, as well, and has been adding new varieties, such as 'Sharon Roberts' lavender with edible flowers. Nichols is famous for its selection of mints and its elephant garlic, too, though I'm not sure that qualifies as an ornamental garden plant.

Keane is a former math professor. He and Rose Marie love to travel and recently went to China with an Oregon delegation. They are also working on a sister city arrangement with Uzhgorod in Ukraine. Cheers for Rose Marie, who volunteers for the local library! There is a nice herb garden behind the nursery, which is open Monday through Saturday all year. Albany is about fifteen miles south of Salem on Interstate 5.

Nichols Garden Nursery, Inc.
1190 N. Pacific Highway
Albany, OR 97321
E. R. Nichols, Keane and Rose Marie McGee
(503) 928-9280
Catalog: Free, CAN, cn/bn

■ *Other sources of herbs are:*

Fieldstone Gardens, Inc., Vassalboro, ME
Rabbit Shadow Farm, Loveland, CO
Surry Gardens, Surry, ME
Winter Greenhouse, Winter, WI

SUNNYBROOK FARMS NURSERY
Artist: Jay Szabo

Holly

■ The varieties of holly available are an amazement to me, and there are new hybrids being introduced all the time. Harold Elmore of **Holly Haven Hybrids** in Knoxville, Tennessee, has a collection of 600 hollies! His collection is so big that he had to buy land ten miles out of town to plant it out. Of these hollies, he lists about 70 varieties each year, but those listed vary from year to year. The hollies on his current list are all very unusual, so here's a source of real collector's plants. He says he will propagate to order from your want-list but that it might take some time to get your plants.

Harold is retired from the Tennessee Valley Authority, where he worked as a chemist. He uttered that familiar phrase, "a hobby which got out of hand." Isn't it wonderful that there are so many victims of plant mania! Visitors are welcome but should call ahead for an appointment; it's sometimes hard to catch Harold between trips to his holly farm.

> **Holly Haven Hybrids**
> 136 Sanwood Road
> Knoxville, TN 37923
> Harold Elmore
> (615) 690-3410
> Catalog: Long SASE, bn

■ *Other sources of holly are:*

Appalachian Gardens, Waynesboro, PA
Beaver Creek Nursery, Knoxville, TN
Bull Valley Rhododendron Nursery, Aspers, PA
Colvos Creek Nursery, Vashon Island, WA
Foxborough Nursery, Street, MD
Louisiana Nursery, Opelousas, LA
Magnolia Nursery & Display Garden, Chunchula, AL
Owen Farms, Ripley, TN
Roslyn Nursery, Dix Hills, NY
Twombly Nursery, Monroe, CT
Wavecrest Nursery and Landscaping Company, Fennville, MI
Woodlanders, Inc., Aiken, SC

Hostas and Other Shade Plants

STOECKLEIN'S NURSERY   *Artist: Carol A. Stoecklein*

Even the smallest garden will probably have areas that get limited sun, and if it doesn't, you'll probably plant trees and shrubs to create a bit of shade. Some of the loveliest of garden plants want woodland conditions, and it would be painful indeed to have to give them up, to say nothing of having to live without the trees and flowering shrubs that shade them. Aren't we agreed that trees and woodland plants are a good thing? By now, you've noticed that whatever I'm writing about at the moment is one of my very favorite plant groups, and it's not that I'm fickle, only very easily seduced.

I'm lucky that I have a lot of trees in my garden, and I've even cleared away some to make room for others I've always wanted, so eventually there will be ample opportunity to plant shade lovers. I haven't yet tried hostas, which I'm afraid would disappear overnight to the depredations of snails (God's little joke on California gardeners, who have other blessings in abundance — his little joke on me personally is the pocket gopher, on whom I lavishly blame everything wrong with my garden).

Many other shade plants are found in the catalogs of nurseries that specialize in native plants and wildflowers and perennials, and many shrubs such as azaleas also like shade.

STOECKLEIN'S NURSERY   *Artist: Carol A. Stoecklein*

■ Marc and Carol Stoecklein of **Stoecklein's Nursery** in Renfrew, Pennsylvania, started growing a variety of hardy shade plants to use in their landscaping business. They say that running a nursery takes twenty-four hours a day and is a labor of love. Marc has a degree in horticulture, and in his landscape work he uses as many tough and hardy native plants as he can; Stoecklein's makes a point of offering plants that perform well for them. There are some shipping restrictions to western states.

Offered are more than 60 varieties of hostas, ornamental grasses, dwarf conifers and other shrubs, and shade-loving perennials. Carol says their display garden is "gorgeous" and at its best in spring and summer. Visitors are welcome Monday through Saturday but should call ahead to be sure someone will be there. Renfrew is thirty miles north of Pittsburgh.

> **Stoecklein's Nursery**
> 135 Critchlow Road
> Renfrew, PA 16053
> Marc and Carol Stoecklein
> (412) 586-7882
> Catalog: $1, bn/cn

■ Sam Jones of **Piccadilly Farm** in Bishop, Georgia, is a botany professor emeritus at the University of Georgia and an author with the late Len Foote of *Native Shrubs and Woody Vines of the Southeast* and *Gardening with Native Wild Flowers,* both published by Timber Press. With his wife, Carleen, he now runs a nursery specializing in plants for shade. They offer more than 120 varieties of hostas and 2 species of *Helleborus* (*orientalis* and *foetidus*) by mail order. They also offer about 380 perennials for both sun and shade, only at the nursery. They have a lovely big display garden, where they welcome visitors Thursday through Saturday from April to mid-June. Bishop is about ten miles south of Athens.

> **Piccadilly Farm**
> 1971 Whippoorwill Road
> Bishop, GA 30621
> Sam and Carleen Jones
> (404) 769-6516
> Catalog: $1

■ Ursula Herz got her training and apprenticeship in horticulture in Germany and Switzerland. Rudy was a watchmaker from Chicago who met and married her in France. She converted him to plants, and they ended up running **Coastal Gardens & Nursery** in Myrtle Beach, South Carolina. They're dog lovers, too, with four Airedales to help them with their work.

The Herzes specialize in hostas, ferns, native plants, Japanese and Siberian iris, and daylilies. They are also collecting gingers, crinum lilies, and salvias, which they will be offering as they build up stock. Plants to California must be shipped bare-root.

There's no room for a display garden, but Rudy says there's always something of interest to a plant lover. Visitors by appointment only. Myrtle Beach is ninety-two miles north of Charleston and seventy-two miles south of Wilmington, North Carolina.

> **Coastal Gardens & Nursery**
> 4611 Socastee Boulevard
> Myrtle Beach, SC 29575
> Rudy and Ursula Herz
> (803) 293-2000
> Catalog: $2d, CAN/OV, bn

■ The **Homestead Division of Sunnybrook Farms** is the retirement business of Peter and Jean Ruh, who used to run Sunnybrook Farms in Chesterland, Ohio. Peter is a lifelong expert on hostas and offers more than 200 varieties, including introductions from Europe, Canada, Japan, and New Zealand; the Ruhs actually grow more than 1,100 varieties. They also collect and offer seed from nearly 1,000 varieties of hosta, offered on a separate seed list. They offer about 75 daylilies from their collection of 350, and 7 epimediums from their collection of more than 30. They have a two-acre display garden that sounds lovely. Visitors should make an appointment; the best seasons are late spring to fall. Chesterland is about twenty miles east of Cleveland.

> **Homestead Division of Sunnybrook Farms**
> 9448 Mayfield Road
> Chesterland, OH 44026
> Peter and Jean Ruh
> (216) 729-9838
> Catalog: $1, CAN/OV, bn

■ **Savory's Gardens** in Edina, Minnesota, is another nursery growing a very broad selection of hostas; the Savory family grows more than 800 varieties at the nursery and offer over 100 varieties in their catalog. Robert Savory started his nursery in 1946 and went on to become a celebrated hybridizer and propagator of hostas (the *Hosta Journal* dubbed him "Hosta Pharaoh of Edina"). His wife, Arlene, has always helped him, and his son Dennis, formerly in research forestry, has joined them and is now doing most of the hybridizing. They also offer daylilies on a separate list and other shade plants and perennials at the nursery. Visitors are welcome to visit the nursery and display gardens Monday through Friday or weekends by appointment; the best months are June through August. Edina is a suburb on the southwestern fringe of Minneapolis.

> **Savory's Gardens, Inc.**
> 5300 Whiting Avenue
> Edina, MN 55435-1249
> Arlene, Robert, and Dennis Savory
> (612) 941-8755
> Catalog: $2, CAN, bn
> Daylily list: Long SASE

■ Mike and Jean Heger of **Ambergate Gardens** in Waconia, Minnesota, also specialize in hostas, growing 250 varieties and offering about 50 to 60 in their catalogs. They also specialize in Martagon lilies, growing about 30 varieties and offering a few in each catalog as their supply increases. They offer a nice selection of hardy plants for woodland and shade.

Mike was a landscape gardener at the Minnesota Landscape Arboretum for many years, where he learned to love and grow hostas. The Hegers finally decided to go into the nursery business to support their plant collecting habit; their two young sons give them some help but prefer hiking and baseball.

The Ambergate display garden looks terrific; visitors are welcome by appointment from mid-April through October. Waconia is about thirty miles southwest of Minneapolis on State Highway 5.

> **Ambergate Gardens**
> 8015 Krey Avenue
> Waconia, MN 55387
> Mike and Jean Heger
> (612) 443-2248
> Catalog: $1, CAN, bn/cn

ROBYN'S NEST NURSERY
Artist: Mari Eggebraaten

■ I was greeted at **Robyn's Nest Nursery** by a black and white cat who came to take my measure. Robyn Duback emerged from the house to explain that she found the cat as a tiny kitten that she thought was dead and put on the compost pile in a hailstorm. The next morning it was crying for food. She took it and fed it with an eyedropper and was converted from a dog person to a dog and cat person. The compost seems to have stimulated growth; he's a huge cat now and has been joined by three others. Robyn gets a high Barton Animal Index rating.

Living on the outskirts of Vancouver, Washington, in an old farmhouse, Robyn specializes in hostas and grows more than 200 species and cultivars. She also offers about 30 varieties of astilbe, which like the same growing conditions as the hostas. She lists a nice selection of other perennials and ornamental grasses, most of which like the growing conditions of the Pacific Northwest. There is an acre-and-a-half display garden in front of the house. The nursery is open Thursday through Saturday from mid-March through June and in September and October, or by appointment.

Robyn's Nest Nursery
7802 N.E. Sixty-third Street
Vancouver, WA 98662
Robyn Duback
(206) 256-7399
Catalog: $1d, bn/cn

ROBYN'S NEST NURSERY   *Artist: Mari Eggebraaten*

■ *Other sources of hostas are:*

A & D Peony and Perennial Farm, Snohomish, WA
Busse Gardens, Cokato, MN
Collector's Nursery, Vancouver, WA
Englerth Gardens, Hopkins, MI
Hildenbrandt's Iris Gardens, Lexington, NE
Jernigan Gardens, Dunn, NC
Klehm Nursery, South Barrington, IL
Mary's Plant Farm, Hamilton, OH
Powell's Gardens, Princeton, NC
Seawright Gardens, Carlisle, MA
Sunnybrook Farms Nursery, Chesterland, OH
Andre Viette Farm & Nursery, Fishersville, VA
Gilbert H. Wild & Son, Inc., Sarcoxie, MO

■ *Other sources of plants for shade are:*

Brookside Wildflowers, Boone, NC
Carroll Gardens, Westminster, MD
Eco-Gardens, Decatur, GA
Gardens of the Blue Ridge, Pineola, NC
Ledgecrest Greenhouses, Storrs, CT
Orchid Gardens, Andover, MN
Andre Viette Farm & Nursery, Fishersville, VA

Iris: Bearded

I have to admit that when I begin to speak of iris, I'm in well over my head. Sure, I can tell the difference between dwarf bearded and tall bearded iris, and bearded and beardless iris, blue iris and yellow iris. But there are so many classes and species of iris, and some of the iris hybrids have such complex breeding that I just have to look vague and tell the truth — they really are beautiful!

Iris, like daylilies, are very popular and appear in some form or other in nearly every garden; like daylilies they are fairly easy to grow and increase and are very habit forming. Many hobbyists end up selling their surpluses to friends and neighbors and then going into the nursery business. While some nurseries sell many types of iris, many of them specialize, and some of them offer hybrids of their own breeding. I don't look on any of these nurseries as "just another iris nursery." There are differences in what each offers, and I'll try to be specific so that you'll be able to choose the nurseries that suit you best.

One very nice custom with some bearded iris (and daylily) nurseries is "extras"; many of the nurseries will send extra plants with your order, sometimes your choice and sometimes theirs. Most iris nurseries take reservations (orders) in the spring and then ship in late summer, so plan ahead.

Bearded iris are a particularly confusing group to us neophytes, so here is a little guide to size in approximate bloom sequence: miniature dwarf bearded (to 8 inches), standard dwarf bearded (8 to 15 inches), intermediate bearded (16 to 28 inches), miniature tall bearded (small-flowered, 16 to 26 inches), border bearded (16 to 27 inches), and tall bearded (28 inches and above). The term *median iris* is a catchall category for standard dwarf bearded, intermediate bearded, and border bearded, that is, every size except miniature dwarf bearded and tall bearded.

Reblooming iris are also bearded, come in many sizes, and bloom in the spring and again one or more times during the summer and fall; this is a genetic trait and not just the result of extra food and water! I'm happy to see the rise of reblooming iris. Think of having that wonderful display more than once a year! Arilbred iris are crosses between bearded and aril iris from the Near East and fall into the bearded camp. 'Space age' iris have appendages of various shapes at the end of their beards; why don't they call them beard-plus?

■ A long list of bearded iris of all types and sizes, including reblooming iris, is issued by **Iris Acres** in Winamac, Indiana. Jean and Thurlow Sanders must offer about 1,000 good older varieties at very reasonable prices. Jean used to work at the blue jeans factory in town but wanted to develop a sideline to keep her busy when she retired. Do you suppose she had any idea how much work it would become? Iris Acres welcomes visitors during bloom season, which is usually late May and early June. Winamac is about halfway between Chicago and Indianapolis, not far from Interstate 30.

> **Iris Acres**
> RR 4, Box 189
> Winamac, IN 46996
> Thurlow and Jean Sanders
> (219) 946-4197
> Catalog: $1 or 3 FCS, CAN/OV

■ As a teenager, Roger Miller worked for the widow of one of the founders of the American Iris Society; now he and his wife, Lynda, run **Miller's Manor Gardens** in Ossian, Indiana, and grow 1,000 tall, median, and dwarf bearded iris and another 100 varieties of Siberian iris. Both Millers have hybridized and won awards for their iris; Lynda runs a retail nursery next door specializing in perennials and unusual shrubs. They also offer about 250 daylilies and 40 hostas. Visitors are welcome Monday and Tuesday and Thursday through Saturday or by appointment; bloom time is usually mid-May to mid-June. Ossian is about fifteen miles south of Fort Wayne.

> **Miller's Manor Gardens**
> 3167 E. US 224
> Ossian, IN 46777
> Roger and Lynda Miller
> (219) 597-7403
> Catalog: $1

■ When we get to the list of **Country View Gardens** in Chesaning, Michigan, we see the fine points that divide the bearded iris. Barb Gibson grows about 250 cultivars of miniature dwarf bearded, 300 standard dwarf bearded, 150 intermediate bearded, 150 miniature tall bearded, and some border bearded and tall bearded. Some of the miniature dwarfs and miniature tall bearded are antique varieties. They seem to bloom in the order given above, from smallest to tallest. Barb also grows about 100 Siberian iris cultivars, and nearly 500 daylilies. A good many of all of these are offered on her list; she says many are older varieties and hardy "good doers."

Barb's mother was an avid gardener, and Barb grew perennials for many years before a book from the local library got her interested in hybridizing iris. She also grows about 1,000 varieties of perennials and sells many of them at the farm. She says her farmer husband is very tolerant and will plow for her; she does everything else!

Visitors are welcome to come and walk the field rows; the iris bloom from late April to mid-June, the daylilies and perennials from July onward. Barb says you must call ahead "after dark" the evening before to be sure someone will be there. Chesaning is about twenty miles northwest of Flint.

Country View Gardens
13253 McKeighan Road
Chesaning, MI 48616
Barb Gibson
(517) 845-7556
Catalog: Long SASE with 2 FCS

■ Lu Jasperson of **Jasperson's Hersey Nursery** in Wilson, Wisconsin, is a housewife gone mad with flowers. She says she inherited her green thumb from her farmer father and joined societies to learn as much as she could. She grows about 300 bearded iris of all types and offers about 75 to 100 on her list each year at very reasonable prices; also listed are a few Siberian iris and peonies.

She started her nursery in 1987 and gets as much part-time work as she can out of her husband, a long-haul trucker, and her two young children. Bless her heart, she does most of it herself and welcomes visitors during bloom time, if they "can tolerate less than perfection!" The nursery is actually in the village of Hersey, where Lu has lived all her life. She says you can take the Wilson exit on Interstate 94 and ask anyone the way to Hersey; it's about fifty miles west of Eau Claire.

Jasperson's Hersey Nursery
2915 Seventy-fourth Street
Wilson, WI 54027
Lu M. Jasperson
(414) 772-4749
Catalog: Long SASE with 2 FCS

■ Sharol Longaker runs the **Anderson Iris Gardens** in Forest Lake, Minnesota, and offers about 550 cultivars of tall bearded iris tough enough to stand the Minnesota winter. Most of these are older tried-and-true varieties, including lots of award winners. Sharol inherited her love of iris from her father, who started the nursery. During the fall and winter she does tax and investment planning, but by bloom season she's at the iris farm for the summer, where she's been trying her hand at hybridizing.

Anderson Iris Gardens also offers about 65 herbaceous peonies and some daylilies and Oriental poppies. Visitors are welcome. Bloom time is usually in June, and guests have been known to bring lawn chairs and lunch to enjoy the plantings. Forest Lake is about thirty miles north of Minneapolis and St. Paul near Highway 35W.

> **Anderson Iris Gardens**
> 22179 Keather Avenue North
> Forest Lake, MN 55025
> Sharol Longaker
> (612) 433-5268
> Catalog: $1

■ Jack Worel of Osseo, Minnesota, has changed the name of his iris nursery from Worel's Iris Gardens to **Holly Lane Iris Gardens,** but everything else remains the same. He offers 500 to 600 varieties of bearded iris in various sizes, both old and new varieties, including some Arilbred iris, another 40 Siberian iris, some hostas, and about 100 varieties of daylilies.

Jack is a former social worker who now does landscaping as well as iris growing; his wife, Jan, helps with the iris. As a Minnesotan, fishing is his pastime of choice; it's in the genes. Every Minnesotan has a Lake Wobegon down the road. Visitors are welcome at the garden, but you should call ahead to ask about bloom; early June is the best time for iris, July for the daylilies. Osseo is ten miles northwest of Minneapolis.

> **Holly Lane Iris Gardens**
> 10930 Holly Lane
> Osseo, MN 55369
> Jack J. Worel
> (612) 420-4876
> Catalog: Free

■ Tracy Jennings of **Riverdale Iris Gardens** in Rockford, Minnesota, specializes in hardy dwarf and median iris; she acquired the business from Zula Hanson when Zula retired after thirty years of iris growing. Tracy now finds herself hooked on iris, which she calls a healthy addiction. The catalog offers a good selection of these smaller irises at reasonable prices.

A former landscape designer with a degree in horticulture, Tracy works for the Agricultural Extension Service part-time and is an apprentice garden judge with the American Iris Society. Visitors must call ahead for an appointment; May is the usual bloom period. Rockford is about thirty miles northwest of Minneapolis and St. Paul.

Riverdale Iris Gardens
P.O. Box 524
Rockford, MN 55373
Tracy W. Jennings
(612) 477-4859
Catalog: $1

■ Eric and Bob Tankesley-Clarke of **Adamgrove** nursery in California, Missouri, are true renaissance men: plant breeders, social workers, musicians, artists, voracious readers, and cat lovers. They'd rate at least a nine on the Barton Animal Index for making a home on their farm for about twelve cats and for naming their farm and business for a beloved cat, Adam.

They offer about 350 tall bearded iris from many breeders but their introductions are from specific hybridizers: their own and those of the late David Sindt, Carl and LaRue Boswell, Donovan Albers, Ben Hager, Lothar Denkewitz of Germany, and the late John Taylor of England. They also specialize in dwarf and median bearded iris (about 400 cultivars), species iris (about 50), and some Japanese, Louisiana, Siberian, and spuria iris as well; there are lots and lots of prize winners among their iris offerings.

In addition, they also offer about 300 daylilies, including introductions from Frank Kropf, and about 30 cultivars of herbaceous peony. Visitors must write ahead for an appointment. California is in central Missouri, near Jefferson City.

Adamgrove
Route 1, Box 246
California, MO 65018
Eric and Bob Tankesley-Clarke
Catalog: $3d, CAN/OV

■ Wait until you see a photo of Jim Hedgecock's 'Son of Dracula'! He's bred a lot that are more beautiful, but this purplish black one's a spine chiller. **Comanche Acres Iris Gardens** in Gower, Missouri, grows more than 2,000 tall bearded iris, some antique varieties, increasing numbers of reblooming iris, and about 50 Louisiana iris. The Hedgecocks offer about 250 varieties in their color catalog. They also grow more than 300 median iris; the free median list is available on request. Some daylilies are available at the nursery.

Jim got into hybridizing and started his nursery in 1980. In 1986 he bought out the Iris Division of the Gilbert Wild Nursery. With the help of his wife, Lemoyne, who runs the garden, and some part-time workers, he manages to run a large iris business and work full-time in an auto dealership. Visitors are welcome at the garden Monday to Saturday; during the last two weeks of April and May, the garden is open every day. Gower is halfway between Kansas City and St. Joseph near Highway 169.

Comanche Acres Iris Gardens
Route 1, Box 258
Gower, MO 64454
Jim and Lemoyne Hedgecock
(816) 424-6436
Catalog: $3, CAN/OV

■ Paul Black drives a school bus and loves to cook — in the winter. In the summer it's all iris. He bought his first iris at a plant sale, and the saleswoman told him to leave the labels on so he could enter it in flower shows — the bug bit! He started his **Mid-America Iris Gardens** in Oklahoma City in 1978 and has won many awards for his hybrid bearded iris; he offers bearded iris in all sizes from tall to miniature dwarf bearded as well as reblooming iris. He grows about 1,000 cultivars and offers about 800 in his catalog.

Paul says his friends joke that he will cross anything that has pollen. He's working on daylilies, hostas, and amaryllis just for fun. He's proud of his large display gardens and welcomes visitors; iris bloom time is mid-April to late May. It's best to call ahead if you want to be sure to catch Paul. The garden is about four miles northwest of downtown.

Mid-America Iris Gardens
3409 N. Geraldine Avenue
Oklahoma City, OK 73112
Paul Black
(405) 946-5743
Catalog: $1, CAN/OV

■ Les and Toni Hildenbrandt have spent a lifetime farming and iris growing. Les somehow persuaded Toni that since he didn't smoke or drink it was all right to spend that "saved" money on iris; Toni's allergic to the scent of iris, so they have to keep them all outside. Their **Hildenbrandt's Iris Gardens** in Lexington, Nebraska, offers about 1,000 cultivars of tall bearded iris, including iris grown by their longtime helpers, Mike and Lila Kratzer, who grow under the name Prairie Promise Iris Garden. The Kratzers will gradually be taking over the iris growing and shipping for both nurseries.

The Hildenbrandts will continue to grow and sell hostas, about 120 varieties, and about 60 varieties of herbaceous peonies. One of the things I've always loved about their catalog was the wonderful selection of Oriental poppies in offbeat colors like apricot, lavender, raspberry, and purple. Les says that they've lost a lot of poppies to early storms in recent years, but he's trying to build up stock again. (Ask for the separate poppy list.) Visitors are welcome anytime to come and walk the rows. Lexington is between Kearney and North Platte in central Nebraska, near Interstate 80 and the Platte River.

> **Hildenbrandt's Iris Gardens**
> HC 84, Box 4
> Lexington, NE 68850-9304
> Les and Tony Hildenbrandt
> Catalog: 2 FCS

■ Calvin Reuter is a corn and soybean farmer in Wisner, Nebraska, who bought a few iris in 1982, added a lot more, and, finding it impossible to dump his increases, began to sell them. He now grows more than 1,400 at his **Spruce Gardens**, offering hundreds of bearded iris of all types, many very reasonably priced.

When I asked if his wife, Luetta, helped him, he said that she, too (like Toni Hildenbrandt of Hildenbrandt's Iris Gardens in Lexington) was allergic to iris, so she has to look at them through the window. Cal still farms, but, luckily, iris shipping time comes at a slack season for farming. In the winter he does model railroading, stamp collecting, and he "monkeys around" with his computer — altogether, a year without any boring stretches! Visitors are welcome during bloom time, usually mid-May to early June. Wisner is about ninety miles northwest of Omaha, between West Point and Norfolk on Highway 275.

Spruce Gardens
RR 2, Box 101
Wisner, NE 68791
Calvin and Luetta Reuter
(402) 529-6860
Catalog: $1

■ **Maple Tree Gardens** in Ponca, Nebraska, also offers bearded iris in all sizes. They list about 800 of the 1,200 they grow, including older varieties at very reasonable prices. They also offer about 50 Arilbred iris hybrids, described as very exotic and having some of the most beautiful colors, and some Siberian iris. They also grow 250 daylilies and list about 150 for summer bloom, as well as about 60 hostas.

Larry Harder started his nursery in 1960, and for more than thirty years he's been an office manager for the U.S. Department of Agriculture and an iris hybridizer and grower; he plans to retire soon to devote more time to his plants. He's active in the American Iris Society and the American Hemerocallis Society. He's on the Ponca Library Board (huzzah!) and the Ponca Historical Society. Ponca is the fifth oldest town in Nebraska. Visitors to the nursery are welcome during bloom time, May for the irises and July for the daylilies. Please call ahead to be sure someone will be there. Ponca is located twenty miles west of Sioux City, Iowa.

Maple Tree Gardens
P.O. Box 547
Ponca, NE 68770
Larry L. Harder
(402) 755-2515
Catalog: Free, CAN/OV

■ I don't know what it is about Nebraska, but it must be ideal for growing iris. Chuck and Mary Ferguson of **North Pine Iris Gardens** in Norfolk are not hybridizers but iris nuts who grow more than 750 bearded iris of all types and also some Arilbred and Siberian iris, daylilies, and hosta; the catalog lists hundreds of varieties. Think of the space and effort it would take just to grow one each of more than 1,000 plants, then multiply the plants by ten!

Mary Ferguson's father was an iris hybridizer in Norfolk, so she grew up surrounded by iris and iris talk; her whole family loves to garden. North Pine Iris Gardens is a good source of older and newer varieties, reasonably priced. Visitors are welcome at bloom time, usually May through mid-June; call ahead to be sure that someone will be there. Norfolk is about a hundred miles northwest of Omaha on Highways 275 and 81.

North Pine Iris Gardens
P.O. Box 595
Norfolk, NE 68701
Chuck and Mary Ferguson
(402) 371-3895
Catalog: $1

■ **Long's Gardens** in Boulder, Colorado, was founded in 1905 and offers a selection of "tried and true, old and new." I don't see any cultivars on the list earlier than the 1960s, but with so many introductions every year, the 1960s may well be the dark ages, iris-wise. Long's grows more than 2,000 varieties and lists about 300 tall bearded iris, plus another 100 border, intermediate, standard, and miniature dwarf bearded iris, and some Arilbred iris. They also offer some new introductions by Colorado hybridizers. Grown in the Rockies, these are very hardy varieties.

The nursery was started by Catherine Long Gates's grandparents, and she sent me some iris and seed catalogs from as far back as 1938. The 1951 catalog of flower and vegetable seed was fascinating; one wonders at how fast varieties come and go — the catalog shows a pretty little star-shaped pink petunia called 'Hollywood Star' (15 cents a packet!) that looks much prettier than the monsters of today. The current catalog offers only iris, and Catherine's parents, sister, and husband are all involved in the business, as time allows. Visitors are welcome during bloom time, which is usually late April to early June; Catherine says you should call ahead to see what's in bloom.

Long's Gardens
P.O. Box 19
Boulder, CO 80306
Catherine Long Gates
(303) 442-2353
Catalog: Free

■ By now it's obvious that iris are toughies, since they grow wonderfully on the plains of Nebraska and on the high foothills of the Rockies. Don and Bobbie Shepard have been growing iris in Phoenix, Arizona, for twenty-five years with great success. They started out with a few plants and, "by pure luck," won a show ribbon with their first effort.

They now grow more than 1,000 iris and list about 800 tall bearded, spuria, and Louisiana iris. They introduce the spuria hybrids of Floyd Wickenkamp, the tall bearded hybrids of Charlie Jenkins and Bernard Hamner, whose stock they have taken over and moved from California to Arizona. Don, who will be retiring soon from the construction industry, has been hybridizing, too, and he is beginning to list his own introductions. **Shepard Iris Garden** has so many visitors in April that groups have to make reservations up to a year in advance. Individual visitors are welcome to drop by the garden any day in April.

> **Shepard Iris Garden**
> 3342 W. Orangewood Avenue
> Phoenix, AZ 85051
> Don and Bobbie Shepard
> (602) 841-1231
> Catalog: 1 FCS

KEITH KEPPEL   *Artist: Joe Gatty*

■ **Keith Keppel** of Stockton, California, specializes in all the very newest varieties of tall and median bearded iris and caters to the "iris crowd." These are iris collectors, exhibitors, and hybridizers who want to try hybridizing with the very latest introductions. Keith and his late partner, Joe Gatty, introduced many of their own hybrids. Keith has won many prizes here and abroad, including the Dykes Medal, the highest award of the American Iris Society.

His iris descriptions include pedigrees, some of which are very complex. In his spare time he does iris genealogy, and he's traced some cultivars back more than twenty generations to their original species iris ancestors. When I asked him how hybridizers think up names for hundreds of new introductions every year, he told me that they raid the daylily and daffodil lists!

Keith has a degree in horticulture and has recently retired from a thirty-year career with the post office — which very kindly subsidized his iris interests. Visitors should call ahead (evenings only) to be sure he'll be there and to check on bloom time, which varies depending on rainfall. Stockton is about thirty miles south of Sacramento on Interstate 5 and an hour and a half east of the San Francisco Bay Area.

Keith Keppel
P.O. Box 8173
Stockton, CA 95208
(209) 463-0227
Catalog: $1

■ **Roris Gardens** in Sacramento, California, is a fairly new but already quite large grower of tall bearded iris. Most of its varieties are recent introductions, many of them prize winners, and many from renowned California hybridizers. Every variety offered is shown in the color catalog.

General Manager Joe Grant told me that Roris has also opened a very popular tall bearded iris nursery in Japan. The catalog will soon list Japanese iris. Visitors are welcome in late April and early May. The nursery is on the south side of Sacramento.

Roris Gardens
7851 Carmencita Avenue
Sacramento, CA 95829
Joseph B. Grant II, Mgr.
(916) 689-7460
Catalog: $2d, CAN/OV

■ Jack and Phyllis Dickey of Healdsburg, California, have taken over **Moonshine Gardens** and all the stock and seedlings of the late Monty Byers. They will be introducing his hybrids and also hybridizing themselves. Monty specialized in reblooming iris and felt that the future of iris lay in that direction. The catalog offers many rebloomers, as well as "novelty" (space age) iris and bearded iris of all sizes.

Jack works at a winery, Phyllis is a school bus driver and mechanic, and they spend almost every other waking moment on the iris. Visitors are welcome to come to their display garden in April and May during bloom time, or by appointment. They live in the Alexander Valley, the heart of the wine country; Healdsburg is about fifteen miles north of Santa Rosa, an hour and a half north of San Francisco on Highway 101.

> **Moonshine Gardens**
> 5080 West Soda Rock Lane
> Healdsburg, CA 95448
> Jack and Phyllis Dickey
> (707) 433-8408
> Catalog: Free

Oregon is the home of two iris growers referred to by a friend of mine as "entry level." By this he meant that they issue beautiful color catalogs full of popular varieties of tall bearded iris and are responsible for luring many innocent people into growing their first iris. Offerings include both new and older varieties and a number of mixed collections. Collections usually lead to the desire to try a few more, and . . .

■ Those of you who have driven through the Willamette Valley on Interstate 5, past the blooming fields of **Schreiner's Gardens** in Salem, Oregon, have had a real treat. Schreiner's has been in business since 1925, started by the father of Robert and the grandfather of Ray and David Schreiner. Schreiner's offers hybrids from many breeders, and they are proud of the many hybrids they've introduced themselves; they have an active breeding program. Visitors are welcome. The last half of May is usually bloom time.

> **Schreiner's Gardens**
> 3625 Quinaby Road N.E.
> Salem, OR 97303
> David Schreiner
> (503) 393-3232
> Catalog: $3

■ **Cooley's Gardens** in Silverton, Oregon, has also been in business for more than sixty years. Started by Rholin and Pauline Cooley in 1928, it's now run by their grandchildren, the Ernsts. Cooley's has also been active in hybridizing and offers its own introductions as well as those of many other hybridizers. Visitors are welcome daily during bloom time, which is usually mid- to late May. Cooley's grows 250 acres of iris. Silverton is fifteen miles east of Salem.

Cooley's Gardens
P.O. Box 126
Silverton, OR 97381
Richard Ernst and Georgie Johnson
(503) 873-5463
Catalog: $4d, CAN/OV

■ Roger Nelson moved his **Iris Country** from eastern Nebraska to Brooks, Oregon, about five years ago. He is an active hybridizer and says that he's emphasizing tough, well-branched, and vigorous iris that will be rot-resistant and do well in all parts of the country. He's introducing three or four new iris a year and lists plants that meet his criteria from many other hybridizers, too; he's growing about 450 tall bearded iris and lists about 300 that have passed his tests in a wide range of climatic conditions.

Roger's been growing iris for more than a quarter of a century and describes himself as a true product of the sixties. He says he loves rock 'n' roll music and carries the human concerns and environmental ethic of that decade in his baggage. For fun, he's planting part of his land as an arboretum. Visitors are welcome by appointment. Brooks is twelve miles north of Salem, east of Interstate 5.

Iris Country
6219 Topaz Street, N.E.
Brooks, OR 97305
Roger Nelson
(503) 393-4739
Catalog: $1

■ Austin Morgan of **Iris Test Gardens** in College Place, Washington, grew up weeding his mother's iris and detested them. He started growing them only when he had nothing in bloom between his tulips and roses. Now he grows 4,000 varieties and lists several hundred each year, including older varieties at very reasonable prices. For thirty years he has also been hybridizing what he calls "double rimmers": iris with two bands of color around the fall.

Now retired, Austin has been a newspaper reporter and

editor, landscaper, judge, carpenter, and security guard since he graduated from Walla Walla College. Visitors are welcome; Austin has a big iris garden one block west of Lions Park on Eighth Street in College Place and an iris display garden around his home. Bloom time is usually mid-May. College Place is three miles south of Walla Walla.

Iris Test Gardens
1010 Highland Park Drive
College Place, WA 99324
Austin and Ione Morgan
(509) 525-8804
Catalog: $.50

■ *Other sources of bearded iris are:*

Aitken's Salmon Creek Garden, Vancouver, WA
Bay View Gardens, Santa Cruz, CA
Borbeleta Gardens, Faribault, MN
The Iris Pond, McLean, VA
Mary's Plant Farm, Hamilton, OH
Maxim's Greenwood Gardens, Redding, CA
Nicholls Gardens, Gainesville, VA
Pleasure Iris Gardens, Chaparral, NM
Powell's Gardens, Princeton, NC
Ramona Gardens, Ramona, CA
Sunnyridge Gardens, Knoxville, TN
Andre Viette Farm & Nursery, Fishersville, VA

■ *Other sources of reblooming iris are:*

The Iris Pond, McLean, VA
Nicholls Gardens, Gainesville, VA
Pleasure Iris Gardens, Chaparral, NM

■ *Other sources of Arilbred iris are:*

Nicholls Gardens, Gainesville, VA

Iris: Beardless

When we get to beardless iris, I'm really dancing on the ice floes! This group includes some of the most interesting and beautiful blooms in the plant world. The people who can keep it all straight have to be smarter than rocket scientists.

■ **The Iris Pond** in McLean, Virginia, specializes in Japanese and Siberian iris, species iris, historic (antique) and reblooming bearded iris, and tall and intermediate bearded iris. Clarence Mahan, who works for the Environmental Protection Agency, is the president of the Historic Iris Preservation Society and is actively working to find and propagate historic varieties, which are in great demand for restoration of historic gardens in this country and abroad.

He's also working on a joint project to register all of the Japanese iris cultivars sold in this country and helped to set up the National Collection of Japanese Iris in England. Visitors are welcome by appointment in May and June; there are Japanese and historic iris display gardens. McLean is across the Potomac River from Washington, D.C.

The Iris Pond
7311 Churchill Road
McLean, VA 22101
Clarence Mahan
(703) 893-8526
Catalog: $2, CAN/OV, bn

■ Diana Nicholls admits that she's ninety percent of **Nicholls Gardens** in Gainesville, Virginia; she's a former school teacher who began to sell her surplus iris to support her hobby. Now her garden is an official display garden for the Society for Japanese Iris and also the Median Iris Society.

She offers Siberian, Louisiana, and Japanese iris, some species iris, bearded, reblooming, and antique bearded iris of all types, and some Arilbreds. She is hybridizing reblooming and Japanese iris, with no introductions yet, and introduces Japanese iris hybridized by Dr. William Ackerman, who's retired from the U.S. Department of Agriculture. Diana grows more than 2,000 iris and offers about 800 in her catalog. In case that's not enough to do, she also offers more than 100 daylilies, both small- and large-flowered.

This is a two-person business. Diana's husband, the other ten percent, sometimes mows and rototills; her mother occasionally visits in the summer to help out. Diana is also an enthusiastic member of the Embroiderers Guild. Like me, she says she's felt compelled to turn down many urgent invitations to join the Perfect Housekeepers Guild. Her garden looks very beautiful, and visitors are welcome from April through first frost; you should call ahead in the early morning or after dark if you plan to come a distance to visit. Gainesville is eight miles north of Manassas and about forty miles southwest of Washington, D.C.

Nicholls Gardens
4724 Angus Drive
Gainesville, VA 22065
Diana and Mike Nicholls
(703) 754-9623
Catalog: $1d, CAN/OV

ENSATA GARDENS
Artist: John Coble

■ **Ensata Gardens** of Galesburg, Michigan, specializes in Japanese and Siberian iris. John Coble and Robert Bauer run a stained-glass studio and discovered Japanese iris in 1981. By 1985 they'd opened their nursery and now create stained glass only in the winter. In their spare time they are renovating a fourteen-room brick farmhouse built in 1858. Both stained glass and iris are career switches — John's trained as a wildlife biologist and Bob as an inorganic chemist.

Currently they're growing more than 400 cultivars of Japanese iris, have 1,000 seedlings waiting for evaluation, and hope that some of them will be worthy of introduction. They've also been importing iris from Japan and Europe and want to collect all of the known cultivars; they currently offer more than 200 in the catalog. They also offer about 50 cultivars of Siberian iris. Visitors are welcome during bloom time, which is mid-June to mid-July; there is a Japanese display garden as well as the growing rows to see at the farm. Please call ahead the evening before to be sure someone will be there and to get directions; like all of the iris growers, John and Bob are outside until dark every day while the iris are in bloom. Galesburg is between Battle Creek and Kalamazoo.

Ensata Gardens
9823 E. Michigan Avenue
Galesburg, MI 49053
Bob Bauer and John Coble
(616) 665-7500
Catalog: $2

■ Joan Cooper of **Cooper's Garden** was well known among iris collectors as a source of species iris. She's recently sold her nursery to Penny Aguirre of Golden Valley, Minnesota, who will keep the name Cooper's Garden. Like Joan, she will offer about 75 species iris and selections, some hardiness-tested Louisiana iris for the north, and 40 varieties of Siberian iris. Also offered are many daylilies, and some hostas, woodland wildflowers, and perennials.

Penny is a molecular geneticist with a master's degree in horticulture. She's very excited about her new venture. She'll have a display garden around her home and growing fields on a farm. Visitors are welcome to come to the display garden but should call ahead to see that someone will be there. Golden Valley is a northwestern suburb of Minneapolis.

Cooper's Garden
2345 Decatur Avenue North
Golden Valley, MN 55427
Penny Aguirre
(612) 591-0495
Catalog: $1, CAN, bn

■ **Borbeleta Gardens** in Faribault, Minnesota, is run by Julius Wadekamper, who grows about 200 varieties of Siberian iris, as well as hundreds of standard dwarf bearded, intermediate, border bearded, and miniature tall bearded iris, offering a good variety of each type. In addition, Wadekamper also grows 200 varieties of daylilies and the same number of Asiatic lilies. About 50 varieties of each are listed in the catalog each year, but you can write and ask about plants on your want-list.

A former teacher with a master's degree in horticulture, Julius grew up reading *National Geographic,* so in the winter he takes off for such warmer climes as Africa, South America, and New Zealand. He's been hybridizing prize-winning Asiatic lilies for years and has registered 65 cultivars. He has been achieving new colors — his latest lily is white and purple. He also introduces the efforts of amateur hybridizers whose plants deserve wider distribution. Visitors are welcome anytime; the best bloom is from May through July. There's a display garden, and you can walk through the planting rows too. Faribault is forty miles south of Minneapolis on Interstate 35W.

Borbeleta Gardens
15980 Canby Avenue
Faribault, MN 55021
Julius Wadekamper
(507) 334-2807
Catalog: $3, CAN/OV

■ Luella Danielson of Chaparral, New Mexico, runs **Pleasure Iris Gardens,** a source of iris for collectors, particularly oncocyclus species and hybrids, oncogelia, regeliocyclus, regelia, Siberian, bearded, reblooming and antique bearded iris of all types, Arilbred crosses and bearded iris of all sizes, including reblooming. We're talking extremely complex crosses here, plants that are truly rare and special; most customers are probably very expert or looking for spectacular blooms for the show bench. Many are Luella's introductions and those of her late husband, Henry.

Visitors are welcome during bloom season, which is usually March and April. Please call for an appointment. Evenings are the best time to catch iris people; they're outside all day, every day, during bloom season, making crosses. Chaparral is three miles northeast of El Paso, Texas. Luella says the roadrunner, which is the state bird, is called the chaparral in New Mexico.

Pleasure Iris Gardens
425 East Lune
Chaparral, NM 88021
Luella Danielson
(505) 824-4299
Catalog: $1d, CAN/OV

■ **Bay View Gardens** in Santa Cruz, California, is run by Joseph Ghio, a former high school teacher and former mayor of Santa Cruz. Joe is known all over the world as the hybridizer of what he calls "Pacifica iris" (Pacific Coast iris hybrids), beautiful crosses of various native iris of the Pacific Coast. He is the winner of many awards for his introductions.

Many of Joe's Pacificas have California place names. His 1991 introductions have names associated with the Loma Prieta earthquake (remember the 1989 Bay Bridge World Series?). He also offers tall bearded iris introductions of his own and others (if there's ever been a prettier iris than his 'Bubbling Over', I've never seen it), Louisiana iris (including Mary Dunn originations and the award winners of John Taylor of Australia), and spuria iris from many different hybridizers. Mail order only.

> **Bay View Gardens**
> 1201 Bay Street
> Santa Cruz, CA 95060
> Joseph Ghio
> (408) 423-3656
> Catalog: $1.50

■ Another source of Pacific Coast iris hybrids is **Portable Acres** in Penngrove, California. Colin Rigby has an extensive collection of new and old varieties from many hybridizers and also offers species iris. He suffered very badly from the Great Freeze of 1990, but he's been able to rebuild his stock.

When he was eight, Colin got a job weeding for a disabled neighbor in Utah who was crazy about plants and taught him a lot about them. One of his fondest memories was seeing the begonia bulb they planted come into bloom — as exotic as any orchid! He's now retired as a graphics artist in the printing industry and loves being able to work with plants all the time. Visitors are welcome during bloom time, which is early April to mid-May, but should call ahead to be sure someone will be there. Penngrove is east of Highway 101, about an hour north of San Francisco.

> **Portable Acres**
> 2087 Curtis Drive
> Penngrove, CA 94951
> Colin Rigby
> (707) 795-5851
> Catalog: Long SASE with 2 FCS, bn

■ Another nursery offering a very wide range of iris types is **Maxim's Greenwood Gardens** in Redding, California. Georgia Maxim's late husband, Paul, was given some tall bearded iris and was soon collecting and hybridizing them. Georgia has continued his interests and has become active in show judging for the American Iris Society as well.

Offered are hundreds of cultivars of spuria, Louisiana, Siberian, Japanese, and Pacific Coast hybrid iris, as well as tall bearded, median, space age, and Arilbred cultivars. She also offers a few daylilies and, every few years, puts out a daffodil list. Visitors are welcome, but if you want to see Georgia, you should call ahead. Bloom starts in early March and continues into early June. Redding is at the north end of the Sacramento Valley.

> **Maxim's Greenwood Gardens**
> 2157 Sonoma Street
> Redding, CA 96001-3008
> Georgia Maxim
> (916) 241-0764
> Catalog: $1, CAN

■ Well known to iris aficionados is **Laurie's Garden** in Springfield, Oregon. Lorena Reid offers unusual iris: crested (Evansia), Sino-Siberians, hybrids between Sino-Siberians and Pacific Coast iris called Cal-Sibes, Japanese iris, a number of *Iris laevigata, I. pseudacorus* and *I. versicolor* for growing in water, and many beardless species iris. She has introduced a number of hybrids and crosses of her own and has won national and local awards for them.

Started in 1964, this is a small nursery with very special plants which wants to stay small, but if you're looking for Lorena's specialties it's a real find. Visitors are welcome any time. The best season is late May through early July; call ahead if you want to be sure someone will be there. The nursery is located about eighteen miles east of Interstate 5 in Eugene on Highway 126.

> **Laurie's Garden**
> 41886 McKenzie Highway
> Springfield, OR 97478
> Lorena M. Reid
> (503) 896-3756
> Catalog: Long SASE, bn

■ Perched high on a hill in Oregon's wine and filbert country, **Chehalem Gardens** near Dundee has a beautiful view and a wonderful setting. Tom and Ellen Abrego have a lovely garden around their house, and on the slope below they have rows and rows of Siberian and spuria iris. When I arrived they were digging and preparing to replant and putting in some landscape features so that they could host an iris society tour coming up in two years. Just standing in a field of blooming iris and looking out over the vineyards and nut groves ought to give the iris tour an unforgettable experience.

Both Ellen and Tom work for Schreiner's, one of the biggest tall bearded iris growers, but they fell in love with spuria iris and felt that there was so much more that could be done to make them better known and used in gardens. Their goal is not to become a large business but to offer Siberians and spurias that they consider really superior. They are growing and trying many varieties to judge their garden value; they offer about 50 cultivars of each type. They don't ship to Florida. Ellen has won honors as Rodent Queen of their local July-O-Rama; she gave me a pep talk and told me about the new Cinch Gopher Trap, which is supposed to be the ultimate answer. We'll see.

Visitors are welcome on weekends during bloom time in May (call for directions) and other times by appointment only. Dundee is on Highway 99W, between Newberg and McMinnville.

> **Chehalem Gardens**
> P.O. Box 693
> Newberg, OR 97132
> Tom and Ellen Abrego
> (503) 538-8920
> Catalog: Free

■ **Aitken's Salmon Creek Garden** in Vancouver, Washington, offer Pacific Coast iris hybrids, Siberian and Japanese iris, and about 1,000 bearded iris of all types; many are shown in color in the catalog. Terry Aitken, an architect, and Barbara Aitken, a real estate agent, became fascinated by iris. Terry began to hybridize all the bearded types and has won top national awards for his efforts. During the winter he hybridizes orchids! Visitors are welcome to walk through the Aitkens' three acres of display plantings from April to June, but you should call ahead to make an appointment if you want to see Terry or Barbara. The garden is six miles north of Vancouver.

Aitken's Salmon Creek Garden
608 N.W. 119th Street
Vancouver, WA 98685
Terry and Barbara Aitken
(206) 573-4472
Catalog: $1d, CAN

ENSATA GARDENS
Artist: John Coble

■ *Other sources of species iris are:*

Adamgrove, California, MO
Appalachian Wildflower Nursery,
Reedsville, PA
Collector's Nursery, Vancouver, WA
Edgewood Farm & Nursery, Stanardsville, VA
Sunnyridge Gardens, Knoxville, TN

■ *Other sources of Japanese iris are:*

Adamgrove, California, MO
Caprice Farm, Sherwood, OR
Porterhowse Farms, Sandy, OR
Tranquil Lake Nursery, Rehoboth, MA
Andre Viette Farm & Nursery, Fishersville, VA

■ *Other sources of Siberian iris are:*

Adamgrove, California, MO
Busse Gardens, Cokato, MN
Caprice Farm, Sherwood, OR
Country View Gardens, Chesaning, MI
Fieldstone Gardens, Inc., Vassalboro, ME
Holly Lane Iris Gardens, Osseo, MN

Klehm Nursery, South Barrington, IL
Miller's Manor Gardens, Ossian, IN
North Pine Iris Gardens, Norfolk, NE
Sunnyridge Gardens, Knoxville, TN
Tranquil Lake Nursery, Rehoboth, MA
Andre Viette Farm & Nursery, Fishersville, VA

- *Other sources of Louisiana iris are:*

Adamgrove, California, MO
Bay View Gardens, Santa Cruz, CA
Comanche Acres Iris Gardens, Gower, MO
Cordon Bleu Gardens, San Marcos, CA
Louisiana Nursery, Opelousas, LA
Shepard Iris Garden, Phoenix, AZ

- *Other sources of spuria iris are:*

Adamgrove, California, MO
Bay View Gardens, Santa Cruz, CA
Cordon Bleu Gardens, San Marcos, CA
Shepard Iris Garden, Phoenix, AZ

CAPRICE FARM
Artist: Elizabeth Rocchia

Kalmias

■ Richard Jaynes retired from the Connecticut Agricultural Experiment Station after twenty-five years of plant breeding to devote his efforts to hybridizing kalmias; to say that he's been successful is an understatement. Many of you know him as the author of *Kalmia: The Laurel Book* (Timber Press); others just know and love his hybrids. His **Broken Arrow Nursery** in Hamden, Connecticut, offers about 30 cultivars of kalmias, another 50 species and cultivars of rhododendrons and azaleas, and a very nice list of unusual conifers and ornamental trees and shrubs, including dogwoods, larches, pines, and species lilacs.

First, read his book and check out all the variety and beauty of mountain laurels, which demand the same sort of growing conditions as rhododendrons and azaleas, then think how you might use some! They surely deserve to be more used. Visitors are welcome to come and stroll through the Jaynes' woodland garden from April through October; the best season to see the kalmias is late May and early June. It's best to call ahead and check that someone will be at the nursery. Hamden is just north of New Haven.

> **Broken Arrow Nursery**
> 13 Broken Arrow Road
> Hamden, CT 06518
> Richard and Sally Jaynes
> (203) 288-1026
> Catalog: $2, bn/cn

■ Another source of kalmias is **Brown's Kalmia & Azalea Nursery** in Blaine, Washington. Ed Brown is a former airline pilot and blueberry grower who loved kalmias and found that very few nurseries were offering them. He and his wife, Barbara, like to travel and are always looking for interesting new plants. They offer about 30 species and cultivars of kalmia, and they also propagate azaleas, rhododendrons, and heather, which they sell at their nursery. Visitors are welcome to come to the nursery, Monday through Saturday and Sunday afternoon. May and June are the best months; they're closed from Christmas to mid-February, but you can visit then by appointment. Blaine is eighty miles north of Seattle, right on the British Columbia border.

Brown's Kalmia & Azalea Nursery
8527 Semiahmoo Drive
Blaine, WA 98230
Ed and Barbara Brown
(206) 371-2489
Catalog: Long SASE, CAN/OV

■ *Other sources of kalmias are:*

Carlson's Gardens, South Salem, NY
Coenosium Gardens, Aurora, OR
The Cummins Garden, Marlboro, NJ
Rice Creek Gardens, Blain, MN
Roslyn Nursery, Dix Hills, NY
Schild Azalea Gardens & Nursery, Hixson, TN
Twombly Nursery, Monroe, CT
Washington Evergreen Nursery, Leicester, NC
Whitney Gardens & Nursery, Brinnon, WA

Lilacs

Most of us have plants that make us sentimental, and I'll bet that for many people it's lilacs. My parents had a lilac bush in back of their house, and every time we visited the ranch at Easter, a commemorative photo was taken in front of that bush. In every part of the country one sees old lilacs growing by country houses. Some seem to have been abandoned for years, and yet they must have been well loved generations ago. If you have room to grow a lilac it will repay you every year with a heart-stopping welcome to spring.

■ The late Brother John Fiala of Falconskeape Gardens in Medina, Ohio, was introduced to plants by an elderly aunt whom he helped to garden; she taught him Latin plant names. By the time he was in high school he had his own orchard; he went on to become a priest and educator but spent all of his life working with plants, particularly lilacs and flowering crab apples. His lilac hybrids have been attracting lots of attention. He wrote the book *Lilacs: The Genus Syringa* (Timber Press) and was one of the organizers of the International Lilac Society. His hybrids are now being propagated and introduced by **Ameri-Hort Research** in Medina; at present they are offering 10 cultivars. Visitors can see the lilacs in bloom at Falconskeape Gardens, which will be open to the public. Medina is about twenty-five miles south of Cleveland.

> **Ameri-Hort Research**
> P.O. Box 1529
> Medina, OH 44258
> Dr. Karen R. Murray
> (216) 723-4966
> Catalog: $2

■ **Wedge Nursery** in Albert Lea, Minnesota, grows about 150 varieties of lilacs and lists anywhere from 40 to 70 varieties of "French" hybrids, Josiflexa crosses, Hyacinthiflora and Prestoniae cultivars, and species lilacs, depending on how propagation efforts have fared the year before. The catalog gives the official color class for each variety. The Wedge Nursery was started in 1878 and is now run by Donald and Bradford Wedge. Don's father started propagating the lilacs; the Wedges are just beginning to offer peonies on the list as well. Mail order only.

> **Wedge Nursery**
> Route 2, Box 114
> Albert Lea, MN 56007
> Don and Brad Wedge
> (507) 373-5225
> Catalog: Free, cn/bn

■ **Heard Gardens, Ltd.,** in Johnston, Iowa, has been specializing in lilacs since 1928; it was recently purchased by Robert Rennebohm, Jr., a landscape architect who wanted to carry on the tradition. He grows about 90 varieties in his display garden (and will propagate unlisted varieties by special request) and offers about 45 varieties and species of lilacs, listed by bloom color. Included are 3 "low-chill" cultivars, which will reliably bloom in southern climates.

Visitors are welcome to come to nursery and display garden; bloom time is late April through late May. Johnston is a northern suburb of Des Moines, and the nursery is located at the "crossroads of the nation," the intersection of Interstates 35 and 80.

> **Heard Gardens, Ltd.**
> 5355 Merle Hay Road
> Johnston, IA 50131
> Robert B. Rennebohm, Jr.
> (515) 276-4533
> Catalog: $2d, cn/bn

■ *Other sources of lilacs are:*

Arborvillage Farm Nursery, Holt, MO
Carroll Gardens, Westminster, MD
Colvos Creek Nursery, Vashon Island, WA
Hartmann's Plantation, Grand Junction, MI
Smith Nursery Company, Charles City, IA
Twombly Nursery, Monroe, CT

Native Plants
and Wildflowers

In the time that I've been collecting catalogs for writing and revising *Gardening by Mail,* two strong trends have become obvious: one is the interest in growing native plants; the other is the interest in growing heirloom varieties of both ornamental and edible plants.

The heartening thing about both trends is the turn away from the new-every-year pressure and toward using plants that have proved themselves superior over a long period, plants that have both practical and sentimental reasons for use. For those of us still living near our native heath (pretty rare in these days), it means using plants we have known and loved all our lives. Is there a heart so hard that seeing the wildflowers of our childhood is not a thrill? It suddenly occurred to me that not everyone reading this grew up in the country — life is so *unfair!*

It used to be that the sort of people who were interested in native plants were academics and amateur botanists who liked to explore the outback botanizing and keying plants along the way. Thanks to them there are good handbooks to native flora for most of the country, and native plant societies in nearly every state open to all who are interested, offering education, plant sales, and field trips.

Thanks also to these native plant enthusiasts, native plants crept into gardens, proved themselves to be attractive and appropriate, and especially tolerant of regional climatic conditions without a lot of fuss. The funny thing is that many of our overlooked native plants have been considered garden gems in England for centuries; many have been "improved" and returned to us as rarities!

Several years ago I was jaunting around southern England visiting gardens with my friend Daniel Campbell of the Botanical Garden at the University of California at Berkeley. Dan had discovered a pink flowering *Zauschneria californica* at the Solidarity Mine in the mother lode area of the Sierra foothills and had brought three plants to give to the great English plantsman Graham Stuart Thomas. On the day we were to take the plants to him it was obvious that two were dead and the third was barely holding on.

Dan did what he could to make it look lively, and as we drove up we could see Graham Thomas puttering in his front garden. When we got out of the car he rushed forward with his hand outstretched — not to shake but to receive the treasure without delay. First things first; having got the plant he very kindly showed us his garden and gave us a cool drink. Luckily the plant lived and got a nice mention in the third edition of his wonderful *Perennial Garden Plants or the Modern Florilegium;* you might also like the very pretty *Zauschneria* 'Solidarity Pink'.

One of the most important things to consider when buying native plants from any nursery is the source of the plants. Years ago plant collectors roamed at will, digging up plants and bulbs to sell to gardeners, or gardeners went collecting for themselves. Louise Beebe Wilder makes many references to Carl Purdy, who wandered around California for many years, digging wild bulbs and shipping them off to climates where they were unlikely to grow. Now we're trying to save plants endangered due to overcollecting, and you should always check to see that the native plants you buy are truly grown from seed or propagated from nursery stock. It's important to check; some nurseries offer "nursery-grown" native plants that are really wild collected plants or bulbs grown in pots at the nursery for a few months. Be sure to ask very firmly if the plants are *nursery-propagated,* and find another source if you don't get a straight answer. Each of the nurseries mentioned here has assured me that they don't do any wild collecting and that their plants are nursery-propagated.

While many of the native plants in this section are native to some part of this continent, some are related species from other parts of the world or species plants just beginning to make their way into gardens and not yet subject to years of selection and hybridizing. Some don't fit into any category except that they are closer to being plants that grow in the wild than cultivated garden plants.

In writing about sources of native plants and wildflowers, I'll try to mention the region where the plants are native. There's a wonderful nursery in New Mexico called Bernardo Beach Native Plant Farm, which stopped shipping because the plants it sold did not thrive in other parts of the country. I need hardly point out that the same is true of nearly all native plants put into inappropriate situations; if you have doubts, why not call the grower and discuss your own specific growing conditions before ordering plants from a different climate.

Single-flowered Kerria   Double-flowered Kerria

TRIPPLE BROOK FARM   *Artist: Betty Stull Schaffer*

■ By now, you know that I love catalogs that are packed with plant information and that seem to be the product of an individual sensibility; the more personal the opinions and point of view, the more I like them. One I have always enjoyed is that from **Tripple Brook Farm** in Southampton, Massachusetts. Stephen Breyer was studying ecology and horticulture in college at the time his parents were winding down their poultry business on the family farm; he decided that using the farm as a nursery for hardy edible, useful, and ornamental plants was a good idea.

His catalog is in tiny print, crammed with plants of all kinds, as his parameters are very broad, very informative, and opinionated; he offers hardy kiwis and bamboos, ornamental grasses, many northeastern native plants, some trees and shrubs, rock garden plants and ground covers, hardy cactus and aquatic plants. Stephen's consuming interest is landscaping, and visitors can come to the farm to walk through his display areas but must call ahead; visits are possible on weekends in the spring and daily from July through the fall. Southampton is in the Connecticut River valley of western Massachusetts on Highway 10, ten miles south of Northampton.

> **Tripple Brook Farm**
> 37 Middle Road
> Southampton, MA 01073
> Stephen R. Breyer
> (413) 527-4626 (evenings)
> Catalog: Free, CAN/OV, bn

■ Phyllis Farkas of **Wildginger Woodlands** in Webster, New York, lives on twenty acres of woodland full of native plants. She began to collect seed and grown-on seedlings and then to sell plants and seeds because she couldn't bear to throw away her surplus. She's very proud of having found a method of growing fringed gentian from seed and sends detailed instructions with the seed; one of her customers told her he'd been trying to grow fringed gentian for forty years and doing it at last was his proudest achievement. She offers a good selection of northeastern native wildflowers and hardy ferns; shipping is difficult to California. Mail order only.

Wildginger Woodlands
P.O. Box 1091
Webster, NY 14580
Phyllis Farkas
Catalog: $1d, bn/cn

■ Don Hackenberry of the **Appalachian Wildflower Nursery** in Reedsville, Pennsylvania, specializes in natives of the Virginia–West Virginia border, the western U.S., Central Asia, the Caucasus, the Russian Pacific coast, and other areas of the former Soviet Union. He's got a long list of phlox (23 on the current list and many more unlisted), species iris, many galanthus, primulas, penstemons, scutellaria, and many species in the ranunculaceae. The catalog gives very good descriptions of the plants; a twice-yearly availability and price list keeps the catalog up-to-date.

A former federal government employee, Don finally gave in to the call of the plant world and quit to do what he loved best. He's crazy about plants, so his list tends to feature plants he's recently discovered, including plants grown from seeds exchanged with botanical gardens all over the world. Visitors are welcome Thursday through Saturday; call ahead for directions and to be sure Don will be there. Reedsville is in central Pennsylvania, about halfway between Harrisburg and State College.

Appalachian Wildflower Nursery
Route 1, Box 275A
Reedsville, PA 17084
Don Hackenberry
(717) 667-6998
Catalog: $2d, bn

■ A nursery high on my list to visit is **Niche Gardens** in Chapel Hill, North Carolina; the enthusiasm that spills out of the catalog is intoxicating. Kim and Bruce Hawks started their nursery in 1986 to offer nursery-propagated native plants instead of the wild-collected plants generally available. Kim, who has a degree in horticulture, runs the nursery and does garden designs. Bruce has a full-time job in air pollution testing and helps out as much as he can. Somehow they find time and energy to produce two catalogs a year, a newsletter, and to offer workshops on garden design with native plants at the nursery. Their list is strong in southeastern native plants, trees and shrubs, and ornamental grasses, everything from bog plants to drought-tolerant plants and some unusual perennials. They have lovely display gardens and are open by appointment only, except for several open weekends in the spring and fall.

Niche Gardens
1111 Dawson Road
Chapel Hill, NC 27516
Kim and Bruce Hawks
(919) 967-0078
Catalog: $3, CAN/OV, bn/cn

NICHE GARDENS　*Artist: Dot Wilbur*

■ One of the most specialized growers of near-wildflowers is Thurman Maness of **The Wildwood Flower** in Pittsboro, North Carolina; he's made a number of crosses between two eastern native plants, *Lobelia cardinalis* and *L. siphilitica*, which he calls *L. hybrida*. These have stunning colors; I saw some of them in the garden at Heronswood Nursery, and they really stood out as superior plants in the border. Thurman lists about 30 cultivars and is introducing a few English cultivars. He also has 3 forms of *Lobelia cardinalis alba* and several forms and hybrids of *Athyrium nipponicum* 'Pictum', the Japanese painted fern; other good ground cover ferns, several good garden shrubs, and *Begonia grandis alba*. Plants shipped to California and Arizona are subject to agricultural inspection, which may cause some delay.

When I asked Thurman if he'd won any awards for his lobelia hybrids, he said he'd given himself a hundred pats on the back — deservedly so, as his plants are really lovely! He grew up in central North Carolina and is a country antiques dealer as well as a part-time amateur plant breeder who has created seventy-five percent of the available perennial lobelia hybrids. He says his is not a conventional nursery. He is very pressed for time, so visitors are welcome by appointment only. Pittsboro is fifteen miles south of Chapel Hill on Highway 15.

The Wildwood Flower
Route 3, Box 165
Pittsboro, NC 27312
Thurman Maness
(919) 542-4344
Catalog: Long SASE, bn

■ Does the Southeast have the best wildflowers and native plants? They certainly have a lot of nurseries specializing in native plants! **Gardens of the Blue Ridge** in Pineola, North Carolina, offers a fine selection of wildflowers and other natives for shade and rock gardens. The nursery was started in 1892 by Harlan Kelsey and bought by Edward Robbins's father in 1913 (he started working there as a boy of thirteen in 1898). Now Edward Robbins's family has inherited the nursery and will be running it. Visitors are welcome to visit Monday to Saturday noon where the plants are grown in acres of raised beds; May through October are the best months. The nursery is located about thirty miles north of Boone, near the Blue Ridge Parkway.

Gardens of the Blue Ridge
P.O. Box 10
Pineola, NC 28662
The Robbins Family
(704) 733-2417
Catalog: $2, CAN/OV, bn/cn

■ How about another wildflower nursery in North Carolina? Surprised? **Brookside Wildflowers** in Boone is run by Jo Boggs, a former interior designer who spent a lot of time photographing wildflowers while her husband fished. When he retired they moved to the mountains so that she could run a nursery. She specializes in native perennials of the East and South; she's recently added some wildflowers from the Pacific Northwest. She lists about 150 perennial wildflowers, grouped by season of bloom. The plant descriptions are excellent, and the catalog includes lists of plants for special uses such as winter interest, plants for shade, flowers for cutting, and so forth. The only state Jo can't ship to is California. The setting of the nursery looks lovely, surrounded by hills and with a pond, an old barn, and display beds. Visitors are welcome daily from May through Labor Day. Boone is west of the Blue Ridge Parkway in western North Carolina. Jo says it's lovely and cool in the summer.

> **Brookside Wildflowers**
> Route 3, Box 740
> Boone, NC 28607
> Jo Boggs
> (704) 963-5548
> Catalog: $2, bn/cn

■ **Eco-Gardens** is a botanical collection in Decatur, Georgia, which specializes in natives and exotic plants hardy in the Piedmont region (USDA Zones 7 and 8). Exotic plants are not "tropical" plants but plants not native to the area. Plants are exchanged with botanical gardens and plantsmen all over the world, and surplus plants are sold to raise operating funds. Don Jacobs has a Ph.D. in ecology and is a former college professor who taught in both Minnesota and Georgia; he also ran a pet supplies business for many years before starting his plant collection.

The Eco-Gardens plant list includes intriguing arisaemas, asarums, epimediums, tiarellas, trilliums, violas, phlox, tricyrtis, and many more. This is definitely a plant source that does not want to grow, only to be self-supporting, so it may take some time to get newer plants added to the list. Visitors must call for an appointment and directions. The gardens are about fifteen miles east of Atlanta.

> **Eco-Gardens**
> P.O. Box 1227
> Decatur, GA 30031

Don L. Jacobs, Ph.D.
(404) 294-6468
Catalog: $1, CAN/OV, bn

■ Gail Barton and Richard Lowery of **Flowerplace Plant Farm**
specialize in plants that will survive the extreme conditions of
their garden in Meridian, Mississippi; this means wildflowers
of their area and ornamental herbs and grasses that can take
extreme heat, heavy clay soil, and have few, if any, pests.
Flowerplace also offers tried-and-true heirloom perennials,
hardy hibiscus, and some tough old garden roses. Gail and
Richard test each plant over several seasons, so gardeners with
similar "impossible" growing conditions can consider these
plants pretested; this way you can let Gail and Richard suffer
the heartbreaks for you. You can be sure that anything you
find on this list is really tough! Among the plants offered are
native asters, rudbeckias, salvias, and some native woody
plants and vines.

Gail is a horticulture instructor at the local community college, and Richard is a former optician who was her student
when he decided to change careers. Richard works at the nursery full-time, assisted by several cats and dogs (good for a
high Barton Animal Index rating). Visitors should call for an
appointment. Meridian is in southeastern Mississippi, near the
Alabama border; Richard says the plant farm is located on
the toenail of the foothills of the Appalachian Mountains.

Flowerplace Plant Farm
P.O. Box 4865
Meridian, MS 39304
Gail Barton and Richard Lowery
(601) 482-5686
Catalog: $3, cn/bn

FLOWERPLACE PLANT FARM
Artist: Gail Barton

■ Bob and Julie Holland live in the White River valley of northwestern Arkansas. Bob learned about wildflowers from his grandmother, Lucy Puckett (doesn't she sound like the perfect gardening granny?). He studied wildlife research and plant pathology in college and wrote environmental impact statements. In the early eighties he and Julie began to experiment with wildflower propagation techniques and were so successful that they started their **Holland Wildflower Farm** in the southern Ozarks.

Bob's now a plant pathologist for the Cooperative Extension Service and a bluegrass musician; Julie has quit teaching high school science, and they are helped by their young daughters, Laurel and Connell, so the nursery is a family project. Their specialties are southeastern and midwestern wildflowers, and they are expanding into native shrubs and trees and some unusual perennials. The catalog describes the plants well (they're sold in quantities of six). Visitors are welcome to visit the farm from Thursday through Saturday or by appointment and see the display garden. The best months to visit are April through June. Elkins is twelve miles southeast of Fayetteville on Highway 16.

Holland Wildflower Farm
290 O'Neal Lane
Elkins, AR 72727
Bob and Julie Holland
(501) 643-2622
Catalog: $2, CAN, bn/cn

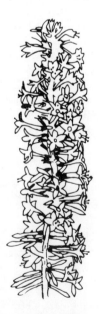

HOLLAND WILDFLOWER FARM
Artist: Bob Holland

■ Meredith Bradford managed a large goat dairy, but when she got interested in wildflowers and married her botany professor, Ed Clebsch, the goats had to go (actually, the goats were in Apple Valley, California, Ed in Tennessee). Together Meredith and Ed Clebsch run **Native Gardens** in Greenback, Tennessee. They offer a good selection of nursery-propagated Eastern native plants and wildflowers of all types for meadow and natural landscaping in sun or shade, including a few shrubs and trees. Their catalog is a marvel of useful information packed into a concise table. Visitors must make an appointment to visit the nursery, located about thirty miles southwest of Knoxville. The Clebsches also have a retail outlet in Townsend, Tennessee (near Gatlinburg and the Great Smoky Mountains) called Wildflowers by Native Gardens.

> **Native Gardens**
> Route 1, Box 464
> Greenback, TN 37742
> Edward and Meredith Clebsch
> (615) 856-3350
> Catalog: $2, cn/bn

■ Andrea Sessions and Marty Zenni rate high on the Barton Animal Index. They both love riding horses and having dogs to help them around the nursery. Andrea is trained as a horticulturist and has worked at the New York Botanical Garden and at the Smithsonian; her husband, Marty, was a city horticulturist in Oak Ridge, Tennessee. They now grow southeastern wildflowers from seeds and cuttings at their **Sunlight Gardens** in Andersonville, Tennessee. They offer more than 150 species of wildflowers and hardy ferns, plus some traditional perennials. Visitors are welcome with an appointment. April through September are the best months to visit. Andersonville is about twenty miles northwest of Knoxville.

> **Sunlight Gardens**
> Route 1, Box 600-A
> Andersonville, TN 37705
> Andrea Sessions and Marty Zenni
> (615) 494-8237
> Catalog: $2, bn

In recent years there has been a movement to preserve and restore the native prairies of the Midwest. In Wisconsin I visited two botanical gardens with demonstration prairies. In one I walked on paths with grasses growing higher than my head;

someone on horseback would have had trouble seeing very far on flat land. The variety of plants within the grass community was surprising, and, of course, plant communities vary with soil moisture and type.

There are several nurseries offering plants and seeds for native prairie plants as well as advice on how to establish the plants and maintain your own prairie — sometimes it even involves burning the grasses in the fall before the snow falls.

Bottle Gentian

PRAIRIE NURSERY *Artist: Helen Mortenson*

■ Neil Diboll of **Prairie Nursery** in Westfield, Wisconsin, wants to encourage the restoration of the prairie and the growing of prairie plants. A former park and forest ranger, Neil also managed the Arboretum of the University of Wisconsin at Green Bay before becoming a nurseryman.

Neil specializes in native midwestern wildflowers and grasses, some of which will also grow well in many other areas except for the Deep South. He publishes a beautiful and informative catalog and is also involved in site analysis, design, and installation of prairie restorations. Visitors may join nursery tours on specific Saturdays in June, July, and August (call for dates) or may make an appointment two weeks in advance. Westfield is about sixty miles north of Madison.

> **Prairie Nursery**
> P.O. Box 306
> Westfield, WI 53964
> Neil Diboll
> (608) 296-3679
> Catalog: $3 (2 years), CAN/OV, cn/bn

Pasque Flower - A. pulsatilla
flowers and seed head

PRAIRIE NURSERY   *Artist: Helen Mortenson*

■ **Prairie Ridge Nursery** in Mount Horeb, Wisconsin, offers a good selection of nursery-propagated native plants for wet prairie, woodland, and prairie, as well as seed mixes so that you can grow your own; the catalog gives a lot of cultural information.

The proprietor, Joyce Powers, is a biologist who has taught for the National Wildlife Federation, the University of Wisconsin Extension Service, public schools, and other groups and who consults on prairie restorations. The nursery has demonstration prairie plantings and is open Monday to Saturday from mid-April to mid-October, and Monday to Friday the rest of the year. Mount Horeb is eighteen miles west of Madison.

> **Prairie Ridge Nursery**
> 9738 Overland Road
> RR 2
> Mount Horeb, WI 53572-2832
> Joyce Powers
> (608) 437-5245
> FAX (608) 437-8982
> Catalog: $1, bn/cn

■ **Prairie Moon Nursery** in Winona, Minnesota, offers a broad selection of seeds and plants for prairies, large and small, and detailed advice on how to plant them; information on the plants is given in concise tables. Alan Wade came by his interest from his mother, Dorothy, who was a pioneer in the reintroduction of prairie plants and who ran the Windrift Nursery in Illinois.

Alan became a member of a land co-op in the "Driftless Area" of southeastern Minnesota; missed by the last glaciers, the land is deeply fissured with steep hillsides and, unfortunately for the co-op, exhausted soil. Now many of the members help with the nursery, where they have twenty acres in the production of native plants and plants for seed. Visitors may visit by appointment only. Winona is east of Rochester near the Mississippi River.

> **Prairie Moon Nursery**
> Route 3, Box 163
> Winona, MN 55987
> Alan Wade
> (507) 452-5231 or 1362
> Catalog: $2, CAN, bn/cn

■ **Landscape Alternatives** in St. Paul, Minnesota, is a source of about 150 native wildflowers and grasses for many garden situations and prairie plantings. It also offers collections of plants for various situations; all of its plants are nursery-propagated.

Partners Karl Ruser and Roy Robison worked together as teacher and student in the Horticulture Department at the University of Minnesota and saw a need for prairie plants for landscape use. The nursery is located in Roseville at 691 W. Larpenteur Avenue. Visitors are welcome from Tuesday through Sunday but should call ahead, as hours are variable.

> **Landscape Alternatives, Inc.**
> 1465 Pascal Street
> St. Paul, MN 55108
> Karl Ruser, Gen. Mgr.
> (612) 488-3142
> Catalog: $1, CAN, cn/bn

LANDSCAPE ALTERNATIVES
Artist: Roy Robison

■ **Orchid Gardens** in Andover, Minnesota, is not a prairie plant nursery but one specializing in native woodland plants and wildflowers. Offered are violets, mosses, hardy ferns, dwarf shrubs, and other native trees and shrubs, as well as a good selection of wildflowers.

Carl Phillips is the son of Norma Phillips, the founder of Orchid Gardens and the author of *The Root Book* and *Adventures of a 'Wild' Plants Woman*. Both books are about growing and knowing native plants and their special cultural requirements and are available from Orchid Gardens. Carl is a landscaper who travels frequently to northern Minnesota, where he and his wife, Yvonne, own woodland property that they use for growing their plants. Mail order only.

Orchid Gardens
2232 139th Avenue N.W.
Andover, MN 55304
Carl and Yvonne Phillips
(612) 755-0205
Catalog: $.75, cn/bn

■ From one extreme to another: **Desert Moon Nursery** in Veguita, New Mexico, is located at 4,800 feet and offers hardy cactus, good selections of yuccas and agaves, and other hardy native plants and wildflowers of the Southwest and the Chihuahuan desert, most of which are perfect for hot, dry gardens. Plants to California have to be shipped bare root; some do not travel as well as others.

Ted Hodoba grew up in Pennsylvania and was an art major in college, but by the fluke of knowing Russian landed a job in a library working with Russian publications. On a trip to New Mexico he walked into a library and got a job, got interested in native plants, became president of the New Mexico Native Plant Society (are you beginning to see a trend here?), and ended up running a native plant nursery. His wife, Candy Croft-Hodoba, is a herpetologist at the Rio Grande Zoo in Albuquerque. Visitors should call ahead to be sure someone will be at the nursery and to get directions.

Desert Moon Nursery
P.O. Box 600
Veguita, NM 87062
Ted and Candy Hodoba
(505) 864-0614
Catalog: $1, bn/cn

It will be a happy day when my fellow Californians bite the bullet and start planting gardens that are in sync with our climate. About two years ago, the papers were full of stories about a zillionaire in the Santa Barbara area willing to pay in the neighborhood of $10,000 a month for water to keep his very large lawn green!

■ **Wildwood Nursery** in Claremont, California, is a source of native and Mediterranean plants for the dry summer climate. Ray Walsh is a landscape architect who wanted to use more native plants and decided to grow them himself. Now he does environmental restorations all over California. His designs feature drought- and fire-resistant plants. He offers plants and seeds of native trees, shrubs, grasses, ground covers, and other plants. There's no room for a display garden, so Ray suggests a visit to the Rancho Santa Ana Botanic Garden in Claremont, famous for its native plant displays. The nursery is in nearby La Verne and is open Monday through Saturday.

> **Wildwood Nursery**
> P.O. Box 1334
> Claremont, CA 91711
> Ray Walsh
> (714) 593-4093 or 621-2112
> Catalog: $1, bn/cn

■ **Las Pilitas Nursery** in Santa Margarita, California, was started by Bert and Celeste Wilson in their back yard while they were still students at Cal Poly in San Luis Obispo. They say that they have become "the nursery of last resort for California native plants" and now offer the largest selection in the world; looking at their plant lists I couldn't argue. Bert says that they've been increasingly successful at working with plants that have previously been considered almost ungrowable.

Their densely packed plant list runs to over a hundred pages and contains a lot of useful cultural information. They also sell separate lists of "deer-proof," edible, drought-resistant, butterfly- and bird-attracting, high-altitude, and fire-resistant plants; each of these lists costs a dollar. The Wilsons can't ship to Arkansas, Florida, Georgia, Louisiana, Mississippi, Tennessee, or Virginia.

Bert is a busy landscape contractor and is proud of a number of his "walk-away" landscapes: plantings that required only one good initial watering to grow on and thrive. Celeste works with the help of only two young children on weekends and a part-time helper, so be patient when you write for a catalog or order plants. Santa Margarita is half an hour south of San Luis Obispo and two hours north of Santa Barbara. Visitors are welcome on Saturdays.

Las Pilitas Nursery
Star Route, Box 23X
Santa Margarita, CA 93453
Bert and Celeste Wilson
(805) 438-5992
Catalog: $6, bn/cn
Price list free

■ **Plants of the Wild** in Tekoa, Washington, is a source of Pacific Northwest native plants, including trees, shrubs, and perennials to conserve water and attract wildlife; the nursery specializes in supplying plants for habitat restoration and has also been working with the Mariposa Foundation in Moscow, Idaho, to propagate and increase two species of calochortus. The nursery is also propagating two species of camassia which have become rare and plans to add more endangered species of native plants. Visitors can see the plants displayed around the nursery office; Tekoa is halfway between Pullman and Spokane in eastern Washington.

Plants of the Wild
P.O. Box 866
Tekoa, WA 99033
Kathy Hutton, Mgr.
(509) 284-2848
FAX (509) 284-6464
Catalog: $1, bn/cn

■ *Other sources of native plants*
and wildflowers are:

Collector's Nursery, Vancouver, WA
Colvos Creek Nursery, Vashon
  Island, WA
Donaroma's Nursery, Edgartown, MA
Forestfarm, Williams, OR
Lamtree Farm, Warrensville, NC
Owen Farms, Ripley, TN
Siskiyou Rare Plant Nursery,
  Medford, OR
Transplant Nursery, Lavonia, GA
Woodlanders, Inc., Aiken, SC
Yucca Do Nursery, Waller, TX

LANDSCAPE ALTERNATIVES
Artist: Roy Robison

Peonies

CAPRICE FARM
Artist: Elizabeth Rocchia

Almost the first plants I ordered when I moved to the country were herbaceous peonies. I'd never lived anywhere where it got cold enough in the winter for peonies. Truth be told, I grew up a few miles from the beach at Malibu in southern California. In those days it was real country, and we had horses, cows, and goats; now it's all rock stars and zillion-dollar houses. I saw my first snow and first peonies in Europe and had been dying to grow peonies ever since (snow, I can easily do without).

In early spring I'm out checking to see if the red shoots are starting to come up. When they're in bloom I stop at their bed every day to enjoy them. When they're done I feel sad. Over five years I've moved the peonies several times. They seem to be more forgiving than they should be; they now have lots of space, sun, and water, and I expect orgies of enjoyment for many springs to come. It's obvious that if I can grow peonies, anyone who lives in USDA Zone 8 or lower can do the same. Just a few in a vase will make you feel like a wealthy seventeenth-century Dutch burgher.

■ David Reath of **Reath's Nursery** in Vulcan, Michigan, was introduced to peonies by Sylvia Saunders, the daughter of the legendary A. P. Saunders, a hybridizer of many spectacular herbaceous and tree peonies while a professor at Clinton College in New York State. Now a veterinarian, David and his son Scott, who has a degree in horticulture, are running a nursery that offers hundreds of peonies, both tree and herbaceous cultivars. They have been hybridizing their own tree peonies with great success but also offer the hybrids of Professor Saunders and Nassos Daphnis, tree peonies from Japan, the very rare *Paeonia suffruticosa* var. *Rock* (both single and double), and the double fern leaf peony. The nursery is located on Michigan's Upper Peninsula and is not open to visitors. The Reaths have one open weekend every year; call for the date.

Reath's Nursery
P.O. Box 521
Vulcan, MI 49892
David Reath
(906) 563-9777
Catalog: $1

■ There's no nursery more closely identified with peonies than **Klehm Nursery** in South Barrington, Illinois. Its thick catalog is a feast for the winter-weary. The nursery was founded in 1852; Roy Klehm is the third generation of peony hybridizers in his family, and his son Kit has recently joined the company. They call their own Klehm family introductions "Estate Peonies." They offer about 325 herbaceous and tree peonies of their own and from many other hybridizers and import some choice varieties from Japan. The nursery also offers many perennials, including daylilies, Siberian iris, hostas (including the introductions of Paul Aden), and other plants for shade.

Klehm Nursery
Route 5, Box 197
South Barrington, IL 60010-9555
Roy Klehm
(217) 373-8400, (800) 553-3715
Catalog: $4d, CAN/OV, bn

■ Kent Crossley is a doctor who grew up in the southern Minnesota community that was home to the largest peony garden in the United States. He started going to peony shows with his parents when he was in grade school, and when the famous old peony nursery closed in 1979, he couldn't resist buying many of the old cultivars to preserve them from going out of commerce.

Kent started **The New Peony Farm** in St. Paul, Minnesota, in 1980; he's now growing 300 cultivars of herbaceous peonies and offers a good selection in his catalog. He's a past president of the American and Minnesota Peony Societies and is now hybridizing peonies and hopes to introduce his own cultivars soon. Visitors may walk through the growing areas in May and June but must call to make prior arrangements and to get directions to the fields, which are near Faribault, forty miles south of St. Paul.

> **The New Peony Farm**
> P.O. Box 18105
> St. Paul, MN 55118
> Kent Crossley
> (612) 457-8994
> Catalog: Free, CAN

■ **Brand Peony Farm** in St. Cloud, Minnesota, was started in the late nineteenth century and passed through several owners. Gerald and Irene Lund bought it in 1983. They offer both newer varieties and a number of older, hard-to-find varieties, some hybridized by one of the original owners, Oliver Brand, and some newer cultivars by the late Ben Gilbertson. The Lunds sell by mail order only but are a good source of heirloom varieties for restoring a historical garden.

> **Brand Peony Farm**
> P.O. Box 842
> St. Cloud, MN 56302
> Gerald and Irene Lund
> Catalog: $1d

■ **Caprice Farm** in Sherwood, Oregon, is known for its peonies. The "caprice" in the name refers to Al and Dorothy Rogers' move to the country to raise their children. Al was a medical researcher in Portland for many years, and the couple found, within commuting distance, a farm with a wonderful old farmhouse where they could raise children, goats, and peonies.

They've now moved out of the old house to a newer house at the top of their peony field and, since Al retired, they have devoted their time to collecting and growing the plants they love. Al Rogers got his first peony as a birthday gift when he was eight. He's now writing a book on peonies which will be published by Timber Press. Their son Richard and daughter Robin Blue work with them. They now grow 200 peony cultivars, both herbaceous and tree types, 250 daylilies, and 150 cultivars of Japanese and Siberian iris. These plants make the Rogers' fields a joy to walk through, starting with the peonies in May through the late daylilies in August. The nursery is about twenty-five miles southwest of Portland and is open Monday through Saturday; call for directions if you don't have a catalog.

Caprice Farm
15425 S.W. Pleasant Hill Road
Sherwood, OR 97140
Al, Dorothy, and Richard Rogers, Robin Blue
(503) 625-7241
Catalog: $2

■ The **A & D Peony and Perennial Farm** in Snohomish, Washington, attracts many visitors in the spring to see its peonies in bloom. The nursery grows more than 500 cultivars and 15 species in the display gardens, including a number of the famous Saunders hybrids, which were brought to the Northwest many years ago by one of Saunders's assistants, as well as about 130 tree peonies. They offer about 180 to 200 varieties in their catalog, and the selection changes from year to year.

Don Smetana is a free-lance advertising whiz, and Keith Abel is a horticulturist and landscaper. In their free time they like to collect mushrooms in the northwestern forests. They also grow more than 400 daylily cultivars and 350 hosta cultivars; about 150 of each are offered in their catalog. They're open daily from April to June for the peonies, and from Wednesday to Sunday all summer for the daylilies. The nursery and display gardens are about twenty miles north of Seattle.

A & D Peony and Perennial Farm
6808 180th S.E.
Snohomish, WA 98290
Don Smetana and Keith Abel
(206) 485-2487
Catalog: $1.50d

■ *Other sources of peonies are:*

Adamgrove, California, MO
Anderson Iris Gardens, Forest Lake, MN

Busse Gardens, Cokato, MN
Carroll Gardens, Westminster, MD
Hildenbrandt's Iris Gardens, Lexington, NE
Andre Viette Farm & Nursery, Fishersville, VA
Wedge Nursery, Albert Lea, MN
Gilbert H. Wild & Son, Sarcoxie, MO

Perennials
and Vines

Many nurseries mentioned in other sections of this book also offer specific garden perennials. There are also many nurseries that sell a broad selection of perennials, but in each specific genera the selection is not broad enough to list them as specialists.

The nurseries described here offer broad selections of perennials, some quite choice or rare, and I have tried to mention nurseries in all parts of the country so that many of you will be able to visit them and see the plants yourselves.

■ **Surry Gardens** in Surry, Maine, offers more than 600 varieties of perennials, herbs, and rock garden plants. The nursery doesn't issue a catalog but rather a plant list with information in a very compact table; among the groups of plants with good selections are campanulas, primulas, platycodons, dianthus, verbascums, and veronicas. James Dickinson, a trained horticulturist, spent summers in Maine in his youth, went to college there, and started his nursery right out of college in

1978. The nursery is open daily from April through October; Surry is west of Ellsworth on Highway 172, not far from Bar Harbor.

Surry Gardens
P.O. Box 145
Surry, ME 04684
James M. Dickinson
(207) 667-4493 or 5589
Catalog: Free, bn

■ Steve Jones of **Fieldstone Gardens** in Vassalboro, Maine, has a broad selection of perennials, herbs, rock garden plants, and ground covers. Listed, among others, are a good selection of aconitums, ajugas, asters, astilbes, campanulas, clematis, hardy geraniums, monardas, peonies, phlox, pulmonarias, veronicas, and vincas. Steve also carries many of the Siberian iris hybrids of Dr. Currier McEwen of South Harpswell, Maine.

Steve has a degree in horticulture from the University of Maine. He started the nursery on the family farm and named it for the many stone walls built by his ancestors. He's the fourth generation to work the farm; his parents still live there and help him with the nursery. Steve is always looking for good plants that will survive in USDA Zone 4 and introduces new ones every year.

Visitors are welcome every day except Monday; there's a large display garden around the nursery. It's open from April to mid-November. Vassalboro is ten miles north of Augusta, off Route 201.

Fieldstone Gardens, Inc.
620 Quaker Lane
Vassalboro, ME 04989-9713
Steven D. Jones
(207) 923-3836
Catalog: $2, CAN/OV, bn/cn

■ **Perennial Pleasures Nursery** in East Hardwick, Vermont, specializes in plants and seeds for period gardens and garden restorations. So committed are Rachel Kane and her mother, Judith, that their plants are listed by period of introduction so that you can choose plants from the appropriate century. They even offer suggestions for studying your garden for signs of earlier layout and include a bibliography of good books for further study. Their plants are primarily species plants and herbs.

There's a three-acre display garden, and visitors are welcome. Judith serves English cream teas in the garden from early June to Labor Day and runs a three-room bed and breakfast in their 1840s Federal brick house. East Hardwick is in the northeast corner of Vermont, about thirty miles north of Montpelier.

> **Perennial Pleasures Nursery**
> 2 Brickhouse Road
> East Hardwick, VT 05836
> Rachel and Judith Kane
> (802) 472-5104 or 5512
> Catalog: $2d, bn/cn

■ Martha's Vineyard, off the coast of Massachusetts, may not be accessible to everyone, but it has a good source for perennials. **Donaroma's Nursery** offers more than 450 perennials, both for the sophisticated gardener and for those who want low-maintenance gardens. Michael Donaroma, who wanted good plants for his landscaping jobs, says that most of the plants are summer bloomers for summer dwellers: good selections of campanulas, delphiniums, dianthus, ornamental and native grasses, lupines, platycodons, late-blooming primulas, scabiosas, silenes, veronicas, and native wildflowers, among others. Visitors are welcome to see the display garden on the main street of Edgartown from late June through August.

> **Donaroma's Nursery**
> P.O. Box 2189
> Edgartown, MA 02539
> Michael Donaroma
> (508) 627-8366 or 3036
> Catalog: Free, CAN/OV, bn/cn

■ Paul Hammer has a Ph.D. in floriculture from Ohio State University. Formerly a professor at the University of Connecticut, he's now putting his degree to good use by growing perennials and rock garden plants at his **Ledgecrest Greenhouses** in Storrs, Connecticut.

Offered are more than 100 varieties in three-inch pots. Paul also offers collections of 24 plants for sun, shade, or mixed sun and shade. The retail nursery is open daily all year except for major holidays; larger plants are available there. Storrs is about nine miles northwest of Willimantic.

Ledgecrest Greenhouses
1029 Storrs Road
Storrs, CT 06268
Paul Hammer
(203) 487-1661
Catalog: 2 FCS, bn/cn

■ What is there to say about **White Flower Farm**? Most of us have wallowed in the wonderful catalog and chuckled along with "Amos Pettingill." One has the feeling that here is an almost seamless blend of big business and plant consciousness, but the nursery grows almost every plant on the premises, except for bulbs and a few woody plants. The catalog is very informative (one of my early tutors), and there's even a horticultural help phone line for customers. Offered is a broad selection of perennials, spring and summer bulbs, and some roses, shrubs, and vines, many illustrated in color. The display garden in Litchfield, Connecticut, is open to visitors from mid-April to the end of October, and it looks quite lovely. The nursery is located about twenty-five miles north of Hartford on Route 63, three miles south of Litchfield.

White Flower Farm
Route 63
Litchfield, CT 06759-0050
Eliot Wadsworth II
(203) 567-0801 or 496-9600
Catalog: $5d, bn/cn

■ Several years ago there was a flurry of books on clematis, with beautiful pictures, and the demand for clematis took off. The largest grower of clematis in this country is **Arthur H. Steffen, Inc.** in Fairport, New York. This is a wholesale business, but it does sell more than 200 varieties of clematis by mail order, both large-flowered cultivars and small-flowered cultivars and species. Steffen imports clematis from abroad, but has also introduced a number of its own cultivars.

It's a shame that the nursery doesn't welcome visitors, because Art Steffen is working on a garden railroad. But the catalog is well illustrated in color, and all those clematis books on the market will give you an idea of what each cultivar or species looks like. Mail order only.

> **Arthur H. Steffen, Inc.**
> P.O. Box 184
> Fairport, NY 14450
> Arthur Steffen, Jr.
> (716) 377-1665
> Catalog: $2, CAN/OV, bn

■ **Carroll Gardens** in Westminster, Maryland, is a sixty-year-old nursery, much bigger than many of those listed here, but they produce a fine catalog with a very broad selection of perennials and shade plants, all types of roses, clematis and other vines, and ornamental trees and shrubs. Among those genera with especially good selection are anemones, asters, astilbes, delphiniums, dianthus, hardy ferns and geraniums, ornamental grasses, helianthemums, kniphofias, lilies, peonies, Oriental poppies, phlox, sedums, and veronicas. General Manager Alan Summers is proud of the breadth of selection and the new introductions. The nursery and display garden are open daily all year (except Thanksgiving and Christmas days) until seven in the evening. Westminster is about thirty miles northwest of Baltimore and twenty miles south of Gettysburg, Pennsylvania.

> **Carroll Gardens**
> P.O. Box 310
> Westminster, MD 21157
> Alan L. Summers, Gen. Mgr.
> (301) 848-5422, (800) 638-6334
> Catalog: $2d, CAN, bn/cn

■ There are several well-known perennial growers who offer a broad selection but sell by mail order only. Started by a group of horticulturists in 1979, **Crownsville Nursery** in Crownsville, Maryland, has a very good plant list — about 1,000 varieties of perennials, ornamental grasses, and some woody ornamentals.

One of the partners, Charles Wasitis, told me that it's hard to pick specific plants to highlight because the list is always changing. There are several advantages to an ever-changing list: new introductions, plants you missed the first time around, or different selections from those you already have. Crownsville does not ship to Arizona, California, Oregon, or Washington.

> **Crownsville Nursery**
> P.O. Box 797
> Crownsville, MD 21032
> Charles Wasitis
> (301) 923-2212
> Catalog: $2d, bn/cn

■ Familiar to gardeners all along the eastern seaboard is the **Andre Viette Farm & Nursery** in Fishersville, Virginia. A friend and I arrived the afternoon before the first frost was expected, and there was a great rush by all hands to get plants into greenhouses for the winter! We were still able to walk around the display gardens and enjoy the perennial plants in the lovely Shenandoah Valley.

This nursery is both a major wholesaler of perennials to other nurseries and a retail and mail order source of many hundreds of varieties of plants for the border, rock garden, and woodland. In addition to a choice selection of perennials of all sorts, the nursery has many daylilies, bearded iris, Siberian and Japanese iris, hostas, oriental poppies, and peonies.

Andre Viette's father, Martin, was a well-known nurseryman on Long Island, but Andre wanted more room and moved the nursery to Virginia; his son Mark now works with him at the nursery. They have a cloning laboratory and are always searching for and increasing unusual plants for introduction. They do not ship to California or Oregon. Visitors are welcome Monday through Saturday; the best months to visit are May through July. Fishersville is four miles east of Staunton on Highway 64.

> **Andre Viette Farm & Nursery**
> Route 1, Box 16
> Fishersville, VA 22939
> Andre Viette
> (703) 943-2315
> Catalog: $2, bn/cn

■ Nancy Goodwin is a former piano and harpsichord teacher who fell in love with cyclamen in England, then discovered that they were threatened and that almost no one in the U.S. was producing them from seed. Nancy Goodwin is now a national treasure. Her **Montrose Nursery** in Hillsborough, North Carolina, is now growing 14 species and 25 forms of cyclamen from seed. She and her fellow plantsman Doug Ruhren are also working on hybridizing hellebores and primulas. They are known for offering unusual perennials, including one of the best selections of salvias in the country.

When I visited in October, one of the display gardens was only a year old but sensational; it featured a number of plants with purple and orange flowers or foliage, including a beautiful purple-leafed sweet potato plant and, new to me, the Labab bean vine. Visitors by appointment only; there are no sales at the nursery but you may order plants to be picked up when you visit. Hillsborough is about twenty miles west of Durham.

Montrose Nursery
P.O. Box 957
Hillsborough, NC 27278
Nancy Goodwin
(919) 732-7787
Catalog: $3, bn

HOLBROOK FARM & NURSERY
Artist: Jane Sutton

■ The catalog of **Holbrook Farm & Nursery** in Fletcher, North Carolina, has always delighted me, both because of the plants listed and the humorous rustic cover photos, and I came away from a visit with Allen Bush with every good impression reinforced. Trained at Kew Gardens in England, Allen bubbles over with the love of plants, and we walked through his greenhouses chattering and laughing a mile a minute!

An inveterate traveler, Allen looks for plants at every stop, so his list usually has something new that he's excited about. He introduced the very popular *Heuchera* 'Palace Purple' from

England only a few years ago, and he's introducing lots of new plants from Germany, too; in almost every genus you'll find something new and different.

One of the things I like about his catalog is that he tells us where he's gotten special plants; it's an example of the plantsman's network in action. Both the contents and the cover continue to delight. Orders to Arizona, California, Oregon, and Washington are shipped only during two specific weeks a year, one in spring and one in fall, because of special shipping requirements. Visitors will enjoy the display plantings around the office cottage; they're welcome April through October, Monday through Saturday. Fletcher is halfway between Asheville and Hendersonville, about twenty miles south of Asheville.

Holbrook Farm & Nursery
P.O. Box 368
Fletcher, NC 28732
Allen W. Bush
(704) 891-7790
Catalog: $2d, bn/cn

■ For years the catalog of **Powell's Gardens** in Princeton, North Carolina, was maddening to read — words crossed out, corrected in pen, lots of typos — and yet, what a terrific list! The last catalog was a wonderful change, produced on a computer and clean as a whistle. What still comes through is the true grit and spirit of the owner, Loleta Powell. She's one of a kind: in the last few years she's been hit by storms, a tornado, rain and rot, and serious illness, yet she says nothing could convince her to quit, even though she's seventy. One of the first perennial nurseries in her area, Powell's specializes in iris, hostas, and daylilies, but also offers a large selection of other perennials, even dwarf conifers and other woody plants, some very enticing indeed. Visitors are welcome all year from Monday to Saturday, and Sundays from April 15 to July 15. There are more than three acres of lovely display garden. Princeton is about forty-five miles southeast of Raleigh on Highway 70.

Powell's Gardens
Route 3, Box 21
Princeton, NC 27569
Loleta Powell
(919) 936-4421
Catalog: $2.50, CAN/OV, bn/cn

■ It seems ungrateful not to write more extensively about **Wayside Gardens** in Hodges, South Carolina, since it was a beautiful Wayside catalog that hooked me·on plants in the first place. But the plain truth is that though it is a fine source of perennials, roses, and trees and shrubs, it is not a specialty nursery. Wayside is a plant broker, buying from specialty nurseries and contract growers all over the horticultural world. It frequently introduces new plants, particularly from England and Europe, and has been a major influence on American gardeners. Mail order only.

> **Wayside Gardens**
> 1 Garden Lane
> Hodges, SC 29695-0001
> The Park Family
> (800) 845-1124
> Catalog: Free, bn/cn

■ The Schultz family founded Wayside Gardens in 1916 in Mentor, Ohio. They sold their interest in Wayside in 1945 (before its move to South Carolina) and started a wholesale nursery, Springbrook, the next year. **Garden Place** is the retail mail order division of Springbrook, which specializes in perennials, ground covers, and ornamental grasses; it offers between 500 and 700 varieties every year.

Now run by the third generation of Schultzes, John, a racing sailor, and his brother Dave, a golfer, the nursery offers good selections of anemones, artemisias, asters, Shasta daisies, dianthus, heucheras, ligularias, Oriental poppies, phlox, and veronicas, among other plants. Mentor is twenty miles east of Cleveland on Lake Erie. There are no display gardens, but visitors are welcome to walk the fields in late August and September when many of the plants are at their best.

> **Garden Place**
> P.O. Box 388
> Mentor, OH 44061-0388
> John and Dave Schultz
> (216) 255-3705
> Catalog: $1, CAN, bn/cn

■ Mary Harrison was encouraged to start a nursery by a state plant inspector who came to examine plants to be sold by the local garden club. **Mary's Plant Farm** in McGonigle, Ohio, began when her daughter decided to stay home to help with the nursery after having a baby. Mary says her parents were gardeners, and she's always been the sort of gardener who has to try every unusual plant she finds.

She offers a broad selection of perennials, including daylilies and hostas, tall and miniature bearded iris, ferns, ivies, thyme, lilac, and box, flowering shrubs, and 7 varieties of beech. Mary also likes offering regional native plants and grasses hardy in USDA Zone 6. At present she's not shipping to Texas. Her gardens are landscaped with perennial borders, a rock garden, and an herb garden, and visitors are welcome from April through October. The nursery is open Tuesday through Sunday except for July and August when it is closed on Sunday. McGonigle is four miles northwest of Hamilton, Ohio, about twenty miles northwest of Cincinnati.

Mary's Plant Farm
2410 Lanes Mill Road
Hamilton, OH 45013
Mary and Sherri Harrison
(513) 892-2055 or 894-0022
Catalog: $1d, bn/cn

■ A fat catalog from a new nursery called **Perpetual Perennials** in Springfield, Ohio, contains a bewildering selection of plants, nearly 2,000 species and cultivars of perennial plants, listed in categories like "everlastings" or "daisy collection" instead of alphabetically by botanical name. Tipping the balance in Perpetual Perennial's favor is a huge and interesting selection of plants, some available in more than one size. Worthwhile, if you don't mind the frustration of trying to find what you want; there's an incomplete botanical name index at the front of the catalog.

Tony and Brenda Pennington and their three children live on a family farm that has become surrounded by "progress," so they opened Perpetual Perennials nursery in response; the whole thing grew much faster than expected, and there have been some growing pains, but the Penningtons are very determined! Visitors are welcome to visit the nursery, which is open Monday through Saturday in April and October, and daily from May through September. Springfield is between Dayton and Columbus on Interstate 70.

Perpetual Perennials
1111 Upper Valley Pike
Springfield, OH 45504
Brenda Pennington
(513) 325-2451
Catalog: $2d, bn/cn

■ Well known to many gardeners is **Bluestone Perennials** in Madison, Ohio. The nursery offers about 500 different perennials in "liner" size at very reasonable prices. Liners are the size of plants you buy in six-packs, bigger than seedlings, with better root development, and hardened off, ready for planting; they grow fairly rapidly after planting, and by the end of the first season they should have bloomed and become well established.

Bluestone lists a very nice selection of good cultivars and now offers about 65 varieties of cutting-grown shrubs as well. The nursery has started shipping larger perennial plants in the fall for early bloom in spring: these fall plants cannot be shipped to Arizona, California, Oregon, and Washington (plants from the spring catalog can be shipped to all states). Richard Boonstra founded his nursery in 1972 and now works with his son Bill and his daughter Jan and their spouses. Richard saw a need for low-cost, high-quality perennial plants long before they became so popular. Visitors are always welcome. Bluestone has a spring clearance sale after Memorial Day (call for the date). Madison is east of Cleveland on U.S. Interstate 90.

Bluestone Perennials
7211 Middle Ridge Road
Madison, OH 44057
R. N. Boonstra
(800) 852-5243
Catalog: Free, bn/cn

INDIGO KNOLL PERENNIALS
Artist: Stephen G. Harsy

■ Steve and Linda Harsy started propagating plants to fill a large garden, got hooked, and started **Indigo Knoll Perennials** in 1986. They loved it so much that Steve quit his job as a research chemist, and they sold their Maryland home and nursery and moved back to Wisconsin, where a former dairy farm near Albany is now their headquarters. Among many other plants, they offer about 20 varieties of dianthus and have another 50 under evaluation for possible introduction (they're even breeding them), as well as about 6 heleniums and several nepetas. Their specialties are sure to change somewhat with their change in location, but the emphasis is on good border plants showing longevity and cold tolerance. The Harsys are planting a display garden at their new location and say that any time but winter is a good time to visit. Albany is thirty miles south of Madison and about an hour and a half northwest of Chicago.

> **Indigo Knoll Perennials**
> N 6258 Edmunds Road
> Albany, WI 53502
> Steve Harsy
> (301) 489-5131
> Catalog: Free, bn

■ Ken and Connie Clifford have been specializing in flowering vines for years. Their **Clifford's Perennial & Vine** in East Troy, Wisconsin, offers large- and small-flowered clematis (both climbing and shrubby), wisteria, ampelopsis, honeysuckle, and others, as well as many field-grown garden perennials. Ken wanted to be a landscape architect, but due to the turmoil of the sixties he didn't finish his studies. He got a job as a bread delivery man and started collecting plants. He and Connie opened their nursery in 1982 and now have a farm where they run a wholesale nursery and sell to gardeners by mail order. They don't ship to Arizona, California, or Hawaii.

> **Clifford's Perennial & Vine**
> Route 2, Box 320
> East Troy, WI 53120
> Ken and Connie Clifford
> (414) 968-4040 Apr.–Sept.
> (414) 642-7156 Oct.–Mar.
> Catalog: $1d, CAN, bn/cn

■ **Winter Greenhouse** in Winter, Wisconsin, is the joint project of two non-Catholic monasteries who chose growing and selling perennials as the best way to support their communities. Started in 1984, they now offer about 700 perennials, wild-flowers, and herbs, and most are hardy to USDA Zones 3 and 4. The plants are listed in tables that give cultural preferences, bloom color and time, hardiness, height, and uses, and are offered in various sizes from liners to larger pots at very reasonable prices. Winter Greenhouse also has an attractive display garden and welcomes visitors daily from mid-April to mid-August, from Monday to Saturday until mid-October. Winter is about twenty-eight miles north of Ladysmith on Highway 70.

Winter Greenhouse
Route 2, Box 24
Winter, WI 54896
Mikael Wilsdahl and Jim Wilson
(715) 266-4963
Catalog: $2, CAN, bn/cn

■ **Milaeger's Gardens** in Racine, Wisconsin, offers nearly 1,000 perennial plants, so it's hard to pin down a specialty. Started in 1960 by Kevin Milaeger's parents, the nursery still involves parents Joan and Dan, as well as Kevin's brother Kent, and his sister Kris and her husband, Dan Reisdorf; it looks as if it keeps them all busy. They publish their catalog twice a year, and they don't call it the "Perennial Wishbook" for nothing. They have good selections of asters, astilbes, campanulas, chrysanthemums, clematis, and other ornamental vines, delphiniums, eupatoriums, ornamental grasses, daylilies, hostas, phlox, sedums, thalictrums, clematis, and old and new roses. Visitors are welcome to come and see the plants in the display garden from May through September. Racine is on Lake Michigan, twenty-five miles south of Milwaukee and ninety miles north of Chicago.

Milaeger's Gardens
4838 Douglas Avenue
Racine, WI 53402-2498
Kevin D. Milaeger
(414) 639-2371 or 2040
Catalog: $1d, bn/cn

■ Ainie Busse started her **Busse Gardens** in Cokato, Minnesota, to supply gardeners with hard-to-find and cold-hardy perennials. It's grown into a large business, and Ainie is one of the founders of the Perennial Plant Association, traveling, lecturing, and writing quite a bit, but she still does what she set out to do. She offers a broad selection of very hardy perennials, including introductions from other countries: more than 500 daylily cultivars (she grows more than 1,000), more than 300 hostas, about 85 astilbes, 25 bergenias, 125 Siberian iris, and asters, hardy geraniums, heucheras, anemones, peonies, epimediums, and much more. No shipping to California.

There are thirty display gardens at the nursery; visitors are welcome Monday through Friday from June through August, other times by appointment. Cokato is sixty miles west of Minneapolis on U.S. Highway 12 (take the County Road 3 turnoff and go north).

Busse Gardens
Route 2, Box 238
Cokato, MN 55321
Ainie H. Busse
(612) 286-2654
Catalog: $2d, bn/cn

BUSSE GARDENS
Artist: M. Heidi Nelson

■ Gail Korn is a former high school English teacher in Nebraska who has found her true calling; when she saw a collection of 300 daylilies in her native Iowa, she started growing and learning all about them. She became friends with the Iowa collector, and when he passed on she bought his collection and moved it to her home in a big cow trailer with each cultivar and its label packed in a grocery bag.

Gail's **Garden Perennials** in Wayne, Nebraska, offers a nice selection of hardy perennials of all types, but her heart still seems to belong to daylilies. She grows about 600 cultivars and offers about 300 in her catalog. She so hates to see the daylily bloom season end that she is adding very late blooming varieties as she finds them. Her display garden looks very nice, and visitors are welcome daily from April to mid-October; July is the best month. Wayne is in northeastern Nebraska, a hundred miles north of Omaha and forty-five miles west of Sioux Falls, Iowa.

Garden Perennials
Route 1
Wayne, NE 68787
Gail Korn
(402) 375-3615
Catalog: $1d, bn

■ Pawnee City, Nebraska, is not a horticultural center, but the enthusiasm of Harriett "Pinky" Dokken may turn people in that area into devoted perennial gardeners. Pinky grew up in Panama, where her father worked for the Panama Canal Company, but she went to university in Nebraska (talk about culture shock!). Even though she considered it an arctic wasteland at first, she married a Nebraska dentist and settled down. At first, a greenhouse was a must. Then she started a flower shop, expanded that into a garden center. Now **Pinky's Plants** publishes a catalog offering about 700 perennials of all kinds. Because gardeners in her area are not used to growing a wide variety of perennials, the catalog contains a lot of basic growing information.

Pinky will be moving the nursery to ten acres in the country in 1993 and is planting display gardens at that site. In the meantime, her nursery in town is open Monday to Saturday from mid-April to mid-October. Pawnee City is in southeastern Nebraska near the Kansas border, about ninety-five miles south of Omaha.

Pinky's Plants
P.O. Box 126
Pawnee City, NE 68420
Harriett Dokken
(402) 852-2195
Catalog: Free, CAN, bn/cn

■ Just when I think I must know about every nursery in America, another one pops up under my nose — perhaps because people who love plants and gardening find it easy to start offering a few surplus plants and suddenly find themselves in the nursery business. Carolyn Singer of **Foothill Cottage Gardens** grew up in my neighborhood, western Sonoma County, but after several moves around the country now lives in Grass Valley in California's Sierra foothills. She soon found herself teaching gardening classes and growing unusual plants that were not locally available. She came to love tough plants while living in Colorado and Montana and especially favors dianthus, artemesias, achilleas, and campanulas; her list offers hundreds of perennials.

Carolyn also does garden designs and has arranged her display to demonstrate a rock garden, shade plants, color combinations, and drought-tolerant plants. The nursery is open Tuesday, Thursday, and Saturday mornings, or by appointment. Visitors should be sure to call first to get directions. The best months to visit are May through October.

Foothill Cottage Gardens
13925 Sontag Road
Grass Valley, CA 95945
Carolyn Singer
(916) 272-4362
Catalog: $2d, bn/cn

CANYON CREEK NURSERY
Artist: Susan Marie Whittlesey

■ John and Susan Whittlesey started **Canyon Creek Nursery** in Oroville, California, in 1985. One of their first specialties was fragrant violets and violas, and they still have a good selection, but they also have many other fine plants as well, including some historic dianthus varieties, erysimums, hardy geraniums, salvias, and other treasured genera in ones and twos.

John fell in love with plants as a child. By the time he was in high school he was traveling around the state visiting nurseries and plantsmen. He says that Marshall Olbrich of Western Hills Nursery was one of his early mentors. After five years of experience with a perennial nursery in Washington, he moved home to California to start his own. His family helps at shipping time; a friend back East told me he'd never seen plants so beautifully packed as those from Canyon Creek. Visitors are welcome but should call ahead for directions and to be sure someone will be there. The nursery is closer to Chico and Paradise than Oroville, roughly fifty miles north of Sacramento.

Canyon Creek Nursery
3527 Dry Creek Road
Oroville, CA 95965
John and Susan Whittlesey
(916) 533-2166
Catalog: $1, bn

■ **Joyce's Garden** in Bend, Oregon, is not around the corner for ninety-nine percent of you, perhaps more, but Joyce Macdonald Glimm grows a nice selection of very hardy perennials. She says that there is frost danger every night of the year; it even froze on July Fourth a few years ago. When she built a solar house, it had an attached greenhouse, so she began raising plants for other nurseries. One thing led to another and now she has three solar greenhouses and her own nursery. Among the plants offered are nice selections of arabis, asters, Shasta daisies, dianthus, *Phlox subulata,* veronicas, thymes, and various ground covers; Joyce says that plants that like good drainage do well for her. Visitors should call ahead. The nursery is six miles from the center of Bend, which is in central Oregon, about eighty miles east of Eugene.

Joyce's Garden
64640 Old Bend Redmond Highway
Bend, OR 97701
Joyce Macdonald Glimm
(503) 388-4680
Catalog: $2, bn/cn

■ When I went to the Northwest to visit nurseries, a friend suggested that I try to find **Collector's Nursery** in Vancouver, Washington. She'd seen the Collector's stand at a Berry Botanical Garden plant sale and had been very impressed. Turning off the highway and into the driveway was like entering an enchanted world — Bill Janssen and his wife, Diana Reeck, have created a garden around their house to die for! Bill was a plant broker, traveling to nurseries up and down the West Coast; Diana considers herself an amateur botanist. They have been in the nursery business for only a few years but are already thinking of looking for more space. Their specialties include gentians, hostas, tricyrtis, species iris, epimediums, daphne, species clematis, dwarf conifers, and native plants of the Northwest.

They are hybridizing hostas, tricyrtis, and Pacific Coast iris and are introducing plants as they prove garden-worthy. Standing in their garden, I saw a eucryphia with deeply cut leaves that stayed in my mind for weeks. So far, Bill and Diana have only that one plant. By the way, the "Collector's" in the name does not mean that they collect plants in the wild, but that plant collectors love their plants! This is still a young nursery, but it looks like a real winner. Visitors should call ahead to see if a visit is convenient and to get directions.

Collector's Nursery
1602 N.E. 162d Avenue
Vancouver, WA 98684
Bill Janssen and Diana Reeck
(206) 256-8533
Catalog: $2, bn

■ *Other sources of perennials are:*

Kurt Bluemel, Baldwin, MD
Edgewood Farm & Nursery, Stanardsville, VA
Forestfarm, Williams, OR
Heronswood Nursery, Kingston, WA
Limerock Ornamental Grasses, Port Matilda, PA
Maple Leaf Nursery, Placerville, CA
Perennial Plantation, Fowlerville, MI
Robyn's Nest Nursery, Vancouver, WA
Roslyn Nursery, Dix Hills, NY
Twombly Nursery, Monroe, CT
Woodlanders, Inc., Aiken, SC
Yucca Do Nursery, Waller, TX

Rhododendrons and Azaleas

There seem to be more nurseries for rhododendrons and azaleas than for any other woody plant class, but this is a bit deceiving. There are so many different species and cultivars of rhododendron and so many different hybridizers that each nursery seems to have its own niche. One may be specializing in very hardy plants for the North and Midwest, or azaleas for the Southeast, another offering varieties selected for plant habit or size. Another nurseryman might be a hobbyist who took on the care of a famous collection when it became available. Other nurseries specialize in rhododendron species or native American azaleas and rhododendrons, some in offering as many varieties as possible.

In describing rhododendron and azalea nurseries, I've tried to emphasize the hybridizers featured when this is an indication of plant hardiness. Most books on rhododendrons give the name of the hybridizer for each, so that if you're looking for a specific cultivar, you're most likely to find it from a nursery that specializes in that hybridizer's plants. Lots of nurseries offer the plants of many hybridizers, and, of course, some offer good selections of species rhododendrons and native azaleas as well.

■ **Eastern Plant Specialties** in Georgetown, Maine, is a source of very hardy species and hybrid rhododendrons, deciduous azaleas, kalmias, pieris, and other unusual trees, shrubs, and dwarf conifers for tough climates. Mark Stavish has a horticulture degree and had worked with the eminent plantsmen Donald Smith of Watnong Nursery and Tom Dilatush before starting his own nursery in 1984 to grow dependable plants for his landscaping jobs. He says he specializes in the "better good doers," including new Yakushimanum hybrids (called "Yaks" or "Yakus" by the cognoscenti).

In 1988 Mark moved the nursery to Maine, where he has a lovely location on a large pond. He loves botanizing in the wild and exploring the coast of Maine. In the winter he noodles on his computer and prepares his catalog, which includes excellent plant descriptions and cultural information. Winters must be long and cold indeed: Mark even has time to think up devious little contests for his readers.

Visitors are welcome from May through October but should call ahead to be sure someone will be there. There are display gardens, and you can picnic near the pond. Georgetown is one hour north of Portland on the coast.

> **Eastern Plant Specialties**
> P.O. Box 226
> Georgetown, ME 04548
> Mark Stavish
> (207) 371-2888
> Catalog: $2d, CAN, bn

■ **Briarwood Gardens** in East Sandwich, Massachusetts, specializes in the hardy rhododendrons bred by Charles Dexter of Sandwich and Jack Cowles of the Dexter Estate and Heritage Plantation, as well as varieties from other hybridizers. Briarwood offers 250 varieties, some sound very special indeed, including some that are very fragrant.

Jonathan Leonard, a medical editor, was originally inspired by the rhododendrons grown by a cousin who was active in the American Rhododendron Society, then by the idea of preserving the work of Dexter and Cowles. He encourages visitors to tour Heritage Plantation, which has a large collection of these and other rhododendrons. The best bloom time is usually the last two weeks of May. Visitors are welcome Monday to Friday from March to November but should be sure to call ahead. East Sandwich is about an hour southeast of Boston, and fifty-six miles east of Providence, Rhode Island.

> **Briarwood Gardens**
> RFD 3
> East Sandwich, MA 02537
> Jonathan Leonard
> (508) 888-2146
> Catalog: $1

■ **Carlson's Gardens** in South Salem, New York, specializes in hardy and smaller azaleas and rhododendrons: Robin Hill, Gartrell, Gable, Great Lakes, Glenn Dale, and North Tisbury evergreen azaleas, and Shammarello, Mezitt, Leach, and Dexter rhododendrons, both small- and large-leaved. Carlson's has also been selecting and naming special clones of native and evergreen azaleas grown from seed and has hybridized "Carlson's Face 'Em Down" evergreen azaleas. The nursery offers some kalmias as well. All of the plants are grown outside all year in USDA Zone 6a. Carlson's does not ship to California.

Bob and Jan Carlson started their nursery in 1969. From the beginning they have been hybridizing for both scent and hardiness with great success. Bob is a former computer software salesman and enthusiastic jazz pianist. The catalog is filled with the Carlsons' own light verse. Visitors are welcome by appointment. They sell plants "too big to ship" and "way too big to ship" at the nursery. South Salem is about fifty miles north of New York City in northeastern Westchester County, near the Connecticut line.

Carlson's Gardens
P.O. Box 305
South Salem, NY 10590
Bob Carlson
(914) 763-5958
Catalog: $3d, bn/cn

■ Another stout rhododendron catalog comes from **Roslyn Nursery** in Dix Hills, New York. The proprietor, Dr. Philip Waldman, is a dentist with a talent for propagation. He started the nursery with his wife, Harriet, in 1984 as a hobby when he couldn't bear to toss his extras. He's become an award-winning hybridizer and lists about 800 rhododendrons and 300 azaleas. Many of his plants are from other northern hybridizers and are very hardy. The catalog indicates hardiness for each plant, as well as lineage or hybridizer, size at maturity, and bloom season.

As with other nurseries, Dr. Waldman's list has gradually broadened to include a variety of other trees and shrubs and some grasses and perennials. He lists about 200 conifers, kalmias, pieris, camellias, hollies, and many other ornamentals and plants for ground cover. There are some restrictions on shipping to western states. Visitors are welcome daily. Dix Hills is near Huntington on Long Island.

Roslyn Nursery
211 Burrs Lane
Dix Hills, NY 11746
Philip and Harriet Waldman
(516) 643-9347
Catalog: $3, bn

Shepherd Hill Farm in Putnam Valley, New York, is another source of many hardy rhododendrons for the Northeast. The nursery offers hybrids by the "hardy boys": Leach, Dexter, Shammarello, Gable, Hobbie, and Mezitt. It also offers evergreen azaleas, kalmias, and pieris. Shepherd Hill does not ship to Arizona, California, Oregon, or Washington.

Gerry Bleyer worked for years for a supplier of packaging for biscuits and candies (including Reese's peanut butter cups!), but felt that something was missing. While working in San Francisco, he fell in love with the rhododendrons in Golden Gate Park. When he moved east again to build a house on his father-in-law's chicken farm, he couldn't find unusual rhododendrons for his garden so he started to propagate them himself. (But, oh dear, Gerry and Myra Bleyer are Mets fans; we could chat happily about plants but not about baseball teams!) Visitors are welcome by appointment only. The display garden and countryside look lovely. The best season is, of course, spring. Putnam Valley is across the Hudson River from West Point.

Shepherd Hill Farm
200 Peekskill Hollow Road
Putnam Valley, NY 10517
Gerry and Myra Bleyer
(914) 528-5917
Catalog: Free

■ Betty Cummins of **The Cummins Garden** in Marlboro, New Jersey, was a homemaker who taught herself propagation out of the old *Wise Garden Encyclopedia* and ended up as chief propagator at a wholesale nursery. She started her own nursery in 1974, and now she teaches propagation to her customers at an annual workshop. She must be a dynamo: in her spare time she reads, does aerobics, bicycles, ice skates, and is a photography buff.

Betty specializes in small plants and feels that there's a real need for them in small gardens and in rock gardens. She offers rhododendrons, azaleas, dwarf conifers, and other small and dwarf shrubs, with eventual size, leaf size, color, season of bloom and hardiness indicated in her catalog. Betty lists 114 hybrids and 46 species of rhododendrons, many evergreen and deciduous azalea cultivars, 62 dwarf conifers and a number of companion plants such as kalmias, heaths, and heathers, pieris, and plants used as ground covers. She doesn't ship to Arizona, California, Oregon, or Washington. Larger plants such as Exbury azaleas are available at the nursery.

Visitors are welcome daily by appointment, except for April, when Betty is open only Friday through Sunday. If you're interested in Betty's propagation workshop, call her for the date. Marlboro is in central New Jersey, about forty miles southwest of New York City and an hour and a half northeast of Philadelphia.

> **The Cummins Garden**
> 22 Robertsville Road
> Marlboro, NJ 07746
> Elizabeth K. Cummins
> (201) 536-2591
> Catalog: $2d, CAN/OV, bn/cn

■ **Hillhouse Nursery** in Voorhees, New Jersey, specializes in the Linwood hardy azaleas, with a few other varieties from Girard, Robin Hill, and Glenn Dale.

Theodore Stecki, the proprietor, was a personal friend of G. Albert Reid, the hybridizer of the Linwood hardy azaleas, and when Reid died in 1986, Stecki took all of the plants and continued to propagate and distribute them. He says that while they are excellent garden plants, there is no typical plant; there are tall, prostrate, and compact growers, early summer and fall bloomers, and flowers of all colors. He offers more than 80 cultivars. There are some difficulties with shipping to California.

In his nonplant life, Ted Stecki is an engineering manager for General Electric and plays the accordion. I told him that he should form a local chapter of "Those Darned Accordions," a San Francisco group that will show up at any event and play "Lady of Spain." Nursery visitors should call ahead to be sure someone will be there and to get directions. Voorhees is about fifteen miles east of Philadelphia.

> **Hillhouse Nursery**
> 90 Kresson-Gibbsboro Road
> Voorhees, NJ 08043
> Theodore S. Stecki
> (609) 784-6203
> Catalog: Free

■ **Bull Valley Rhododendron Nursery** in Aspers, Pennsylvania, offers the very hardy hybrids of Dexter, Leach, Pride, Consolini, Gable, and several others, and new introductions of Dr. William Rhein of Pennsylvania. The nursery grows about 500 cultivars and offers about 100 in the catalog. You may also specially request custom propagating.

Ray Carter is a heating and cooling contractor; his wife, Faye, says he just got "carried away." They started out as collectors and ended up propagating for others, even doing tissue culture. Their daughter Kim Altice has joined them in the business. They also offer about 35 hardier species and cultivars of magnolias and about 50 species and cultivars of holly from the collection of Robert K. Peters, including several new introductions. They do not ship to California, Oregon, or Washington.

Visitors are welcome on weekends in May or by appointment. Aspers is in south central Pennsylvania, about ten miles northeast of Gettysburg.

Bull Valley Rhododendron Nursery
214 Bull Valley Road
Aspers, PA 17304
Faye and Ray Carter, Kim Altice
(717) 677-6313
Catalog: $2

■ The **Cardinal Nursery** in State Road, North Carolina, specializes in introducing new hybrids. Among the hybridizers that Bill Storms is excited about are Weldon Delp of Harrisburg, Pennsylvania, and Russ and Velma Haag of Brevard, North Carolina. Bill also lists hybrids from many others, some well known (Leach, Dexter, Gable, Pride, Shammarello) and others less well known, with fairly short lists but whom he thinks worthy of distribution. Most of the hybridizers are from the East Coast, but Bill offers older varieties from West Coast, British, and German sources, as well, and many Yakushimanum varieties and hybrids. Because many of the hybrids are recent introductions, supplies are usually limited. Cardinal does not ship to Arizona, California, Oregon, or Washington.

Bill Storms worked with rhododendron greats Warren Balsiefen and Guy Nearing in New Jersey in the fifties and sixties, then moved to North Carolina and started his own nursery in 1968. He's helped by his wife, Barbara, a retired librarian. Every plant is described by eventual size, flower color, bloom time, and hybridizer. Quality ratings are given when the hybrid has been rated by the American Rhododendron Society. Visitors are welcome on Saturday or by appointment. State Road is near Elkin, about forty miles west of Winston-Salem, off Interstate 77.

Cardinal Nursery
Route 1, Box 316
State Road, NC 28676

Bill and Barbara Storms
(919) 874-2027
Catalog: Free

■ Just as the Northwest seems to be the mecca of rhododendrons, the Southeast seems to be the center of azalea hybridization and culture. The **Transplant Nursery** in Lavonia, Georgia, does offer a good selection of rhododendrons, including the hardy hybrids of Dexter, Leach, and Consolini as well as the introductions of Olin Holsomback of Georgia.

However, it's the azalea listings that dazzle. Transplant specializes in the native deciduous azaleas of the Southeast and offers many selections and some crosses. The nursery also sells the azalea hybrids of Glenn Dale and Back Acres, James Harris, Kehr, North Tisbury (Polly Hill), Pennington, and Robin Hill; Kiusianum hybrids; and new and old Kurume and Satsuki cultivars. The catalog lists some camellias and woody companion plants as well, mostly southeastern natives. For each plant size at maturity, hardiness and bloom season are given, with good color descriptions. Transplant cannot ship to California, Oregon, or Washington.

The nursery was started in 1975 as the hobby of Mary Beasley's late husband, George, who was an ardent collector, and she has now turned it into a real business with her son Jeff and his wife, Lisa. Visitors are welcome to visit the nursery and display garden during the bloom season, March through May; call ahead at other times. Lavonia is about ninety miles northeast of Atlanta on Interstate 95, close to the South Carolina border and Lake Hartwell.

Transplant Nursery
Parkertown Road
Lavonia, GA 30553
Mary, Jeff, and Lisa Beasley
(404) 356-8947
Catalog: $1, CAN/OV, bn

■ **Schild Azalea Gardens & Nursery** in Hixson, Tennessee, went professional in 1988, after Joseph Schild, Jr., had been fooling around with azaleas for twenty years. His mentor was Clifton Gann, a nurseryman and plant breeder and an expert in the native azaleas of the Southeast, who took him out into the field and started him on his breeding programs. All of Schild's native plants are nursery-grown, but every spring he searches for outstanding plants in the wild and makes crosses on the spot, going back to collect the seed in the fall. In the spring and fall, he leads field trips to see native azaleas, wild-flowers, and other native plants; call him for the dates.

Joseph Schild offers seed-grown native and Asian species azaleas and rhododendrons, evergreen azalea hybrids, North Tisbury evergreen azaleas, Exbury and Knap Hill deciduous azaleas, unnamed crosses from his breeders corner, and a selection of his new introductions. He also lists kalmia cultivars. No shipping to Alaska, California, Hawaii, Oregon, or Washington. Visitors are welcome by appointment; bloom time is April through July. Hixson is a northern suburb of Chattanooga.

> **Schild Azalea Gardens & Nursery**
> 1705 Longview Street
> Hixson, TN 37343
> Joseph E. Schild, Jr.
> (615) 842-9686
> Catalog: $1d, bn

■ Another source of very hardy rhododendrons is **Mowbray Gardens** in Cincinnati, Ohio. Christopher Trautmann is a landscaper, a former tennis pro, and the grandson of the "Onion King" of Texas, A. E. Trautmann.

He's introducing the very hardy hybrids of Dr. Tom Ring of Ohio, offering new Ring hybrids every year, and is hybridizing himself. He's also beginning to offer Kiusianum azaleas from Japan, prostrate small-leaved plants that grow in volcanic craters; he says they're popular for bonsai. No shipping to California, Oregon, or Washington. Visitors are welcome by appointment only to come to the display garden and arboretum planted around Christopher's home; he sells some dwarf conifers there.

> **Mowbray Gardens**
> 3318 Mowbray Lane
> Cincinnati, OH 45226
> Christopher Trautmann
> (513) 321-0694
> Catalog: Free

■ **Girard Nurseries** in Geneva, Ohio, is another source of hardy azaleas and rhododendrons, as well as many flowering trees and shrubs, conifers, and ground covers. Started in 1946 by Peter Girard, Sr., it's now run by his son Peter, Jr., and his wife, two daughters, and son-in-law. Over the years, both Peters hybridized many hardy deciduous and evergreen azaleas and rhododendrons. The majority of the deciduous azaleas are sterile, with double flowers, large-flower tresses, and fragrance; the evergreens are mostly compact-growing with large flowers. The rhododendrons have been bred for hardiness and color; Pete mildly brags about a blue variety and some new "Yaku" hybrids.

Also offered are a number of dwarf conifers, including some of the Girards' own selections, flowering and ornamental trees and shrubs, and some plant collections for those who have the luxury of space to fill. They even offer seed of rhododendrons, conifers, and ornamental trees. Many of the plants are shown in color in the catalog. Girard does not ship to Arizona or California. The nursery is open daily from March to July, and Monday to Saturday the rest of the year. Visitors are welcome to come to the display garden whenever the nursery is open. Geneva is between Cleveland and Ashtabula on Highway 20.

> **Girard Nurseries**
> P.O. Box 428
> Geneva, OH 44041
> Peter Girard, Jr.
> (216) 466-2881 or 969-1636
> Catalog: Free, bn/cn

Why is the Northwest such a mecca for rhododendron growers and breeders? It seems to have perfect growing conditions for many acid-loving plants and a climate ideal for propagating and growing rhododendrons (the Washington State flower); it's also a wonderful place to live and garden.

■ **Westgate Garden Nursery** in Eureka, California, lists more than 600 species and hybrid rhododendrons, about 75 azaleas, and several dozen companion trees and shrubs. These are rhododendron collectors' treasures as well as old favorites, miniatures to large-tree forms. Where else but in a rhododendron catalog would a plant with a spicy New World name like Jalipeño be descended from Old World aristocrats like the Earl of Athlone and Jean Marie de Montague?

Catherine Weeks started out as a housewife who loved plants, particularly rhododendrons and the woody plants like Japanese maples and dwarf conifers, which thrive under the same growing conditions. She taught herself how to propagate and grow them on. I doubt if she ever sees the inside of her house now! Visitors are welcome any day but Wednesday, but should call ahead. There are hundreds of plants in the ground (Catherine laughed when I asked about a display garden);

March through May are the best months to visit. Eureka is about halfway between San Francisco and the Oregon border on the California coast.

Westgate Garden Nursery
751 Westgate Drive
Eureka, CA 95501
Catherine Weeks
(707) 442-1239
Catalog: $4d, bn

■ The three Kelley brothers bought the Hall Rhododendron Nursery in Drain, Oregon, several years ago and have changed the name of the retail division to **Kelleygreen Rhododendron Nursery.** To my delight, the approach to the nursery is an old covered bridge that leads into a clearing in the fir forest where the Kelleys are growing a huge selection of rhododendrons.

They are changing slightly from the Hall list to emphasize their broad selection of species rhododendrons, but with nearly 1,600 species and hybrids listed, it's hard to imagine what they don't have. The catalog gives lineage, eventual size at maturity, season of bloom, and American Rhododendron Society quality rating. The lowest quality rating I could find was 2/3 for an old ponticum hybrid. My guess is that older hybrids of lower quality are dropped as newer varieties are introduced. Species rhododendrons are described in the same way, with quality ratings for the species; some are available in a variety of color selections. Kelleygreen also offers some deciduous and evergreen azaleas and pieris.

The Kelleys have a big display garden that they are renovating because both the display plants and the trees that shelter them have gotten too large. It should be lovely when it's finished. Visitors by appointment only; Drain is thirty-eight miles southwest of Eugene, Oregon.

Kelleygreen Rhododendron Nursery
P.O. Box 62
Drain, OR 97435
Jan D. Kelley
(503) 836-2290
Catalog: $1.25, bn

■ I've never visited **Greer Gardens** in Eugene, Oregon, at the proper time of year, but it must be wonderful. There is a lovely woodland garden behind the nursery which displays rhododendrons and azaleas, and many of the other unusual trees and shrubs Greer offers.

The Greer catalog is a labor of love and continues to grow and offer more special plants every year. Harold Greer is one of our rhododendron greats, the author of several books and hybridizer of many popular cultivars. His catalog is full of glowing descriptions and wonderful color pictures. It's detailed and informative, an education on rhododendrons. Greer had the incredible luck of hybridizing 'Trude Webster' while he was still a teenager and, according to an article in *Horticulture,* for years he laid carpets in the winter so that he could stay with rhododendron growing.

The Greer catalog lists most hybrids without the name of the hybridizer, but it's clear that the nursery offers plants from many sources, based on Greer's own liking for them. The lineage is given for most plants, and the name of the hybridizer is given for recent introductions. Greer also offers many species rhododendrons and special selections of species, Vireya rhododendrons, and evergreen azaleas from many hybridizers.

These days almost half the catalog is taken up by "companion plants": camellias, redbuds, clematis, daphnes, hamamelis, magnolias, pieris, stewartias, Japanese maples, conifers, dogwoods, many other ornamental trees and shrubs, and a selection of plants for bonsai. The "back of the book" seems to be growing robustly every year. This year there are thirty-one pages of trees, shrubs, vines, Japanese maples and conifers, even rock garden plants and bulbs — more pages than Greer devotes to rhododendrons.

Greer Gardens
1280 Goodpasture Island Road
Eugene, OR 97401-1794
Harold E. Greer
(503) 686-8266
Catalog: $3, CAN/OV, bn

■ Dick "Red" Cavender of **Red's Rhodies** in Sherwood, Oregon, has what my brother, a lifelong train lover, would consider his dream job — he's been a brakeman on the Union Pacific for thirty years. Rhododendron growing was a hobby he learned from other enthusiasts; like many of the newly converted, he propagated lavishly for his own garden and began to sell his extras around 1975.

Red's enthusiasm is always far-reaching. When I visited several years ago he was selling *Rhododendron occidentale* and sempervivums; now he's growing about 125 species and hybrids of Vireya rhododendrons and listing about 20. He'll propagate to order. Vireyas are native to the Malay archipelago and are much more tender than the rhododendrons from India and China. Many are very vibrant in color. They make good greenhouse plants (or even houseplants during the winter).

And Red has also fallen in love with pleiones (ground orchids) and offers 3 species and 3 cultivars by mail; when we spoke he was planning a trip to the Chelsea Flower Show in England and hoped to bring more pleiones home with him. He also sells *Rhododendron occidentale* selections and other rhododendrons and azaleas at the nursery.

Visitors should call ahead; the best months are March through early June, though the Vireyas bloom intermittently all year. Sherwood is twenty miles southwest of Portland.

> **Red's Rhodies**
> 15920 S.W. Oberst Lane
> Sherwood, OR 97140
> Dick and Karen Cavender
> (503) 625-6331
> Catalog: Long SASE, CAN, bn/cn

■ Art Stubbs, a former letter carrier, and his wife, Eleanor, once a teacher, were gradually sucked into the vortex; since 1975 their **Stubbs Shrubs** in West Linn, Oregon, has been specializing in evergreen azaleas and offers more than 400 hybrids from Linwood, Robin Hill, Girard, North Tisbury, and Greenwood. They also offer Kurume and Satsuki varieties.

Eleanor says they attract a lot of collectors, bonsai people, and landscapers looking for special plants. They have been active on the long-range planning committee of the Crystal Springs Rhododendron Garden in Portland. Visitors are welcome to visit the nursery in its lovely country setting but should call ahead to be sure someone will be there. West Linn is fifteen miles south of Portland and five miles east of Interstate 5.

> **Stubbs Shrubs**
> 23225 S.W. Bosky Dell Lane
> West Linn, OR 97068
> Arthur and Eleanor Stubbs
> (503) 638-5048
> Catalog: $2d

■ Another well-known rhododendron nursery is **The Bovees Nursery** in Portland, Oregon. Started as a retirement venture by Robert and Gertrude Bovee in 1953, the nursery has been owned by Lucille Sorensen, a former neighbor of the Bovees, and George Watson since 1972. Lucy's daughter Kathy Sorensen also works at the nursery. Many of the hybrids they offer are those of Robert Bovee, but the catalog lists lineage and hybridizer for almost all the hybrids, along with hardiness, color and bloom time, and general size. The Bovees Nursery lists a number of species rhododendrons grouped according to classification. The catalog also lists both the Yakushimanum hybrids of Shammarello and the "Yak" species selections of Robert Bovee. Lucy and George grow about 300 species and hybrid Vireya rhododendrons and offer about 100 in the catalog.

Finally, they list some deciduous and evergreen azaleas, both species and hybrids, and a mixed bag of "companion plants," good trees and shrubs, vines, and perennials for similar growing conditions. Visitors are welcome to come to the nursery and the display garden, which is deservedly famous. The Bovees Nursery is open Wednesday through Sunday or by appointment.

The Bovees Nursery
1737 S.W. Coronado
Portland, OR 97219
Lucille Sorensen and George Watson
(503) 244-9341
Catalog: $2, CAN/OV, bn/cn

■ **Whitney Gardens & Nursery** in Brinnon, Washington, was started in 1955 by Bill and Faye Whitney. Bill was a camellia grower and rhododendron hybridizer who wanted more space to expand his rhododendron collection. George and Anne Sather bought the nursery in 1970; their daughter Ellie, an artist and photographer, now helps run the nursery.

They grow about 2,500 rhododendrons in their collection and display garden and will propagate to special order if you send your want-list. They offer about 1,200 for sale at the nursery and list many of them in the catalog.

Hybrid rhododendrons are listed with parentage, growing preferences, eventual size, bloom period, flower color, and hardiness. Hybridizer and year of introduction are given for almost every plant. They also offer a broad selection of species rhododendrons, pages of *R. yakushimanum* hybrids, deciduous and evergreen azaleas, camellias, magnolias, kalmias, Japanese maples, and some ground covers and choice deciduous trees and shrubs. Whitney sells lots of colorful hanging baskets and some perennials at the nursery.

There's a seven-acre display garden that attracts thousands

of visitors for spring bloom and again in the fall for the autumn color from a variety of trees; visitors are welcome daily from February through November or by appointment. Brinnon is on the west side of the Hood Canal, about an hour and a half north of Olympia and two and a half hours west of Seattle by ferry and road.

> **Whitney Gardens & Nursery**
> P.O. Box F
> Brinnon, WA 98320
> Anne Sather
> (206) 796-4411
> Catalog: $3, CAN/OV, bn

■ Sometimes I'm overwhelmed by what people do when they love a certain type of plant. David and Joan Hammond of **Hammond's Acres of Rhodys** in Arlington, Washington, grow nearly 7,000 varieties of species and hybrid rhododendrons and offer nearly 1,000 in their catalog. The catalog describes each plant as to size, habit, hardiness, flower and bloom season, and quality rating. There are also some hybrid and species azaleas and a few kalmias. Dave says you should send him your want-list, as he will propagate plants on special request.

Dave is a former consultant in the door industry; Joan is a registered nurse. As a hobby, they buy new toys for disadvantaged children at Christmastime. They also sell flowering trees, Japanese maples, fruit trees, and other plants at the nursery. They say their whole property of seven acres is their display garden; visitors are welcome (groups should call ahead), and April and May are the best months. Arlington is sixty miles north of Seattle.

> **Hammond's Acres of Rhodys**
> 25911 Seventieth Avenue N.E.
> Arlington, WA 98223
> David and Joan Hammond
> (206) 435-9206 or 9232
> Catalog: $2, bn

■ *Other sources of rhododendrons and azaleas are:*

Appalachian Gardens, Waynesboro, PA
Colvos Creek Nursery, Vashon Island, WA
Lamtree Farm, Warrensville, NC
Nuccio's Nurseries, Altadena, CA
Woodlanders, Inc., Aiken, SC

Rock Garden and Alpine Plants

SISKIYOU RARE PLANT NURSERY
Artist: Baldassare Mineo

■ Marjorie and George Walsh run **Daystar** in Litchfield, Maine, a treasure trove of rock garden plants: heaths and heathers, small rhododendrons, dwarf conifers and other small shrubs and trees, and lots of primulas. They also have started offering other "interesting" flowering and ornamental small trees and shrubs. With New England reticence, they list plants by name only, with color of bloom or foliage, but there's an excellent book list so that customers who don't know them can look them up. Visitors must make an appointment to visit the nursery. Litchfield is about ten miles southwest of Augusta.

Daystar
Route 2, Box 250
Litchfield, ME 04350
Marjorie and George Walsh
(207) 724-3369
Catalog: $1d, CAN, bn

■ Naturally, **The Primrose Path** in Scottdale, Pennsylvania, offers a good selection of primulas, as well as other rock garden plants and plants for the border and woodland. Charles Oliver has been a biologist; both he and his wife, Martha, are passionate gardeners, too. They used to run a water-testing service, but all they really wanted to do was get out into the garden, so they switched careers.

They have very nice offerings of astilbe, hardy geraniums, heucheras, penstemons, a large selection of phlox and primulas, tiarellas, and hardy ferns. They also specialize in native plants of the local shale barren. Visitors are welcome at the display garden and nursery, Thursday to Saturday in April and May, Monday to Saturday through October; it's best to call ahead. Scottdale is on the edge of the Appalachians in southwestern Pennsylvania, about forty miles south of Pittsburgh.

The Primrose Path
RD 2, Box 110
Scottdale, PA 15683
Charles and Martha Oliver
(412) 887-6756
Catalog: $1.50d, bn/cn

WE-DU NURSERIES
Artist: Richard E. Weaver, Jr.

We-Du Nurseries in Marion, North Carolina, is the only nursery rating a full ten on the Barton Animal Index. I visited We-Du on an October morning after a violent storm when most of the plants were covered by fallen leaves — but the animals!! There were cats of all ages and descriptions, pygmy goats, exotic quail, partridges, and pheasants, bantam chickens, wild ducks on a large pond, and of course, dogs. Wherever we walked, there were animals to greet us or to be admired;

it was obvious that Dick Weaver and Rene Duval (the We-Du of the name) are almost as crazy about animals as they are about plants. Their place is called Polly Spout after the historic spring on their property.

However, they are very serious collectors and propagators of rare plants. Dick Weaver has a Ph.D. in botany and worked at the Arnold Arboretum for many years. We-Du is a source of rare plants, both perennials and rock garden varieties, particularly North American and Far Eastern wildflowers. Among the specialties are epimediums (10 species and 25 varieties), more than 50 varieties of species iris, lobelias, penstemons, phlox, tricyrtis, trilliums, violas, and rare bulbs. This list doesn't even begin to do justice to the catalog, which is a joy to read and beautifully illustrated by Dick, and which offers plants so special and rare that you have to read it next to your reference shelf. The nursery does not ship to Arizona, California, or Hawaii.

Visitors must call ahead to find out when it would be convenient to visit; the best time of year is mid-April to mid-May. The nursery is about eight miles south of Marion, which is about halfway between Asheville and Hickory in western North Carolina. You'll find the proprietors, plants, and animals all to be first-rate.

We-Du Nurseries
Route 5, Box 724
Marion, NC 28752
Richard Weaver and Rene Duval
(704) 738-8300
Catalog: $2d, CAN/OV, bn

■ Jerry Hopkins went to work for Beldon Saur at **Rocknoll Nursery** while still a college student; he and his wife, Jan, went into the nursery and landscaping business after he quit being a research engineer. In 1991, twenty years after going to work for the Saurs, he bought Rocknoll Nursery from Eleanor Saur, then eighty-five years old. Jerry lists a good selection of alpine and rock garden plants, native plants, and other plants for shade and borders. There may be inspection delays on shipments to California.

Jerry and Jan have been developing the Gardens of Sawyer Point, a riverfront park and recreational area in Cincinnati. In their spare time they try to catch up on sleep. Visitors are welcome to come to their display garden and nursery Saturday to Tuesday in April to mid-June and September through October, or by appointment. Early summer is the best season.

Hillsboro is an hour east of Cincinnati and about an hour and a quarter south of Columbus.

Rocknoll Nursery
7812 Mad River Road
Hillsboro, OH 45133
Jerry and Jan Hopkins
(513) 393-5545
Catalog: $1, bn/cn

■ The last time I talked to Bob Stewart, he ran a nursery called Life-Form Replicators. He's now merged with the nursery of his bride, Brigitta, and they are going to use the name of her nursery, **Perennial Plantation**. They specialize in perennials and alpine and rock garden plants and have been growing many unusual varieties from seed collected all over the world. Bob says he may eventually make a video catalog so that customers can see what the plants look like. Visitors are welcome from Monday to Saturday, from April through June, or by appointment. You can see the plants in the fields and dig the ones you want. Fowlerville is halfway between Lansing and Ann Arbor, off Interstate 96.

Perennial Plantation
P.O. Box 857
Fowlerville, MI 48836
Bob and Brigitta Stewart
(517) 223-8750
Catalog: $2, bn

■ Rock gardeners in the Minneapolis area must know **Rice Creek Gardens** in Blaine; even outside Minnesota many have heard talks by Betty Ann Addison. She and her husband, Charles, grow an extensive collection of hardy alpine plants, rarer perennials, hardy daylilies, and dwarf shrubs, and propagate woody ornamentals, hardy rhododendrons, shrub roses, and kalmias. They like to travel, looking for the best plants, and they design gardens.

Betty Ann and Charles met at a plant propagation seminar, and he moved his tissue culture lab to Minnesota to marry her; they are very active in the Woody Plant Society (an excellent source of plant hardiness information), and in the winter they study plants! They offer limited mail order. The display garden on their five-acre nursery is really very beautiful. If you live in the area, plan to visit in several seasons. Blaine is a northern suburb of Minneapolis; the nursery is open daily from May through October.

Rice Creek Gardens
11506 Highway 65
Blaine, MN 55434
Betty Ann and Charles Addison
(612) 574-1197 or 755-8484
Catalog: $2, OV, bn

■ **Colorado Alpines** in Avon, Colorado, is in the true American Alps, just seven miles west of Vail at 7,500 feet. The nursery offers a broad selection of alpine plants, mostly seed-grown from seeds collected all over the world and wintered outside in cold frames — these are the real toughies. Among the larger classes offered are androsaces, aquilegias, campanulas, dianthus, gentians, penstemons, phlox, pleiones, primulas, saxifragas, sempervivums, silenes, and a few dwarf conifers. Colorado Alpines is adding native trees, shrubs, wildflowers, and dry land plants for the West.

Marty and Sandy Jones were inspired to live in the Rockies and have been doing landscaping around Vail since 1973; in 1983 they started growing alpine plants, which they love. They're also involved in the creation of the Betty Ford Alpine Gardens in Vail, which they highly recommend to visitors to the area. Their own display garden is at its best in June; visitors are welcome daily at the nursery from April to October.

Colorado Alpines, Inc.
P.O. Box 2708
Avon, CO 81620
Marty and Sandy Jones
(303) 949-6464 or 6672
Catalog: $2d, CAN/OV, bn

■ Another nursery known to rock gardeners all over the country is **Siskiyou Rare Plant Nursery** in Medford, Oregon. Founded in 1963 by Boyd Kline and Lawrence Crocker and bought by Baldassare Mineo and Jerry Colley in 1978, the nursery is now run by Mineo alone. The catalogs, definite "take-to-bedders," offer nearly 1,100 rock garden and alpine plants, many of which are special selections of native plants of Oregon and northern California. Among the treasures are good selections of androsaces, arctostaphylos, campanulas, daphne, dianthus, erodiums, genistas, gentians, hardy geraniums, lewisias, penstemons, phlox, primulas, saxifragas, tricyrtis, vacciniums, violas, and zauschnerias. And, oh yes, add dwarf conifers and other small shrubs, hardy ferns and dwarf forms of Japanese maples.

Two catalogs a year (spring and fall) means two long evenings curled up in bed, reading and looking at illustrations by the multitalented Baldassare Mineo, a former architect from California. In addition to running the nursery, Baldassare has been working on a worldwide color photo encyclopedia of 1,500 alpine plants for the rock garden, to be published by Timber Press.

My only visit to the nursery was on a day when he was away, but a display garden in front of the nursery gave me plenty to wonder over. Visitors are welcome on Saturday from nine to two, March through October, or by appointment. Medford is on Interstate 5, thirty miles north of the California border and near the Ashland Shakespeare Festival.

Siskiyou Rare Plant Nursery
2825 Cummings Road
Medford, OR 97501
Baldassare Mineo
(503) 772-6846
Catalog: $2d, CAN, bn

SISKIYOU RARE PLANT NURSERY
Artist: Baldassare Mineo

■ I love some plant lists for their quirkiness and eclecticism; sometimes it's pretty hard to decide how to categorize a nursery. **Nature's Garden** in Scio, Oregon, offers some perennials, lilies, hardy opuntia cactus, and a selection of rock garden plants: sedums and sempervivums, species iris, hardy ferns and primroses; the plants are small and very reasonably priced.

Frederick Held is an Austrian who started working with plants in Salzburg at age fourteen and has worked in many countries. He started Nature's Garden in Oregon in 1974. Frederick has recently moved from Beaverton to Scio, and is building up stock again. He gets seed from many plant society exchanges and from friends in Germany and Czechoslovakia. He says that primulas and cats give him great joy. Frederick won an award for his *Primula juliana* 'Friday', which is hardier than 'Wanda', and a national trophy for *Primula frondosa* in 1990. He's not set up for visitors or on-site sales, so mail orders only, please.

Nature's Garden
40611 Highway 226
Scio, OR 97374
Frederick W. Held
Catalog: $1.25d, CAN, bn/cn

■ Rick Lupp of **Mt. Tahoma Nursery** in Graham, Washington, was an air cargo agent and a longtime mountain climber and hiker who became interested in the alpine plants he saw growing at high altitudes. Rick now grows a wide selection of alpine plants from around the world, and shade and rock garden plants, including 50 species of campanulas, 20 species and cultivars of lewisia, 50 species and cultivars of primulas, and 15 species and cultivars of daphne.

There is a big display garden at the nursery, and Rick also sells troughs for trough gardens at the nursery (no shipping of troughs). Visitors are welcome on weekends, or by appointment during the week and in the months of July and August (Rick still likes to climb). Graham is about twenty-five miles southeast of Tacoma on Highway 161.

Mt. Tahoma Nursery
28111 112th Avenue East
Graham, WA 98338
Rick Lupp
(206) 847-9827
Catalog: $1, CAN, bn

■ Larry Bailey is an architect who's won national design awards for historic preservation. He's also an artist and a primula maven. Not just any primulas, but the "florist" or exhibition auriculas developed by hobbyists in the Midlands of England in the nineteenth century. He found an old primrose scrapbook and was thrilled when he discovered that the old-fashioned varieties were still being grown.

His **Bailey's** catalog offers more than 100 named varieties, many collected in England from the individual growers. Larry has also won awards for his own hybrids. Also offered are about 20 older Juliana hybrids. This is a very small nursery, and plants are frequently in limited supply; you may have to reserve them for delivery later. Larry's two daughters are helping him grow and ship his primulas. Mail order only.

> **Bailey's**
> P.O. Box 654
> Edmonds, WA 98020
> Larry A. Bailey
> (206) 774-7528
> Catalog: Free, bn

■ Several years ago I went to a wonderful Hardy Plant Society study weekend in Edmonds, Washington, organized in great part by Evie Douglas and her husband, Dan. In addition to keeping things humming, they had a booth offering exquisite rock garden and perennial plants. That they survived the weekend is a miracle. Evie's **Cricklewood Nursery** in Snohomish still sells exquisite plants, including anemones, astilbes, hardy geraniums, primulas, hellebores, woodland plants, plants from New Zealand, some old roses, plants with gold and silver leaves, several alpine willows, and several trilliums. Some unusual plants are available only at the nursery because they are not grown in quantity or are difficult to ship.

Evie started working in a "kid nursery" (Head Start), but after having her own kids, she switched to plants and started her plant nursery. She's taught some classes at Edmonds Community College. Dan, luckily, is an arborist and shares Evie's passion for plants. Visitors may come and see the display garden on Friday and Saturday from April through June. Please call for an appointment. Snohomish is about ten miles southeast of Everett and thirty miles north of Seattle.

> **Cricklewood Nursery**
> 11907 Nevers Road
> Snohomish, WA 98290
> Evie Douglas
> (206) 568-2829
> Catalog: $2d, bn

■ Herb Senft got interested in plants while he was a student at the University of California at Santa Cruz, where he volunteered as a docent at the UCSC Botanical Garden, which specializes in Australian and South African plants. Now he calls himself a plantoholic and runs **Skyline Nursery** in the rainy Northwest, specializing in perennials and rock garden plants, including anemones, aquilegias, arabis, campanulas, antique varieties of dianthus, epimediums, gentians, ornamental grasses, helianthemums, species iris, lewisia, penstemons, pulmonarias, saxifragas, and much more. He's so eager to find new plants that he will happily trade plants with other collectors.

Visitors are welcome at the nursery all year from Monday through Saturday; call ahead (between 8 A.M. and 5 P.M.) if you're coming a distance to be sure that someone will be there. Sequim (pronounced squim) is on the northern tip of the Olympic Peninsula, an hour and a half west of Seattle by ferry and road, between Port Angeles and Port Townsend.

> **Skyline Nursery**
> 4772 Sequim-Dugeness Way
> Sequim, WA 98382
> Herb Senft
> (206) 683-2294 (8 A.M.–5 P.M. PST)
> Catalog: $1, bn

■ **Lamb Nurseries** in Spokane, Washington, has always had an intriguing catalog for lovers of rock garden plants and perennials. It won my heart years ago when I lived in San Francisco and ordered a dozen reblooming iris. Never having heard of "extras," I was thrilled to receive about fifteen plants! They have particularly good selections of alyssum, asters, aubrietas, campanulas, chrysanthemums, hardy fuchsias, helianthemums, phlox, veronicas, and violas. They also offer some choice ornamental shrubs.

Founded around 1930, and run for many years by Dick Sekijima, the nursery was taken over in 1987 by Nicola Luttropp. Nicola says she was a professional student before becoming a nurseryperson; she was a financial analyst before getting degrees in horticulture and landscape architecture.

Visitors may come to the nursery and look around. From Monday to Thursday during shipping season (March through June 15) you will get no service, but you can pick up plants that you've ordered ahead. On Friday and Saturday the staff will help you; the nursery is always closed on Sunday. The best months to visit are March through October. Spokane is in eastern Washington, near the Idaho border.

Lamb Nurseries
101 East Sharp Avenue
Spokane, WA 99202
Nicola Luttropp
(509) 328-7956
Catalog: $1, CAN/OV, bn/cn

■ *Other sources of rock garden and alpine plants are:*

Alpine Gardens & Calico Shop, Stitzer, WI
Appalachian Wildflower Nursery, Reedsville, PA
Bluestone Perennials, Madison, OH
Canyon Creek Nursery, Oroville, CA
Collector's Nursery, Vancouver, WA
Fieldstone Gardens, Vassalboro, ME
Gardens of the Blue Ridge, Pineola, NC
Ledgecrest Greenhouses, Storrs, CT
Miniature Plant Kingdom, Sebastopol, CA
Perpetual Perennials, Springfield, OH
Porterhowse Farms, Sandy, OR
Sandy Mush Herb Nursery, Leicester, NC
Springvale Farm Nursery, Hamburg, IL
Twombly Nursery, Monroe, CT
Andre Viette Farm & Nursery, Fishersville, VA

WE-DU NURSERIES
Artist: Richard E. Weaver, Jr.

Roses

FOREVERGREEN FARM   *Artist: Suzy Verrier*

A number of recent articles and a book have made the rose rustlers of Texas the most famous horticultural desperados in the country. Once or twice a year they fan out into old towns and homesteads, looking for old garden roses that have been scorned by the modern rose trade. These roses are found growing over old farmhouses, in cemeteries, along roadsides, and in old town gardens, many treasured for generations, others gone wild and completely forgotten.

I've heard Fred Boutin from the California mother lode, and Virginia Hopper and her sister Joyce Demits from the northern California coast, talk about scouring old homesteads and pioneer towns for old roses, and there are others all over the country with sharp eyes out for these treasures. The ability of these roses to live neglected for a hundred years and still bloom every year makes them wonderful plants for gardens; the great variety of flowers, from single wild types to huge cabbages, make them sought after by collectors who can somehow crowd dozens to hundreds into their gardens.

The term *old garden roses* has pretty much come to include old hybrids whose origins have been lost to the ages, the crosses and hybrids of the eighteenth and nineteenth centuries, and the early tea roses of the late nineteenth and early twentieth century. It also loosely includes the modern shrub roses, those with complicated breeding that includes the old garden roses and more modern hybrids; nurseries that sell old garden roses usually sell some species roses as well. Until fairly recently breeding records were very poorly kept; when old roses that could not be easily identified were found, they were given a "study name" for the place found or were named after the gardener who grew them. Old rose catalogs are full of name clarifications and corrections as further identifications are made.

Most of these roses are tough and disease-resistant, don't require a lot of pruning or spraying, and once established will grow on for many years, without much care, as demonstrated by the roses growing at abandoned homesteads and cemeteries. Unlike modern hybrids, they are almost always propagated from cuttings instead of grafted or budded. These cuttings develop strong roots of their own and never throw up shoots of different varieties from the rootstock. The flowers can be heart-meltingly beautiful, come in all shades from white to dark red, pale to bright yellow, peach to apricot, or striped, and make sensational bouquets.

I've become addicted to these roses and have about 40 varieties at present, adding a few more each year. When my niece married last summer I took in several big plastic milk jugs full of roses to the caterers for table decorations. You can imagine my distress when I arrived at the reception and saw that my roses hadn't been used; the caterer told me that they'd "found jugs of flowers, but those weren't *roses!*" I guess they thought that all roses came with uniform straight stems and half-opened buds for flowers. My crestfallen look must have melted her heart, for my roses began to appear as romantic decorations on the hors d'oevre trays!

FOREVERGREEN FARM   *Artist: Suzy Verrier*

■ **Forevergreen Farm** in North Yarmouth, Maine, is run by Suzy Verrier, an artist and illustrator of children's books, so of course the rose on the cover is exquisite. She's also the author of the book *Rugosa Roses* (Capability's Books), which sings the praises of those hardy beauties. Her catalog offers a broad selection of old garden roses, English roses, the tough roses hybridized by Griffith Buck in Iowa, shrub and species roses, and of course, a good selection of rugosas. Visitors are welcome daily (only afternoons on Sunday) from June through September; the last ten days of June are the very best. There are more than 500 roses in the display garden. Forevergreen also has an annual Rose Day in June; call for the date. North Yarmouth is about twenty miles north of Portland, Maine.

> **Forevergreen Farm**
> 70 New Gloucester Road
> North Yarmouth, ME 04021
> Suzy Verrier
> (207) 829-5830
> Catalog: Free, bn

■ Mike Lowe, an engineer, started **Lowe's own-root Roses** in Nashua, New Hampshire, in 1979, custom-propagating old roses from his collection of nearly 2,000. He still propagates only to order, and it takes eighteen months to receive your plant, but he may very well have roses that are not available anywhere else. Mike is renowned for his expertise and is looking forward to retiring so that he can devote all his time to roses. Visitors must call ahead for an appointment to visit the display garden; the best month is June. Nashua is in southern New Hampshire, not far from the Massachusetts border.

> **Lowe's own-root Roses**
> 6 Sheffield Road
> Nashua, NH 03062
> Malcolm "Mike" Lowe
> (603) 888-2214
> Catalog: $2, bn

■ **Country Bloomers Nursery** has recently moved from southern California to Udall, Kansas, to take advantage of the room to expand on the family farm. Mike Morton is a former park service employee and landscaper who fell in love with old roses when his horticultural class from UCLA went on a field trip to Descanso Gardens. Country Bloomers started in 1982 as a miniature rose nursery. Mike and his partner, Sharon Gordon, an attorney, became overwhelmed by the demand when their back-yard business blossomed. They grow more than 250 old roses, about 100 miniatures, and also modern shrub roses such as those from David Austin in England. They list about 80 old garden roses and about 40 miniatures, and the list will grow as they get settled in Kansas. They are establishing display gardens; visitors should be sure to call ahead. Udall is thirty miles south of Wichita, near the Oklahoma border.

Country Bloomers Nursery
R.R. 2
Udall, KS 67146
Mike Morton
(316) 986-5518
Catalog: Free, CAN/OV

■ A very new source of old roses in Loveland, Colorado, is **Rabbit Shadow Farm.** Charlie Gibbs was a chemist and his wife, Mary, was in advertising until 1990. They currently have a mail order list of about 30 very hardy old and modern shrub roses and 15 species roses; they offer another 30 varieties at the nursery. The list is sure to grow in the years to come: they also offer scented and specialty geraniums and many varieties of herbs. Visitors are welcome daily. Loveland is forty miles north of Denver.

Rabbit Shadow Farm
2880 E. Highway 402
Loveland, CO 80538
Mary and Charlie Gibbs
(303) 667-5531
Catalog: Free

■ Dr. William Campbell started the **High Country Rosarium** with his daughter Melinda in Denver, Colorado, to offer very hardy roses for the Rocky Mountain area. His parents grew roses in Colorado Springs and sent him a big bundle of rose plants when he bought his first house. His interest in things historical led him to old roses. Melinda has gone into horticultural therapy; he says the new Ralph Moore hybrid, 'Linda Campbell', is named for his wife, not his daughter. His selection continues to grow; he has about 600 varieties and lists the toughest ones. There is a minimum order of ten plants. Also offered are collections for hedges, drought tolerance, high altitudes (hardy and short growing season), and roses with good hips for bird lovers. There are display gardens around his office at 1717 Downing Street and around his home at 162 Ash Street; both are well labeled. Late spring and early summer are the best months.

High Country Rosarium
1717 Downing Street
Denver, CO 80209
William Campbell; John Ray, Mgr.
(303) 832-4026
Catalog: $1, bn/cn

■ Rose central for the famous rose rustlers of Texas is the **Antique Rose Emporium** in Brenham. Mike Shoup stopped in his tracks when he saw a neglected rose called 'Mermaid' growing on a fence. He began to look for more and came into contact with others on the prowl for old roses. His catalog has grown to more than 200 varieties in less than ten years. A number still have Texas "study names"; others are better known. Some have been grown in Texas for 150 years.

Mike has written *Landscaping with Antique Roses* with Liz Druitt (Taunton Press). The book emphasizes roses for the Deep South, and his rose offerings tend toward those that have proven themselves in southern growing conditions. There's a lovely display garden around a pioneer stone house, which is open daily, except for a few holidays; the nursery is in Independence, between Austin and Houston, off of Highway 290.

Antique Rose Emporium
Route 5, Box 143
Brenham, TX 77833
Mike Shoup
(409) 836-9051, (800) 441-0002
Catalog: $5, CAN

■ During the many years that old roses were out of fashion, the torch was carried by **Roses of Yesterday & Today** near Watsonville, California. Founded in the 1930s as Lester Rose Gardens, it was later known as Lester & Tillotson, and finally as Will Tillotson's Roses of Yesterday & Today. Dorothy Stemler, mother of the current owner, Patricia Wiley, was Will Tillotson's right hand and inherited the nursery from him. During those early years they offered roses that could not be ordered through modern catalogs. They now find themselves in a rapidly growing niche of the nursery business.

Roses of Yesterday & Today now offers about 240 varieties, including some modern hybrid teas; unlike most other old rose

nurseries, most of their propagation is by budding and graft-
ing rather than rooted cuttings. Now the whole Wiley family
is involved, including Pat's husband, Newt, daughter, Kathy
Minier, and son, Andy. There's a display garden in a clearing
of the redwood forest around the office. The best months to
visit are May and June. There's a good map and directions in
the catalog (or call for directions); Watsonville is between
Monterey and Santa Cruz on Highway 1.

> **Roses of Yesterday & Today**
> 802 Brown's Valley Road
> Watsonville, CA 95076-0398
> Patricia Wiley and Kathryn Minier
> (408) 724-3537 or 2755
> Catalog: $4, CAN/OV, bn

ROSES OF YESTERDAY & TODAY
Artist: Anne Marie Bonet-Egberg

■ At last! A new source of old roses right here in my home-
town. Philip Robinson and Gregg Lowery of **Vintage Gardens**
in Sebastopol, California, are well known to old rose collectors. Gregg is a landscaper, and Philip tends the famous old
rose garden at the Korbel Winery. They have a collection of
nearly 2,000 old roses and have just started selling by mail
instead of holding a two-day free-for-all at their nursery each
spring. They list several hundred varieties propagated from
their collection, many of which I haven't seen in other old rose
catalogs. They do not encourage visitors but plan to have an

annual open garden during spring bloom (usually May or early June); call for information.

Vintage Gardens
3003 Pleasant Hill Road
Sebastopol, CA 95472
Gregg Lowery and Philip Robinson
(707) 829-5342
Catalog: $2, bn

■ Virginia Hopper and Joyce Demits of **Heritage Rose Gardens** in Fort Bragg, California, were loggers' wives who liked to ride horseback in the redwood forests of the north coast. They began to notice the roses that grew at old homesteads and in old towns, and to collect cuttings as they went along. This led them to reading about old roses to identify their finds, then to growing more and more, and finally to starting a nursery. Some of the roses in their catalog still have their "study names," usually the name of the village or homestead where they were found. The catalog has a list of name corrections and clarifications for roses sold earlier under study names. They offer a number of species roses, and every type of old garden rose, early tea roses, and shrub roses. Visitors may come to their display garden but must make arrangements to do so in advance. Fort Bragg is on the Mendocino County coast, about three and a half hours north of San Francisco.

Heritage Rose Gardens
16831 Mitchell Creek Drive
Fort Bragg, CA 95437
Virginia Hopper and Joyce Demits
(707) 984-6959 or 964-3748
Catalog: $1d, CAN/OV, bn

■ **Greenmantle Nursery** near Garberville, California, is a hold-over from the back-to-the-land movement of the 1970s: Ram and Marisa Fishman moved to redwood country to raise food and children. Ram has become a nurseryman specializing in heirloom apples and other fruit, a writer and lecturer on pomology, and a busy horseshoer. Marisa has become a collector of old roses, offering a wide selection of all types and many species, about 275 in all. Most of the roses offered are cuttings from the mother plants grown in the Fishmans' garden; a few are budded onto *Rosa multiflora* rootstock.

The Fishmans are great growers of heritage plants and children. Their kids, who used to help with the nursery, went off to Reed, Swarthmore, and Amherst colleges — so much for the isolation of the deep country! Marisa warned me that her supplies of plants are sometimes limited, especially the rarer varieties. She also collects species iris and other endangered plants of all types. Visitors are welcome only in late May and early June and must call or write well in advance for an appointment and directions; Garberville is about four hours north of San Francisco on Highway 101.

> **Greenmantle Nursery**
> 3010 Ettersburg Road
> Garberville, CA 95440
> Ram and Marisa Fishman
> (707) 986-7504
> Rose list: Long SASE, bn

■ I pride myself on knowing about almost every mail order nursery, so you can imagine my chagrin when my pen pal, Bill Grant, sent me a list of his favorite rose nurseries, including **Heirloom Old Garden Roses** in St. Paul, Oregon, which I had somehow missed. I quickly sent for the catalog and can truly say I was very impressed by the selection, a total of 700 varieties by Heirloom's count!

John Clements is a retired air traffic controller who's been growing roses for thirty years; his wife, Louise, loves roses but also likes to write, paint, photograph, and travel, though it's hard to imagine that they have time for anything but roses, since they also hybridize and introduce roses of their own. The catalog offers good descriptions of all the roses offered and lists in the back give suggestions for the best roses to suit a variety of growing conditions and special uses.

The Clementses have a display garden with 500 varieties of roses, and visitors are welcome daily from April through September. St. Paul is about thirty miles southwest of Portland near Newburg.

> **Heirloom Old Garden Roses**
> 24062 N.E. Riverside
> St. Paul, OR 97137
> John and Louise Clements
> (503) 538-1576
> Catalog: $1.50, bn

■ Gerry Kruger of Spokane, Washington, knows which roses survive harsh winter climates and says that old garden roses are coming into vogue in her area because so many hybrid tea roses are lost every winter. Her **Blossoms & Bloomers** offers about 40 varieties each year, grown on their own roots, drawn from her collection of almost 300 tough old roses. Gerry says she's got dirt in her veins; her grandfather hybridized roses, and her best seller is a huge once-blooming pink climber passed down in her family and called 'Grandpa's Rose'. Visitors are welcome to call ahead and come to the nursery and display garden, which are open only during the months of May and June; she also sells more than 100 varieties of perennials at the nursery. Spokane is in far eastern Washington.

> **Blossoms & Bloomers**
> 11415 East Krueger Lane
> Spokane, WA 99207
> Gerry and Ron Krueger
> (509) 922-1344
> Catalog: $1

■ *Another source of species roses is:*

Forestfarm, Williams, OR

■ *Other sources of old garden roses are:*

Carroll Gardens, Westminster, MD
Milaeger's Gardens, Racine, WI
Wayside Gardens, Hodges, SC

ROSES OF YESTERDAY & TODAY
Artist: Anne Marie Bonet-Egberg

But, you say, what about "real roses"? Most people still think of roses as the hybrid tea and floribunda roses we see growing everywhere. They are always very popular, and some of them are lovely, but I don't think of them as very beautiful plants with their thorny legs and all the upkeep. But what do I know? They are sold by the multimillions and have millions of admirers! They are very easily available in garden centers and in many general nursery catalogs, but I want to mention a couple of sources that offer more than just the most popular or the current "roses of the year."

■ **Thomasville Nurseries** in Thomasville, Georgia, has been in business since 1898. Paul Hjort is the third generation of his family to run the nursery. He offers both new and older hybrids — teas, floribundas, climbing roses, and a few miniature and tree roses. He also offers azaleas, including some southern natives, and many daylilies, as well as several cultivars of liriope. The nursery has an American Rose Society–sanctioned display garden, which is at its best from mid-April through mid-November. Thomasville is thirty-five miles north of Tallahassee, Florida.

> **Thomasville Nurseries**
> P.O. Box 7
> Thomasville, GA 31799-0007
> A. Paul Hjort
> (912) 226-5568
> Catalog: Free

■ **Edmunds Roses** (formerly Roses by Fred Edmunds) in Wilsonville, Oregon, has just moved on a generation. Fred Edmunds has retired from the business he started in 1949 with his wife, Wini, and their son Phil is taking over. Phil says that Fred is still there every day, working away. The Edmundses offer new introductions from the best hybridizers all over the world, particularly England and New Zealand, as well as many old favorites. Many of their customers must show roses, since performance on the show bench is mentioned in many of the descriptions. Visitors are welcome only during the last two weeks of September, when they may walk through the fields; please call ahead. Wilsonville is located about twenty miles south of Portland.

> **Edmunds Roses**
> 6235 S.W. Kahle Road
> Wilsonville, OR 97070

Philip Edmunds
(503) 682-1476
FAX (503) 682-1275
Catalog: Free

■ **Stanek's Garden Center** in Spokane, Washington, is another source of hybrid teas and floribunda roses, as well as some rugosas, climbers, and English roses. They also offer some perennials and clematis. The nursery was started in 1913 by Tim Stanek's grandfather. The garden center is open daily, all year. Spokane is in eastern Washington.

> **Stanek's Garden Center**
> 2929 East Twenty-seventh Avenue
> Spokane, WA 99223
> Tim Stanek
> (509) 535-2939
> Catalog: Free

Miniature roses have become very popular over the last few years for growing in pots and hanging baskets as well as in gardens. Sometimes you see them planted in front of other roses to hide the awkward legs, or planted in low borders. Most of the miniature rose nurseries seem to be on the Pacific coast, where growing conditions apparently are ideal.

■ Martin and Norma Kelly were public school music teachers until their retirement, got into roses of all kinds, then judged rose shows, tried their hand at hybridizing, and now run **Gloria Dei Nursery** in High Falls, New York, which offers more than 100 cultivars of miniature roses. Visitors are welcome to come to the greenhouse in spring and summer, but please call ahead to be sure someone will be there. High Falls is about thirty miles north of Newburgh, west of the Hudson River.

> **Gloria Dei Nursery**
> 36 East Road
> High Falls, NY 12440
> Marty and Norma Kelly
> (914) 687-9981
> Catalog: 1 FCS

■ Susan O'Brien of **Tiny Petals Nursery** in Chula Vista, California, is the daughter of the late Dee Bennett, an award-winning hybridizer of miniature roses. Of the 200-plus varieties Sue offers, 50 are her mother's hybrids. Dee left Susan and her husband, Pat, a legacy of more than 100 seedlings, which will be introduced as they prove themselves. Every sort of miniature rose, including trees, climbers, hanging varieties, microminiatures, and "bush plants" is available. Susan is a psychiatric nurse; Pat was a welder who now runs the nursery. Visitors are welcome at the nursery Thursday through Monday; late March and April are the best months. Chula Vista is between San Diego and Tijuana, Mexico.

Tiny Petals Nursery
489 Minot Avenue
Chula Vista, CA 91910
Pat and Sue O'Brien
(619) 422-0385
Catalog: Free

■ Earl and Agnes McDaniel of **McDaniel's Miniature Roses** in Lemon Grove, California, are experienced plant propagators who have also gone into hybridizing miniature roses and offer about 125 varieties for sale, their own hybrids and those of many other hybridizers. Earl used to work in the defense industry but has found much more interesting work in his roses. Visitors are welcome, but please call ahead to be sure someone will be there and to get directions. Lemon Grove is just east of San Diego.

McDaniel's Miniature Roses
7523 Zemco Street
Lemon Grove, CA 92045
Earl and Agnes McDaniel
(619) 469-4669
Catalog: Free, CAN/OV

■ Best known of the American hybridizers of miniature roses is Ralph Moore of **Sequoia Nursery** in Visalia, California. He began hybridizing them in 1937 and has created hundreds, many of which have won awards here and abroad. He is considered to have created a whole new class of rose. The Sequoia catalog offers about 100 varieties of miniature roses, and another 75 nonminiature roses, including some old garden varieties and some new hybrids of Moore's own, including 'Topaz Jewel', the first repeat flowering yellow hybrid rugosa rose. Mr. Moore has increasingly turned his interest to hybridizing larger roses and has several that sound wonderful. The nursery is open daily except holidays. Visalia is about an hour south of Fresno.

Sequoia Nursery — Moore Miniature Roses
2519 East Noble Avenue
Visalia, CA 93277
Ralph H. Moore
(209) 732-0190 or 0309
Catalog: Free

■ **Justice Miniature Roses** in Wilsonville, Oregon, offers a very wide selection of miniatures, about 300 varieties from many well-known hybridizers. The nursery has also been importing the hybrids of McCann and McGredy from New Zealand and has tried hybridizing as well. Jerry and June Justice's nursery is just down the road from Edmunds Roses, so you know it's in good rose-growing country. Visitors are welcome daily from mid-April to mid-September. The Justices are twenty miles south of Portland.

Justice Miniature Roses
5947 S.W. Kahle Road
Wilsonville, OR 97070
Jerry, June, and Tara Justice
(503) 682-2370
Catalog: Free

Sedums and Sempervivums

■ In Stitzer, Wisconsin, is **Alpine Gardens & Calico Shop**, a nursery selling sedums, sempervivums, jovibarbas, other alpine plants, and quilting supplies. Run by Charlotte Nelson, an expert in both gardening and quilting, the shop sounds like a fun place to visit in summer and winter. Charlotte grows all of her plants outside all year. She does not ship to Arizona, California, Oregon, Washington, or Texas.

Charlotte likens rock gardening to quilting, planning and laying out plants in pleasing color combinations and patterns. Because she is partially disabled, with knee problems, Charlotte says she's figured out all sorts of low-maintenance gardening techniques for the handicapped, which she calls "throw and grow." The Nelsons live on a lovely farm and have display gardens. Visitors are welcome from April through September but should call ahead to be sure someone will be at the nursery. Stitzer is in southwestern Wisconsin, two and a half miles southeast of Fennimore.

> **Alpine Gardens & Calico Shop**
> 12446 Country F
> Stitzer, WI 53825
> Charlotte Nelson
> (608) 822-6382
> Catalog: $2, bn

■ Micki Crozier in Sedgwick, Kansas, is crazy about sedums and sempervivums and is growing about 650 of them at present. She's also active in the Sedum Society, collects and trades plants with friends overseas, and has on display many plants from her collection at the "Garden on the Rocks" at Botanica in Wichita.

She does not sell all of the varieties she grows by mail, but her **Country Cottage** list offers a good selection and several mixed collections, and she may be able to supply others on a limited basis — send her your want-list. Her list changes from year to year to make other varieties from her large collection available and to allow her to increase others. Because she is so busy, you must call in advance about a visit. Sedgwick is about twenty miles northwest of Wichita.

> **Country Cottage**
> Route 2, Box 130
> Sedgwick, KS 67135
> Micki Crozier
> (316) 976-0496 (evenings)
> Catalog: 1 FCS, bn

■ **Jim & Irene Russ** have been growing and studying sedums and sempervivums for thirty years; of course, it started out as a hobby. Jim was a truck driver and heavy equipment operator. He and Irene now offer more than 250 sempervivums and 75 sedums, with more of their own hybrids under evaluation. They also grow 2 species of lewisia. They do not have a display garden as such, but visitors can come in the spring and early summer to see the many plants growing in flats.

The mailing address is Igo, California, the nursery is in Ono. These are real place names! Jim thinks they are Indian names and says there are many fantastic stories about where they came from. Visitors should call a day or two in advance; late afternoon or early evening is the best time to catch the Russes. Ono is about sixteen miles west of Redding at the north end of the Sacramento Valley.

> **Jim & Irene Russ**
> P.O. Box 6450
> Igo, CA 96047
> (916) 396-2329 (after 5 P.M. PST)
> Catalog: $.50, CAN/OV, bn

■ John and Joyce Hoekstra started **Squaw Mountain Gardens** in Estacada, Oregon, in 1983. After John died their daughter Janis and her husband, Arthur Noyes, joined the nursery. They grow hundreds of cultivars of sempervivums, sedums, other rock garden succulents such as orostachys, jovibarbas and rosularias, and some tender varieties such as adromischus, aeoniums, crassulas, and echeverias. They are working on hybrids of their own, but none have been introduced yet. Also offered are some hardy ferns, ivies, and heathers. They have a big display garden, and just for their own pleasure they have been planting a six-acre arboretum as a memorial to John Hoekstra. Visitors are welcome. The best months to visit are May through September; please call ahead to be sure someone will be there. Estacada is thirty-five miles southeast of Portland in the Mount Hood foothills.

Squaw Mountain Gardens
36212 S.E. Squaw Mountain Road
Estacada, OR 97023
Joyce Hoekstra, Janis and Arthur Noyes
(503) 630-5458
Catalog: Free, bn

■ *Another source of sedums and sempervivums is:*

Porterhowse Farms, Sandy, OR

SQUAW MOUNTAIN GARDENS
Artist: Nicole Barnes

Trees: Conifers

All "collectors' plants" have their passionate partisans, but surely one of the most intense groups of collectors are those who collect dwarf conifers. These trees have the advantage of being compact, lending themselves to use in many garden settings and allowing collectors to build big collections in fairly small spaces. Dwarf conifers can also be grown as bonsai or to their natural size in containers.

There are so many different varieties available that you could make collecting them a life's work and on your deathbed you'd hear of new ones you just had to have. Most of the nursery-people in dwarf conifers began as collectors. Some are still collectors who will propagate from their collections. Most of them will tell you that they started collecting with the help of a generous mentor.

■ **Twombly Nursery** in Monroe, Connecticut, offers a very extensive list of dwarf conifers, mostly newer and hard-to-find cultivars, as well as many ornamental trees and shrubs, such as Japanese maples, beeches, magnolias, hamamelis, kalmias, hollies, lilacs, and many viburnums. This is a marriage of trees and shrubs (Kenneth Twombly) and perennials and rock garden plants (Priscilla Twombly), so the Twomblys also offer a broad selection of the latter, as well. If you're looking for more mature specimens, many of the trees and shrubs are available in larger sizes at the nursery. The Twomblys don't ship to California or Oregon.

Watch out: Kenneth and Priscilla raise Norfolk terriers, too, so don't go near the nursery unless you are immune to adorable dogs. They have several display gardens and regular nursery hours from March through October, but they're closed Sunday in July and August. Monroe is in central Connecticut, between Bridgeport and Danbury, about fifty miles from New York City.

Twombly Nursery
163 Barn Hill Road
Monroe, CT 06468

Kenneth and Priscilla Twombly
(203) 261-2133
Catalog: $3, bn/cn

■ A very Spartan catalog is that of **Michael & Janet Kristick**
in Wellsville, Pennsylvania. It is just a list of dwarf conifers
and Japanese and species maples, but it's a very broad choice
of both. The Kristicks started their nursery in 1968 because
people were asking them to propagate plants from their large
collection. They don't keep a big inventory of plants but will
propagate desired plants for customers if they don't have them
in stock. Because Michael is so busy, there are sometimes
delays in shipping. Western states have agricultural restrictions
on some of these plants.

The nursery is only a part-time occupation for Michael,
who's also a corporate officer at a textile plant. He also likes
to work on old Lancia cars with his son. They have about
eight cars and travel around to vintage auto races. You must
have an appointment to visit, so contact the Kristicks well in
advance. Wellsville is between Harrisburg and York, about
eighty miles west of Philadelphia.

Michael & Janet Kristick
155 Mockingbird Road
Wellsville, PA 17365
(717) 292-2962
Catalog: Free, CAN/OV, bn

■ A more recent addition to dwarf conifer specialists is **Rarifolia** in Kintnersville, Pennsylvania, started in 1985 by collectors Skeeter and Beth Rodd. Their kind mentor was Helene
Bergman, who, with her husband, Fred, owned Rariflora Nursery, at one time one of the largest collections of dwarf conifers
in the world. Beth says that she and Skeeter are compulsive
collectors. They left the refrigeration service business to become nurseryfolk.

Their catalog offers more than 400 dwarf conifers and 100
Japanese maples. They do give you a reading list to help you
bone up. They have a large collection of "witches brooms,"
the chance mutations of both species and cultivars which are
frequently very different in color or habit. Some they find by
driving around looking up into trees! Who says plant collecting
is without risk? Visitors are asked to call for an appointment.
The Rodds say that May through September are the best
months. Kintnersville is near the Delaware River, about halfway between Easton and Doylestown off of Route 611.

Rarifolia
R.D. 2
Kintnersville, PA 18930
Skeeter and Beth Rodd
(215) 847-8208
Catalog: $3d, bn/cn

■ For years one of my favorite catalogs has been the one from **Foxborough Nursery** in Street, Maryland. I didn't know until I talked with David Thompson that his is also a large wholesale nursery. David started his nursery in 1977 with the last plants propagated by the world-renowned plantsman and nurseryman Henry J. Hohman of Kingsville Nursery. David is constantly growing and trying new introductions of conifers and other ornamental trees, and his mail order catalog offers a selection of the rarest, newest, and best of the more than 3,000 varieties he grows. He says people are always sending him their want-lists.

The catalog is a straight listing of dwarf conifers and an increasing selection of ornamental deciduous trees and shrubs by botanical and cultivar name. For those of you who keep *Hilliers Manual of Trees and Shrubs* or even weightier tree manuals on your bedside table, this catalog should pose no problem.

Why do I like such a Spartan catalog? The offerings are wonderful, full of unfamiliar names that send me off to look them up (the catalog does suggest several good books). In addition to his dwarf conifers, David lists Japanese maples, beeches, box, a number of cultivars of dogwood, beech, witch hazel, hollies, the wonderful Camperdown elm, and zelkova.

Shipping plants to California may be difficult due to the agricultural regulations against the Japanese beetle. There is a display garden. David Thompson asks that you call at least a week before you want to visit. Street is about eleven miles north of Bel Air, Maryland.

Foxborough Nursery, Inc.
3611 Miller Road
Street, MD 21154
David Thompson
(301) 879-4995
Catalog: $1d, CAN/OV, bn/cn

■ Driving up to the **Washington Evergreen Nursery** near Leicester, North Carolina, you come around a corner to find the "corporate center," a tumbledown tobacco barn standing at the edge of a pond. We walked through the display garden of dwarf conifers at the far end of the pond, deciding which ones we liked best and thinking that there was room for a dwarf conifer in each of our gardens. Collectors will recoil in horror, but there's no getting around it — they're just plain cute! High-minded, scholarly interest might come later, but everyone must buy the first one because it's irresistible.

Jordan Jack arrived to show us around, followed by a faithful pseudo–Border collie called Scruffy who flops comfortably wherever his master stops. A retired aerospace engineer and self-taught nurseryman and propagator, Jordan has to be the happiest of men; from spring to fall he works by the pond on his plants; in the fall he packs them carefully into greenhouses and goes off to spend the winter near Charleston, where he plays golf and bridge and enjoys his camellias.

The catalog lists about 180 varieties of dwarf conifer and 20 cultivars of kalmia. Jordan is also growing some small-leaved rhododendrons and other dwarf shrubs at the nursery. The catalog offers basic cultural information, a reading list, and a list of dwarf conifer collections so that the amateur can bring some learning to the listings. Plants are offered in various sizes, from small plants for bonsai to plants in three-gallon containers for instant effect. Visitors are welcome from May to October if they call ahead; the best times to call are from 7 to 9 A.M. or between 5 and 7 P.M. (eastern standard time). The nursery is about half an hour north of Asheville.

Washington Evergreen Nursery
P.O. Box 388
Leicester, NC 28748
Jordan Jack
(704) 683-4518 (Apr.–Oct.)
(803) 747-1641 (Nov.–Mar.)
Catalog: $2d, bn

■ Another source of dwarf conifers is **Springvale Farm Nursery** in Hamburg, Illinois, run by Will and Jeanne Gould. They also advertise under the name "Avid Gardener." The Goulds had a wholesale nursery, visited a local dwarf conifer collector, and fell in love! They offer a very good selection, including lots of Chamaecyparis cultivars, Japanese maples and other small shrubs, perennial plants, and ground covers for the rock garden. They don't ship to Alaska, Arizona, California, or Hawaii. Visitors may come to the nursery by appointment. The Goulds are developing a display garden. There are two Hamburgs in Illinois; this one is about eighty miles northwest of St. Louis near the Mississippi River.

Springvale Farm Nursery
Mozier Hollow Road
Hamburg, IL 62045
Will and Jeanne Gould
(618) 232-1108
Catalog: $2d, bn/cn

■ Ho hum, here she comes with another nursery near Sebastopol! Actually, I feel as if I live in horticultural heaven, the proof of which is offered all through these pages. **Miniature Plant Kingdom** was a miniature rose nursery when I first knew it, but Don Herzog fell in love with bonsai, and now he sells many dwarf conifers and other broad-leaved trees and shrubs for bonsai growers, among which are some lovely garden plants. He and his wife, Becky, also offer some perennials, alpines, and rock garden plants. They sell about 250 varieties of miniature roses at the nursery. Don has the first garden railway that I ever saw, though I've never been there when the train came through. The nursery is closed on Wednesday and Sunday morning. It's near Occidental, about twelve miles west of Santa Rosa; call for directions.

Miniature Plant Kingdom
4125 Harrison Grade Road
Sebastopol, CA 95472
Don and Becky Herzog
(707) 874-2233
Catalog: $2.50, bn/cn

■ Robert Fincham was a dwarf conifer collector and a science teacher who started propagating and then selling his extras to other collectors in 1979. Several years ago he moved his collection of nearly 2,000 dwarf conifers to Oregon, went into the nursery business, and is now running a big wholesale nursery. His **Coenosium Gardens** in Aurora is his retail and mail order division, offering about 600 cultivars of dwarf conifers, 30 cultivars of European beech, about as many Japanese maples, and a few other trees and shrubs, including more than 20 kalmias.

The Coenosium catalog falls halfway between those of Washington Evergreen and Foxborough: the plants are described briefly with no information on ultimate size, but hardiness zones are given. The joy of such a listing is the vast variety offered. There are about seven pages of just *Picea abies* — weeping, bun-shaped, globular, conical, cushion-form, contorted, and in every color and shade imaginable. Bob

Fincham expects that his readers have already passed through the freshman and sophomore courses and know where to find more information on the plants listed.

Planted around the office of the nursery and around the house across the street is Bob's collection of dwarf conifers, all perfectly displayed and tended. From smaller than a head of lettuce to the size of medium shrubs, the collection is an encyclopedia of dwarf conifers, their habits and possibilities. Visitors are welcome at any season if they call ahead for an appointment; Aurora is just a few miles east of Interstate 5, near Canby.

> **Coenosium Gardens**
> 6642 S. Lone Elder Road
> Aurora, OR 97002
> Robert and Dianne Fincham
> (503) 266-5471
> Catalog: $3d, CAN/OV, bn

■ Lloyd Porter and Don Howse of Sandy, Oregon, started collecting, propagating, and growing rock garden and alpine plants and dwarf conifers while still working at other jobs, Don at a large wholesale nursery, Lloyd for the U.S. government.

Their **Porterhowse Farms** list offers many choice plants for collectors: dwarf conifers and other plants for bonsai, many sempervivums, jovibarbas, orostachys, rosularias and sedums, saxifragas, dianthus, lewisias and other alpine plants, and Japanese iris. Porterhouse also offers several collections: alpine plants, sempervivums, bonsai companion plants, dwarf shrubs, pre-bonsai plants, and Japanese iris.

Lloyd and Don hope to remain small and to work for their own pleasure without outside help, so don't expect an army of minions replying to your inquiry by return post. Visitors are welcome to come and see the display garden and nursery plants, which are at their best from March to October. Be sure to call ahead the evening before to be certain someone will be there. Sandy is thirty miles east of Portland, halfway between Portland and Mount Hood.

> **Porterhowse Farms**
> 413 S.E. Thomas Road
> Sandy, OR 97055
> Lloyd Porter and Donald Howse
> (503) 668-5834
> Catalog: $2, bn

■ *Other sources of dwarf conifers are:*

Beaver Creek Nursery, Knoxville, TN
Camellia Forest Nursery, Chapel Hill, NC
Collector's Nursery, Vancouver, WA
The Cummins Garden, Marlboro, NJ
Forestfarm, Williams, OR
Girard Nurseries, Geneva, OH
Powell's Gardens, Princeton, NC
Roslyn Nursery, Dix Hills, NY

So now that you've read the listing of the nurseries that sell dwarf conifers, you're wondering where to get the wonderful big conifers? Don't fret: many of these specialists also sell trees that will become monarchs of the forest in addition to the genetic dwarfs that will always stay fairly small. Conifers that grow to be large are also available from many catalogs and from local nurseries.

The following two nurseries are good to know about if you are looking for conifers for a large undeveloped garden, for windbreaks or visual screens, or if you want to grow your own Christmas trees. Both are in Indiana, Pennsylvania, the "Christmas tree capital of the world." Indiana is about sixty miles northeast of Pittsburgh, about halfway between Pittsburgh and Altoona.

■ **Musser Forests** has been selling seedling trees and shrubs since 1928. The nursery offers a good selection of conifers, flowering and shade trees, azaleas, rhododendrons and other flowering shrubs, and some ground covers. Plants are available in quantities of 10, 50, and up. Visitors are welcome at their garden center, open daily except major holidays, from mid-March to mid-November.

> **Musser Forests, Inc.**
> P.O. Box 340
> Indiana, PA 15701
> Fred A. Musser
> (412) 465-5686
> Catalog: Free, CAN/OV, cn/bn

■ **Carino Nurseries** is a source of conifers primarily for Christmas tree growers, but many are fine ornamental trees for gardens, windbreaks, and reforestation. Most are available as seedlings or transplants and in quantities of 100 or 1,000 —

but wait! Carino also sells some specials in quantities of 10 or 20. There are some restrictions on shipping pines to western states. Mail order only.

Carino Nurseries
P.O. Box 538
Indiana, PA 15701
James L. Carino
(412) 463-3350, (800) 223-7075
Catalog: Free, cn/bn

■ **Cascade Forestry Nursery** in Cascade, Iowa, also lists a variety of seedling conifers and broad-leaved trees and shrubs, which are sold in any quantity. They also sell potted and balled-and-burlapped trees in larger sizes at commensurate prices. Started by Leo Frueh in 1974, Cascade specializes in hardy northern nut and hardwood trees, advising on plantings and even helping the woodlot owner to find a buyer for hardwood used for veneers. Cascade doesn't ship to California, Oregon, or Washington. Visitors are welcome, especially after June 15. The nursery is open Monday through Friday, and Saturday morning from March to mid-June. Cascade is between Cedar Rapids and Dubuque on Highway 151.

Cascade Forestry Nursery
Route 1
Cascade, IA 52033
Leo H. Frueh
(319) 852-3042
Catalog: Free, cn/bn

■ *Other sources of conifers are:*

Appalachian Gardens, Waynesboro, PA
Colvos Creek Nursery, Vashon Island, WA
Forestfarm, Williams, OR
Greer Gardens, Eugene, OR
Pacific Tree Farms, Chula Vista, CA
Smith Nursery Company, Charles City, IA
Wavecrest Nursery & Landscaping Company, Fennville, MI
Yucca Do Nursery, Waller, TX

Trees and Shrubs: Hardy

MOUNTAIN MAPLES *Artist: Terry Tanaka*

Now you can stop guessing about which plants I really like the best. If you could come into my house and snoop, you'd find that I keep Michael Dirr's *Manual of Woody Landscape Plants,* third edition (Stipes Publishing Company), *Shrubs* and *Roses* by Phillips and Rix (both from Random House), and *The Gardener's Illustrated Encyclopedia of Trees & Shrubs* by Brian Davis (Viking) right next to my bed. In my heart of hearts, nothing is as beautiful as a tree or shrub; the variety of shapes, habits, foliage and flower, autumn color — these really are my favorites.

When the real estate salesman brought me to see Lafalot, I said to him before we had come all the way up the driveway, "Let's write up the offer right now!" The yard was full of lovely trees, some quite unusual for a California garden. Those trees, and the new treasures that I've planted, are my greatest joy.

■ **Appalachian Gardens** in Waynesboro, Pennsylvania, is a source of maples, box (including some hardy Canadian crosses between English and Korean box), dogwoods, euonymus, forsythias, hydrangeas, hollies, kalmias, crape myrtles, magnolias, pieris, prunus, viburnums, hardy rhododendrons and azaleas, other trees and shrubs and a good selection of dwarf and regular conifers. Appalachian Gardens specializes in USDA introductions from the National Arboretum, especially the plants of the late Dr. Egolf. All the plants are very well described in the catalog, with the best soil pH given when relevant. There are restrictions on shipping to California, Oregon, and Washington.

Tom McCloud and Ezra Grubb started this business in 1985 as the retail division of their wholesale nursery, Appalachian Nurseries. Tom worked at a major nursery in California in production and research before going into business for himself. Ezra was a frustrated nurseryman who has found his calling. Visitors are welcome Monday through Saturday noon; please call ahead. Waynesboro is in south central Pennsylvania, one and a half hours south of Harrisburg or one and a half hours north of the Washington-Baltimore area.

> **Appalachian Gardens**
> P.O. Box 82
> Waynesboro, PA 17268
> Tom McCloud and Ezra Grubb
> (717) 762-4312
> Catalog: $2d, bn/cn

■ **Lamtree Farm** in Warrensville, North Carolina, specializes in southeastern native trees and shrubs: stewartias, franklinias, chionanthus, fothergilla, halesias, kalmias, styraxes, about 14 species of native azaleas and 3 native rhododendrons, as well as other choice woody plants.

Lee Morrison is a former horticulture student and telephone installer. He wants to encourage the use of native plants in landscaping and feels that nursery-propagated natives are much better plants than those collected in the wild. Lee also offers Turk's-cap lilies (*Lilium martagon*) and is trying to increase other native perennials. He does not ship to California, Oregon, or Washington. The nursery is at 3,500 feet, so the plants are quite hardy. In the fall, the staff makes and ships Christmas wreaths and garlands. There is no display garden, but visitors are welcome with a prior appointment. Warrensville is in northwestern North Carolina, thirty-five miles northeast of Boone.

Lamtree Farm
Route 1, Box 162
Warrensville, NC 28693
Lee A. Morrison
(919) 385-6144
Catalog: $2, bn

■ Another catalog with great collector appeal comes from **Woodlanders** in Aiken, South Carolina. Here are nearly 1,000 plants, some which you won't be able to find anywhere else. There's strong emphasis on native North American plants suitable to USDA Zone 8 and above, but also a broad selection of ornamental plants from everywhere else.

Just leafing through the catalog, I'm struck by good selections of hardy citrus, hamamelis, many hollies, magnolias, oaks, native rhododendrons and azaleas, hypericums, sarcococcas and viburnums; these are just the largest groups and don't begin to suggest all of the treasures offered. There are lists of trees, shrubs, yuccas and relatives, bamboos and grasses, vines, perennials and ferns, and finally, odds and ends. The odds and ends are plants that are either rare or not available in enough quantity to offer in the regular catalog. They are available on a first come, first served basis until they're gone; some will no longer be offered, others are new plants just coming into production.

Several of the native plants are offered in a variety of selections: plants selected because of interesting mutations or geographic differences or berries of a different color, different growth habit, or different leaf form and color. These plants are not hybrids, but naturally occurring variations of the species spotted by someone with a good eye; they add immeasurably to the choices available to discriminating gardeners, and it's great to find nurseries willing to try newer selections and offer the best for sale. These are North American native plants from Zone 8 and above.

As with most of the catalogs I love to read carefully, Woodlanders offers a reading list and, even better, a reference to reading for each specific plant.

Run by dedicated plantsmen, Woodlanders was started in 1980 by Robert and Julia Mackintosh, a landscape architect and a teacher who had been living in Grenada. They persuaded George Mitchell, a horticulturally inclined Grenadian, to join them. He is now doing most of the propagating. They were later joined by Bob McCartney, who had worked in wildlife management and as a horticulturist at Colonial Williamsburg. You must have an appointment to visit and must place orders in advance if you want to pick up plants. The nursery is located about fifteen miles northeast of Augusta, Georgia.

> **Woodlanders, Inc.**
> 1128 Colleton Avenue
> Aiken, SC 29801
> Robert Mackintosh, Robert McCartney, and
>   George Mitchell
> (803) 648-7522
> Catalog: $1, CAN/OV, bn

■ **Magnolia Nursery & Display Garden** in Chunchula, Alabama, is owned by Dr. John A. Smith, a dentist and fanatic plant collector. He's currently the president of the American Magnolia Society. Magnolia Nursery is actually a wholesaler with a thirty-acre display garden, but it does sell magnolias and a few other plants. Many are its own introductions, including Gresham hybrid magnolias selected from the Gloster Arboretum, hollies, new selections of redbuds, and other plants. Visitors are welcome on Saturday by appointment; the best months are March to October. The nursery is about thirty miles north of Mobile.

> **Magnolia Nursery & Display Garden**
> 12615 Roberts Road
> Chunchula, AL 36521
> Linda Erdman, Mgr.
> (205) 675-4696 or 8471 (evenings)
> Catalog: $1d, CAN/OV, bn

■ Other farmers who switched from field crops, in this case cotton, soybeans, and cattle, to ornamental trees and shrubs are Edric and Lillian Owen of Ripley, Tennessee. The catalog from **Owen Farms** grows year by year. The selection is not as large as some, but very good. Offered are acer species, a few Japanese maples, a number of crab apples, dogwoods, hollies, viburnums, many of the mildew-resistant crape myrtles from the National Arboretum, Satsuki azaleas, some perennials, and a number of native southern plants. As with other good catalogs, a list of books is included so that you can educate yourself about the plants.

Third-generation farmers, the Owens have been mad for plants for thirty years, and Edric is also a bonsai maven, so it seemed natural to switch from agricultural crops to ornamental plants. They don't ship bonsai, but finished bonsai are for sale at the nursery. When asked what they like to do in their spare time, they just laughed! The Owens ask that you call ahead if you want to visit. The nursery is about sixty-five miles north of Memphis, just off U.S. Highway 51.

Owen Farms
Route 3, Box 158-A
Ripley, TN 38063
Edric and Lillian Owen
(901) 635-1588 (6–9 P.M. CST)
Catalog: $2, CAN/OV, bn/cn

■ **Beaver Creek Nursery** in Knoxville, Tennessee, is another source of unusual trees and shrubs. Mike Stansberry was turned on to rare plants by a college professor, and when he found they weren't readily available, he started growing them himself. Begun with a partner in 1986, the nursery is now run by Mike and his father.

They offer a very nice selection of ornamental trees and shrubs. One of my "test plants" is *Betula albo-sinensis,* which the Stansberrys have on their list. They offer a good selection of hollies (how about 'Old Heavy Berry' or 'Satyr Hill'?), magnolias and dwarf conifers, a number of viburnums, the mildew-resistant crape myrtles from the National Arboretum, and other choice plants. They have been introducing some new magnolia cultivars selected from their own and other crosses. Unfortunately, they can't ship to California, Oregon, or Washington due to the Japanese beetle quarantine. Their new display gardens are coming along and are at their best in spring and fall; visitors should call first. The nursery is in Knox County, north of Knoxville.

Beaver Creek Nursery
7526 Pelleaux Road
Knoxville, TN 37938
Mike Stansberry
(615) 922-3961
Catalog: $1d, bn/cn

■ **Oikos Tree Crops** in Kalamazoo, Michigan, specializes in fruiting native trees. In addition to filberts, chestnuts, walnuts, and other nuts and fruit trees, Oikos offers between 30 to 40 species of oaks and a couple of hybrid oaks. Ken Asmus worked on his family's Christmas tree farm and for wholesale nurseries before starting his own nursery in 1985. He was interested in native food and medicinal plants and especially liked "big" trees like the oaks. He is adding high-altitude evergreen oaks from the Southwest and unusual trees and shrubs from several private collections. His last catalog had a charming drawing by one of his daughters, with the caption "A tree is a friend for life," so he knows how to raise kids as well as trees. Visitors are welcome by appointment. The nursery is about fifteen miles west of Kalamazoo.

Oikos Tree Crops
721 North Fletcher
Kalamazoo, MI 49007-3077
Ken Asmus
(616) 342-6504
Catalog: Free, CAN/OV, cn/bn

■ **Wavecrest Nursery & Landscaping Company** in Fennville, Michigan, considers itself to be in Michigan's "Banana Belt" (USDA Zone 6!). It offers a very impressive "availability list" of woody plants, including Japanese maples, box, conifers (including a weeping larch), dogwoods, beeches, hollies, magnolias, flowering crab apples, viburnums, azaleas and rhododendrons, various flowering shrubs and some perennials. Altogether the nursery grows about 1,000 woody plants and will supply items from your want-list if they're available. There are some agricultural restrictions on shipments to western states.

I never caught up with the proprietor, Carol Hop, so I talked to a pleasant nurseryman instead. Carol's plant list speaks (shouts, actually) for itself. She has a garden center with some of the plants in a display garden. It's open daily from mid-March to Thanksgiving. Fennville is about fifteen miles south of Holland on the eastern shore of Lake Michigan.

Wavecrest Nursery & Landscaping Company
2509 Lakeshore Drive
Fennville, MI 49408
Carol T. Hop
(616) 543-4175
Catalog: $1d, CAN/OV, bn

■ I'm including **Hartmann's Plantation** in Grand Junction, Michigan, because of personal taste. I happen to think that blueberries are wonderful garden plants: lovely in bloom, delicious in fruit, glowing in fall coloring, and their stems are pretty in winter. Nothing beats going out to pick a few berries for your breakfast cereal or sending guests home with fresh berries, but the plants can hold their own with many one-season shrubs. Hartmann's offers many varieties, suited to both North and South, some excellent as ground covers, even varieties for bonsai. It also sells other berrying plants and shrubs, hardy fruits, and some lilacs and miniature roses.

Started in 1944 by Edward and Catherine Hartmann, the nursery is now run by their son Patrick, with help from his son Dan and daughters Patrice and Ann. Visitors are welcome but are asked to call ahead. Hartmann's sells fresh berries at the nursery in summer. Grand Junction is seven miles east of South Haven on Lake Michigan and thirty miles south of Holland.

Hartmann's Plantation
P.O. Box E
Grand Junction, MI 49056
Pat Hartmann
(616) 253-4281
FAX (616) 253-4457
Catalog: $2.25d

■ **Starhill Forest Arboretum** in Petersburg, Illinois, is a private research facility, selecting and hybridizing oaks for collectors and arboreta. Guy and Edie Sternberg have been working with oaks since 1976. Guy is a landscape architect and manager of rights-of-way for the Illinois Conservation Department.

Starhill doesn't sell trees, but it does make acorns and scion wood available, so you can acquire some rare oaks if you're willing to do some of the work yourself. The facility offers seed and/or scion wood of 17 white oaks, 12 white oak hybrids, 14 black oak species, and 5 black oak hybrids. The Sternbergs are actively searching out and selecting natural hybrids, as well as making crosses.

In addition, they sell packets of acorns from the oaks growing around Lincoln's Tomb in Illinois, surprise packets of acorns of very rare oaks, and acorn packets chosen for the buyer's area and climate. They also offer seed of about 20 other ornamental trees and shrubs, mostly North American natives. Visitors may come to their twenty-acre arboretum but must have an appointment. Petersburg is northwest of Springfield.

Starhill Forest Arboretum
Route 1, Box 272
Petersburg, IL 62675
Guy and Edie Sternberg
(217) 632-3685
Catalog: $1 and Long SASE, bn

■ Bill Smith of Charles City, Iowa, puts out a mimeographed list, tightly packed, of trees and shrubs, many of which are desirable ornamentals. These come from liner size to several feet tall and include conifers, amelanchiers, dogwoods, lilacs, physocarpus, potentillas, various prunus, spiraea, viburnums, flowering crab apples, honey locusts, oaks, and for those of you who want a "tapestry hedge," green and purple European beech in liner sizes.

There are many more liner-sized trees and shrubs; if you have lots of space to fill, and time to grow plants on in cans for several years, you may want to contact the **Smith Nursery Company** and request the "Wholesale List." Bill says it's too hard to remember the prices from two lists!

Bill tends to make growing plants sound about as exciting as fixing vacuum cleaners, but his list has many intriguing plants; maybe he's just a kidder. Call for directions if you want to visit. Bill says there's not much to see but lots of liners and little plants. I don't think Bill sees much glamour in the nursery business! Charles City is located in north central Iowa, near the Minnesota border.

> **Smith Nursery Company**
> P.O. Box 515
> Charles City, IA 50616
> Bill Smith
> (515) 228-3239
> Catalog: Free, CAN/OV, bn/cn

■ I count myself a certified tree nut, having planned the Barton Arboretum in my mind for many years. So for such as me there's a high-voltage charge in reading the catalog from **Arborvillage Farm Nursery** in Holt, Missouri. Here are page after page of "show trees," each worth a special place in your garden, or even better, to be planted in groups of five in your arboretum. Hugh Johnson quotes Lord Rothschild as saying that "no garden, however small, should be without its two acres of rough woodland." These days we'd have to say that every garden, however small, deserves to have at least one beautiful tree.

Arborvillage offers a broad selection of collector's trees and shrubs: maples, horse chestnuts, birches, dogwoods, magnolias, flowering crabs, prunus, oaks, mountain ashes, lilacs, elms, viburnums and zelkovas, to mention only the larger groups. A good reading list will help you find out more about each plant.

The proprietor, Lanny Rawdon, is a former airline pilot who fell in love with woody plants and went into the nursery business when Braniff Airlines went out of business. He has the very commendable desire to see a botanical garden/arboretum in every city and town in the U.S. Visitors are welcome at the farm by appointment. Holt is about twenty miles northeast of Kansas City near Interstate 35.

Arborvillage Farm Nursery
P.O. Box 227
Holt, MO 64048
Lanny Rawdon
(816) 264-3911
Catalog: $1, bn

■ No list of tree and shrub sources would be complete without **Louisiana Nursery** in Opelousas, Louisiana. Its catalog "Magnolias and Other Garden Aristocrats" lists hundreds of magnolias, michelias, bamboos, buddleias, camellias, chaenomeles, dogwoods, gardenias, hydrangeas, hollies, crape myrtles, oleanders, osmanthus, palms, viburnums, vines, and many more. The variety of plants is really staggering. Another huge catalog lists daylilies, Louisiana and species iris and tender summer-blooming bulbs. Altogether the nursery grows more than 5,000 plants, all raised on the premises.

Ken and Belle Durio started their nursery in 1950 and have been joined by two of their sons in running all of this themselves with only occasional help. (The Durios think large in every way; they have ten children and twenty-seven grandchildren!) They are working on a fifty-acre arboretum, which will have a two-mile trail. The nursery is open six days a week, except in March and April when the magnolias are in bloom; then it's open seven days a week. It's about three miles south of Opelousas and fifteen miles north of Interstate 10 on State Highway 182.

Louisiana Nursery
Route 7, Box 43
Opelousas, LA 70570
Ken, Albert, and Dalto Durio
(318) 948-3696 or 942-6404
Catalog: $5 (Magnolias and Woody Plants)
Catalog: $3 (Daylilies)
Catalog: $2 (Crinums)
CAN/OV, bn/cn
Call for price of catalogs sent by airmail overseas.

■ William Barber of the **Barber Nursery** in Houston, Texas, lists his seedling trees and shrubs simply by botanical and common name. There are about 75 varieties, including some desirable plants for those with the patience to grow them on; many are southern native trees, including a number of oaks. Bill has recently moved from Oregon back to his native Texas. He says Oregon weather was "too wet and cold." Before moving to Oregon, he worked with Lynn Lowery, a noted plant collector and native plant nurseryman in Texas. Visitors are welcome; the cool season is the best time to visit.

> **Barber Nursery**
> 13118 Patano Drive
> Houston, TX 77065
> William Barber
> (713) 894-2430
> Catalog: Free, CAN/OV, bn

■ It's hard to know how to categorize **Yucca Do Nursery** in Waller, Texas. John Fairey and Carl Schoenfeld are plantsmen with very wide interests, and their list contains not just trees and shrubs, but also perennials. They describe their specialties as "Texas native plants and their Mexican, Asian, and southeastern counterparts." For instance, they offer styrax species from the U.S., Mexico, and Japan. Fairey's beautiful seven-acre garden contains a plant collection of more than 3,000 species and cultivars and has been written about in several gardening magazines. If you order from Yucca Do you'll be invited to one of the two yearly open houses. Waller is northwest of Houston on Highway 290.

If you can't tour the garden, a tour through the catalog gives you a feeling for the rarities Fairey and Schoenfeld have collected and are making available. They've often traveled to Mexico with noted plantsmen and a Mexican botanist and say that new Mexican plants are being found all the time. A number of their plants are selections of Mexican plants, particularly trees such as pines and oaks and cephalotaxus, excellent conifers for the South.

The list has species maples that will do well in Texas and the Southwest, bouvardias, asclepias from Texas and Mexico, species clematis, and a very good selection of salvias. The list gets longer every year and is always changing. I haven't begun to do justice to the offerings. A category called "Odds and Ends" on the last page of the catalog lists a number of intriguing plants.

Yucca Do Nursery
P.O. Box 655
Waller, TX 77484
John Fairey and Carl Schoenfeld
(409) 826-6363
Catalog: $4, bn

■ Bob Barnard of **Maple Leaf Nursery** near Placerville in the Sierra foothills of California started growing plants for bonsai enthusiasts, but other plant lovers found him out, so now you can buy a variety of conifers and other trees and shrubs for use as garden plants, plus a number of perennials (including a good assortment of lavenders and rosemaries). It's hard to characterize the list, but it's the sort on which you'll always find something you've been wanting, or something which you would have wanted if you'd known about it.

Offered are deciduous azaleas, species and Japanese maples, cytisus and cistus, dogwoods (including a *Cornus florida* cultivar called 'Barton'!), some lovely-sounding helianthemums, prunus, a number of perennials, and a few conifers. Many of Bob's plants are drought-tolerant. He says that since drought is a fact of life, you might as well grow the best! He does not ship outside of the fifty U.S. states.

Bob's been working in the nursery business practically since the day he graduated from college with a degree in horticulture. He started Maple Leaf in 1987 and manages to keep it going with help from his family; the last time I called his mother was there weeding. Visitors are welcome on Monday and Thursday by appointment only; plants may be picked up but must be ordered in advance. Placerville is about forty miles east of Sacramento on Interstate 50.

Maple Leaf Nursery
4236 Greenstone Road
Placerville, CA 95667
Bob Barnard
(916) 626-8371
Catalog: $1.50, bn/cn

■ To get to **Mountain Maples** near Laytonville, California, you have to drive seven and a half miles up a twisting gravel road, diving to the side of the road when you see a cloud of dust coming from the opposite direction. You first come to a locked gate and finally to a hand-built house. On the steep hill above are greenhouses full of small maple trees.

Nancy and Don Fiers went into the nursery business to enable them to stay on their remote mountain. In a few years they have become proficient grafters and propagators, and with the help of two well-known maple experts nearing retirement, they have developed a fine collection of stock plants and sources of seed.

Beyond the reach of the electric company, they live comfortably in their snug solar house surrounded by high-fidelity equipment and a computer run on batteries. Like me, they heat in winter with a wood stove, though they must have to stoke faster than I do. Nancy says that one neighbor does engineering drawings which he faxes to the city; one wonders if cities will survive the era of the fax.

Their catalog offers an ever-lengthening list of Japanese maples, 125 cultivars and 8 species at latest count. They are growing for both bonsai fans and "regular" gardeners, so when you order you should tell them how you plan to use the plant. Visitors by appointment only; the best time to call is between 7 and 9 A.M. (Pacific standard time) or on Monday. Laytonville is on Highway 101, about halfway between Ukiah and Garberville.

Mountain Maples
59011 Spy Rock Road
Laytonville, CA 95454-1329
Don and Nancy Fiers
(707) 984-6522
Catalog: $1, bn

MOUNTAIN MAPLES   *Artist: Terry Tanaka*

■ When I told plant friends that I was going to visit nurseries in Oregon, many asked if I was going to visit **Forestfarm** in Williams. This nursery has become legendary among plant collectors for the wide selection of interesting plants it offers. When I first started to get the catalog, it was a collection of loose colored sheets, so that once you'd seen something that interested you it was a real game to find it again as you shuffled. The catalog is now a fine booklet, informative, full of excellent, concise plant descriptions and quotations from plant greats on nearly every page. And this model catalog does it right — plants are listed in alphabetical order by botanical name: one list for perennials and one for everything else, so that wanted plants are easy to find.

Ray and Peg Prag started their nursery in 1973, right out of college at the University of California at Davis, because they wanted to work together in the field they loved, in a rural setting. Ray has degrees in botany and horticulture, and Peg has learned everything from working with Ray, and boy, do they ever work! They started by making some clearings in the fir forest and growing native plants because they felt there was a great need to use them more widely in landscaping, but they're plant mad, and other plants, many quite rare, began to creep in. In order to reach the market for rarer plants, they started mail order. They say there's never any free time anymore, even in winter when they start seeds and work on the catalog. Their dedication and knowledge is really impressive, and they are constantly looking for new plants and sources of seed. They'll even trade with their customers for new items.

What's in their booklet? By their own count, approximately 400 American native plants, about 300 conifers including about 100 pines, about 50 oaks, 50 eucalyptus, 50 prunus, about 45 dogwoods, 85 birches and 85 species maples, 65 viburnums, 40 hollies, 30 sorbus and 30 spiraea, around 50 willows and 40 species roses, to name just the largest groups of woody plants. There are also about 1,000 perennials!

Too good to be true? What's the catch? It's all true, and the plants are well grown and healthy on arrival, but in order to provide such a selection at reasonable prices, most of the plants are quite small. They come in "tubes," paper growing containers about 2 by 2 by 8 inches, which allow good, deep root growth. Many of the customers are other nurseries, who buy and grow on their rare plants, selling them for much more a few years later. Recently they have started to ship a few larger plants in one- and five-gallon pots. Prices reflect the longer time that it takes to bring the plants along.

The Prags are busy shipping early in the week. To visit you must have an appointment toward the end of the week. If you want to pick up plants, please order a week in advance so they can gather your plants for you. Williams is off State Highway 238 between Medford and Grants Pass.

> **Forestfarm**
> 990 Tetherow Road
> Williams, OR 97544-9599
> Ray and Peg Prag
> (503) 846-6963 (9–4 P.M. PST)
> Catalog: $3, CAN, bn/cn

■ As a studier of catalogs, I have several favorites, and I flop down to read them as soon as they arrive. High on my list is the one from **Gossler Farms Nursery** in Springfield, Oregon, perhaps because in my mind's eye I can visualize the farm and almost hear Roger Gossler talking about the plants. He's a terrific plantsman. He reads everything, knows and networks with plant people all over the country, bubbles over with enthusiasm, *and* he loves animals. The Gosslers get an eight on the Barton Animal Index for two lovely dogs and two huge cats, one called Monster, who is orange like my old Tusker.

Originally the senior Gosslers raised sweet corn and peppermint, but they got interested in magnolias and other unusual shrubs, and their son Roger took up their interest as well. Roger and his mother, Marjory, have developed a terrific nursery, specializing in magnolias and most of the genus *hamamelis*. To me, walking through their growing houses is like walking through Tiffany. I stopped once on my way home from Portland. On one quick pass I saw a number of plants I had always wanted and bought a few to take with me. At the motel that evening I settled down to study the catalog and realized that I'd had a very narrow escape from financial disaster — I wanted everything listed, but my slight case of traveling flu had caused me to walk right past a number of musts in the nursery without seeing them!

The catalog seems to lean toward plants that give their best in fall, winter, and early spring. In addition to 60 magnolia varieties (the Gosslers grow more than 200 varieties at the nursery), it lists many species and varieties of corylopsis, hamamelis, michelias, viburnums, and all the species of stewartia. There are many other treasures as well, sometimes just a single shrub or perennial that the Gosslers have fallen in love with. The list is always changing as they develop new interests and tastes, so if you see something you want you'd better order it; it may not be on the list again the next year. Roger is developing an interest in unusual perennials and is offering many of these at the nursery. A good way to see the magnolias in bloom is to go when the Gosslers open the nursery to the public, usually a weekend or two early in April (call to find out when). The rest of the year you must call ahead to visit. Springfield is just east of Eugene.

Gossler Farms Nursery
1200 Weaver Road
Springfield, OR 97478-9663
Marjory and Roger Gossler
(503) 746-3922 or 747-0749
Catalog: $2, bn/cn

■ Lucile Whitman is a paradox. She has the soft southern voice of her native Georgia and the brisk, efficient personality of someone from the coolest parts of the West. This dynamo has a Ph.D. in Latin and Greek and is a former university professor. When she's not working hard at her nursery, she likes to play tennis or golf! She has settled on a ridge west of Salem, Oregon, with her "sort of" dachshund and propagates and sells wonderful small trees.

Whitman Farms grows many of the trees on for other nurseries and landscapers but will sell some of her trees as liners in wholesale quantities as small as 25 at very reasonable prices. It would be impossible for me to suggest that you buy 25 trees and throw away 23, but you could get together with some friends or grow the others on in cans for benefit plant sales or special gifts to gardening friends. Maybe you could even arrange a street tree planting in your neighborhood if someone would agree to grow the trees on in cans for some time.

Among the treasures on her wholesale list are maple species, dogwoods, beeches, magnolias, prunus, ribes, and stewartias. She also has a retail mail order catalog that lists mostly fruiting currants and gooseberries, filberts, and species and Japanese maples and magnolias. Mail order only.

Whitman Farms
3995 Gibson Road
Salem, OR 97304
Lucile Whitman
(503) 585-8728
Catalog: Long SASE, CAN, bn

■ **Colvos Creek Nursery** on Vashon Island, Washington, always has a very interesting list, both unusual trees and shrubs and many northwestern native plants. The proprietor, Mike Lee, is a landscape architect and started a nursery in 1976 to provide uncommon plants for himself and other garden designers. At present he's working on an identification book for native and cultivated trees of the Northwest.

To my great disappointment, when I was in the Seattle area visiting nurseries, Mike was in California doing the same thing, so I didn't get to visit him. Mike's list offers more than 35 species of oaks, 30 species of maples, more than 20 species of pines, about 10 hardy eucalyptus, as well as a number of arbutus, box, dogwoods, cotoneasters, escallonias, hollies, loniceras, photinias, prunus, species roses, willows, mountain ashes, lilac species, viburnums, and, as befits a nursery in Washington, a number of conifers. This is a small nursery and stock is sometimes limited. It's best to order as soon as you get the availability list. The catalog lists everything being propagated, but not all plants are available at the same time. Mail order only.

> **Colvos Creek Nursery**
> P.O. Box 1512
> Vashon Island, WA 98070
> Mike Lee
> (206) 441-1509
> Catalog: $2d, bn

■ The catalog put out by **Heronswood Nursery** in Kingston, Washington, is so delicious and seductive that it's no wonder I went to visit co-owner Dan Hinkley when I was in his area, across Puget Sound from Seattle.

Somehow I miscounted driveways and went down to a house with a black cocker spaniel — all wags. After several false tries, I finally drove into Heronswood to be greeted by an identical dog! I thought he'd run over to greet me again from the house next door, but Dan so liked that dog that he got one of his own. He rates high on the Barton Animal Index because he also coddled along a twenty-year-old dog who walked sideways and needed all of his food blended.

Dan teaches ornamental horticulture at Edmonds Community College just north of Seattle, a direct ferry ride from his nearest town. His discriminating eye is evident in the types of plants he offers and also in the fine specimens in his nursery rows. Through contacts in botanical gardens, other nurseries, and travel abroad, he offers some plants that are new to many gardeners.

Dan and his partner, Robert Jones, an architect, specialize in Asiatic species of trees, shrubs, vines and perennials, and shrubs and trees from the Southern Hemisphere. They have good selections of species maples, rubus, hypericums, hydrangeas, loniceras (both shrubs and vines), sorbus, mahonias, buddeleias, berberis, ornamental grasses, and perennials. Many of their plants are fairly unusual or recently introduced. The display gardens are absolutely beautiful, but because they are so busy, you must call ahead for an appointment and directions to visit. Kingston is across the sound from Edmonds. You can take a ferry from Edmonds to Kingston or from Seattle to Bainbridge Island.

Heronswood Nursery
7530 288th Street N.E.
Kingston, WA 98346
Daniel Hinkley and Robert Jones
(206) 297-4172
Catalog: $3, bn

■ *Other sources of Japanese maples are:*

Coenosium Gardens, Aurora, OR
Foxborough Nursery, Inc., Street, MD
Greer Gardens, Eugene, OR
Michael & Janet Kristick, Wellsville, PA
Rarifolia, Kintnersville, PA
Springvale Farm Nursery, Hamburg, IL
Twombly Nursery, Monroe, CT
Whitney Gardens & Nursery, Brinnon, WA

■ *Other sources of trees and shrubs are:*

The Bovees Nursery, Portland, OR
Camellia Forest Nursery, Chapel Hill, NC
Carroll Gardens, Westminster, MD
Cascade Forestry Nursery, Cascade, IA
Coenosium Gardens, Aurora, OR
Crownsville Nursery, Crownsville, MD
Foxborough Nursery, Inc., Street, MD
Girard Nurseries, Geneva, OH
Greer Gardens, Eugene, OR
Powell's Gardens, Princeton, NC
Roslyn Nursery, Dix Hills, NY
Twombly Nursery, Monroe, CT
Wayside Gardens, Hodges, SC
Whitney Gardens & Nursery,
    Brinnon, WA

MOUNTAIN MAPLES
Artist: Terry Tanaka

Trees and Shrubs: Tender

Gardeners living in the warmest regions of the country, USDA Zones 9 and 10, can grow many of the plants that the rest of us can grow, but there are some plants that just don't like warmish winters and others that can't take hot and humid summers.

During the winter I was talking to Carl Schoenfeld at Yucca Do Nursery near Houston, and he cracked me up by saying that it had been so cold this winter, "Down to fifty degrees both night and day!" The point, of course, is that we all have to deal with our local climate, and if yours is warm in winter, you can grow some plants that the rest of us can't. This is not meant to be a list of sources of plants for subtropical areas but a few suggestions for plants that only gardeners with warm winters can grow.

■ For those who live in Florida, parts of the Gulf South, and southern California, the tender "Chinese" or tropical hibiscus is a popular shrub and is available in wonderful variety. **Fancy Hibiscus**™ in Pompano Beach, Florida, offers grafted hybrids of *Hibiscus rosa-sinensis;* more than 300 varieties are grown at the nursery, and about 200 are listed each year. No plants can be shipped to California.

Winn Soldani is a hybridizer who's won prizes for his introductions. He also imports plants from Brazil, the Caribbean, Malaysia, and Hawaii. Winn says he was a whiskey and wine salesman until he went to a hibiscus show at a local mall. Now he consults with botanical gardens. Visitors are welcome to come and see the plants all year round, but please call for an appointment. Pompano Beach is a northern suburb of Fort Lauderdale.

Fancy Hibiscus™
1142 S.W. First Avenue
Pompano Beach, FL 33060

Winn Soldani
(305) 782-0741
Catalog: $2d

■ Naturally, Florida would have a terrific source of palms.
The Green Escape in Palm Harbor, Florida, grows between
400 and 500 palms representing 60 to 75 genera. Marshall
and Joan Weintraub run an insurance agency. Twenty years
ago they started collecting palms, and in 1986 they started
their nursery.

Marshall says that many palms are quite hardy, and others
make excellent indoor plants. The Weintraubs publish a descriptive catalog and send semiannual availability lists, offering about 300 palms and containing cultural information.
Eventually they will have a display garden — inquire after
1993. At present, sales are by mail order only. They ship
worldwide except to Puerto Rico and Hawaii.

The Green Escape
P.O. Box 1417
Palm Harbor, FL 34682-1417
Marshall and Joan Weintraub
(813) 784-1991
FAX (813) 787-0193
Catalog: $6d, CAN/OV, bn

■ Right now, you're going to complain that my definition of
ornamental plants is pretty elastic! It's true, but I think that
many fruits are very ornamental: blueberries, figs, dwarf citrus, kiwis, persimmons, grapes, olives, and pomegranates. You
should see people stop and gasp when they walk under my
grape arbor; I figure that if it makes people gasp, it's ornamental.

Jonathan Cowley and his daughter Brandy of **Just Fruits** in
Crawfordville, Florida, were organic vegetable gardeners who
became interested in starting a little orchard. They went off
to visit the agriculture department of the state university, spent
an exciting day touring the fruit plantings, and came home
dedicated to starting a nursery selling fruits that would grow
in their area.

The Cowleys grow all of the fruits I've just mentioned, which
will thrive in areas with only 500 to 650 hours of chill (just
short of tropical) and high humidity. They can't ship citrus to
Arizona, Louisiana, or Texas, or any plants to California. Visitors are welcome Thursday to Sunday but should call ahead
to be sure someone will be there. The nursery is closed during

the month of July and is actually located in Medart near Crawfordville, thirty miles south of Tallahassee.

Just Fruits
Route 2, Box 4818
Crawfordville, FL 32327
Jonathan and Brandy Cowley
(904) 926-5644
Catalog: $3d

■ **Air Exposé** in Houston, Texas, grows more than 700 cultivars of *Hibiscus rosa-sinensis,* offering many by mail on their list, which describes only flower color. The nursery ships worldwide and welcomes your want-list. Also listed are more than 12 varieties of bougainvillea and 7 varieties of hardy hibiscus (althea).

George Haynes III is an architect, general contractor, and landscaper whose hobby got out of hand. He says he had 100 cultivars before he knew it, and had to take out a nursery license. His wife and parents help with the nursery. Visitors are welcome by appointment only. There are many plants on display.

Air Exposé
4703 Leffingwell Street
Houston, TX 77026
George Haynes III
Catalog: Long SASE, CAN/OV

■ For those who live in milder climate areas, the selection from **Pacific Tree Farms** in Chula Vista, California, includes a number of trees not available elsewhere. Founder Bill Nelson is a former optometrist who started collecting plants that were unavailable for the challenge of finding and propagating them. His catalog includes a number of unusual fruiting trees from warmer climates, citrus, palms, a broad selection of pines, and various subtropical ornamental trees, many with spectacular flowers. Several of these plants are drought-tolerant.

Most plants come in a five-gallon size and are naturally more expensive than smaller plants; they're shipped bare-root and treated with antitranspirant and the roots are dipped in a water-holding gel. Citrus cannot be shipped to Arizona, Texas, Louisiana, or Florida. I talked to nursery manager Kurt Peacock, who says that visitors are welcome every day but Tuesday; call for directions. Chula Vista is between San Diego and Tijuana, Mexico.

Pacific Tree Farms
4301 Lynwood Drive
Chula Vista, CA 92010
William L. Nelson
(619) 422-2400
Catalog: $2, CAN/OV, bn/cn

■ Also for warm-climate gardeners, **Stallings Exotic Nursery** in Encinitas, California, has a great selection of flowering trees and shrubs; unusual fruits, both subtropical and tropical; bamboos and palms, grasses, jasmines, and *Hibiscus rosa-sinensis*. Stallings actually grows about 3,000 plants, so the catalog only hints at the riches available at the nursery. This may be an opportunity to find things on your want-list.

The nursery was founded in 1945 by Virgil Stallings, with the idea that "hard to find doesn't mean hard to grow." The nursery is now owned by Jack Porter, a plant lover who works for Hughes Aircraft in Tucson and comes to visit his plants on weekends. The nursery is managed by Dale Kolaczkowski and is open daily except for major holidays. Encinitas is twenty-five miles north of San Diego and a hundred miles south of Los Angeles.

Stallings Exotic Nursery
910 Encinitas Boulevard
Encinitas, CA 92024
Jack D. Porter
(619) 753-3079
Catalog: $3d, CAN/OV, bn

■ **Neon Palm Nursery** in Santa Rosa, California, is a source of plants for subtropical climates: 78 species of palms, 11 species of cycads (with some new cycad hybrids just being introduced), and also conifers, bamboos, agaves, and other trees and shrubs. Also offered are a good selection of variegated plants of all types and plants with weeping growth habits. Hardiness is indicated using the zones from the *Sunset Western Garden Book* (Lane Publishing Company); all of the plants are hardy to Sunset Zone 14 (USDA Zone 8).

Dale Motiska started collecting palms because he could find only pictures of them in books. A former letter carrier, he's also a musician and songwriter in his spare time. The nursery has just moved to the south side of Santa Rosa, where there's a display garden, two acres of palms, and a cactus garden in development. Visitors are welcome Tuesday through Saturday and Sunday afternoon except for major holidays. Santa Rosa is an hour north of San Francisco.

> **Neon Palm Nursery**
> 3525 Stony Point Road
> Santa Rosa, CA 95407
> Dale Motiska
> (707) 585-8100
> Catalog: $1, bn

■ Fuchsias are very popular along the coast of northern California, Oregon, and Washington, and there are a few hardy species like *F. magellanica* which will survive elsewhere. **Regine's Fuchsia Gardens** in Fort Bragg, California, is in prime fuchsia-growing country and lists about 400 varieties and another thirty species and selections. The varieties that are not in stock are rooted to order. Regine Plows has finally changed the name of her nursery, which she bought from fuchsia hybridizer Annabelle Stubbs in 1979. Regine is hard of hearing, so she didn't want her phone number listed. No shipments to Hawaii. Visitors may come to the nursery Wednesday through Sunday. Fort Bragg is on the coast of northern California, about fifty miles northwest of Ukiah.

> **Regine's Fuchsia Gardens**
> 32531 Rhoda Lane
> Fort Bragg, CA 95437
> Regine and Bruce Plows
> Catalog: $1, bn

■ A catalog that never fails to grab my attention when it comes is the one from **Trans Pacific Nursery** in McMinnville, Oregon. Jackson Muldoon has worked for years as a custom plant propagator, a profession that has taken him to Africa, Australia, New Zealand, the South Seas, and the Pyrenees in Spain. He's developed a particular liking for the plants of Australia and other countries of the Southern Hemisphere. His plant list changes almost every year as he finds other plants he wants to grow; this year he features plants from the alpine zones (Mount Kilimanjaro) of East Africa. Many of his plants are unusual and some will need a warm climate or a greenhouse; the list includes trees, shrubs, vines, bulbous plants, grasses, and Japanese maples.

It's fun to read a catalog that is so individual. You get the impression that Jack Muldoon pays very little attention to what's popular. In person, Jack looks like a southern California surfer, which it turns out he was in his youth. In addition to running his nursery, he also custom grafts Japanese maples for other nurseries. Visitors should call for an appointment and directions. There is no display garden. McMinnville is about thirty miles southwest of Portland on Highway 99W.

Trans Pacific Nursery
16065 Oldsville Road
McMinnville, OR 97128
Jackson Muldoon
(503) 472-6215
Catalog: $1d, CAN/OV, bn

■ *Other sources of tender trees and shrubs are:*

Woodlanders, Inc., Aiken, SC
Yucca Do Nursery, Waller, TX

■ *Other sources of fuchsias are:*

Antonelli Brothers, Santa Cruz, CA
Merry Gardens, Camden, ME

Alphabetical Index of Nurseries

MCCLURE & ZIMMERMAN

Geographical Index of Nurseries

State and City	Nursery

ALABAMA

Birmingham	Steve Ray's Bamboo Gardens, 23
Chunchula	Magnolia Nursery & Display Garden, 210

ARKANSAS

Elkins	Holland Wildflower Farm, 128

ARIZONA

Phoenix	Shepard Iris Garden, 102

CALIFORNIA

Altadena	Nuccio's Nurseries, 40
Chula Vista	Pacific Tree Farms, 226–27
	Tiny Petals Nursery, 193–94
Claremont	Wildwood Nursery, 134
Clements	King's Mums, 43
Encinitas	Stallings Exotic Nursery, 227
Eureka	Westgate Garden Nursery, 167–68
Fort Bragg	Heritage Rose Gardens, 189
	Regine's Fuchsia Gardens, 228
Garberville	Greenmantle Nursery, 189–90
	Nancy Wilson Species & Miniature Narcissus, 46
Grass Valley	Foothill Cottage Gardens, 155–560
Healdsburg	Moonshine Gardens, 103–4
Igo	Jim & Irene Russ, 197
Laytonville	Mountain Maples, 217–18
Lemon Grove	McDaniel's Miniature Roses, 194
Long Beach	Greenwood Daylily Gardens, 61

McKinleyville	Fairyland Begonia Garden, 33–34
Oroville	Canyon Creek Nursery, 156–57
Penngrove	Portable Acres, 111
Placerville	Maple Leaf Nursery, 217
Pomona	Greenlee Nursery, 71
Ramona	Ramona Gardens, 61
Redding	Maxim's Greenwood Gardens, 112
Sacramento	Roris Gardens, 103
San Francisco	GreenLady Gardens, 32
San Gabriel	Sunnyslope Gardens, 42–43
San Marcos	Cordon Bleu Farms, 60
Sanger	Kelly's Plant World, 31
Santa Barbara	Bio-Quest International, 30–31
Santa Cruz	Antonelli Brothers, Inc., 31–32
	Bay View Gardens, 111
Santa Margarita	Las Pilitas Nursery, 134–35
Santa Rosa	Alpine Valley Gardens, 62
	Neon Palm Nursery, 227–28
Sebastopol	Bamboo Sourcery, 23–24
	Miniature Plant Kingdom, 203
	Robinett Bulb Farm, 32–33
	Vintage Gardens, 188–89
Stockton	Keith Keppel, 103
Upland	Van Ness Water Gardens, 19–20
Visalia	Sequoia Nursery — Moore Miniature Roses, 194–95
Walnut Creek	Pollen Bank, 61
Watsonville	Roses of Yesterday & Today, 187–88

COLORADO

Avon	Colorado Alpines, Inc., 177
Boulder	Long's Gardens, 101
Denver	High Country Rosarium, 186–87
Loveland	Rabbit Shadow Farm, 186

CONNECTICUT

Bantam	John Scheepers, Inc., 27
Gaylordsville	Bloomingfields Farm, 55
Hamden	Broken Arrow Nursery, 116
Litchfield	Van Engelen, Inc., 26
	White Flower Farm, 144
Monroe	Twombly Nursery, 199–200
Storrs	Ledgecrest Greenhouses, 143–44

FLORIDA

Auburndale	Color Farm, 68–69
Crawfordville	Just Fruits, 225–26

Gainesville	Wimberlyway Gardens, 56
Miami	Skula's Nursery, 64–65
Palm Harbor	The Green Escape, 225
Pompano Beach	Fancy Hibiscus™, 224–25
Sanford	Daylily World, 56–57
	Floyd Cove Nursery, 57
Weirsdale	Ivies of the World, 74–75

GEORGIA

Bishop	Piccadilly Farm, 88–89
Decatur	Eco-Gardens, 126–27
Lavonia	Transplant Nursery, 165
Thomasville	Thomasville Nurseries, 192

ILLINOIS

Batavia	Shady Hill Gardens, 68
Hamburg	Springvale Farm Nursery, 202–3
Petersburg	Starhill Forest Arboretum, 213
Riverwoods	The Bulb Crate, 27–28
South Barrington	Klehm Nursery, 137

INDIANA

Crawfordsville	Davidson-Wilson Greenhouses, 67–68
Floyds Knob	Pinecliffe Daylily Gardens, 58–59
Ossian	Miller's Manor Gardens, 94
Valparaiso	Coburg Planting Fields, 59
Winamac	Iris Acres, 94

IOWA

Cascade	Cascade Forestry Nursery, 206
Charles City	Smith Nursery Company, 214
Johnston	Heard Gardens, Ltd., 119

KANSAS

Burlington	Huff's Garden Mums, 42
Radium	The Cactus Patch, 36–37
Sedgwick	Country Cottage, 196–97
Udall	Country Bloomers Nursery, 185–86

KENTUCKY

Lancaster	Sleepy Hollow Herb Farm, 82

LOUISIANA

Opelousas	Louisiana Nursery, 215

MAINE

Camden	Merry Gardens, 78
East Lebanon	Valente Gardens, 52
Georgetown	Eastern Plant Specialties, 159–60
Litchfield	Daystar, 173
North Yarmouth	Forevergreen Farm, 185
Surry	Surry Gardens, 141–42
Vassalboro	Fieldstone Gardens, Inc., 142

MARYLAND

Baldwin	Kurt Bluemel, Inc., 70–71
Baltimore	Wicklein's Aquatic Farm & Nursery, 17–18
Buckeystown	Lilypons Water Gardens, 18–19
Crownsville	Crownsville Nursery, 145–46
Jarrettsville	Maryland Aquatic Nurseries, 17
Owings Mills	Bundles of Bulbs, 27
Street	Foxborough Nursery, Inc., 201
Westminster	Carroll Gardens, 145

MASSACHUSETTS

Carlisle	Seawright Gardens, 53–54
East Sandwich	Briarwood Gardens, 160
Edgartown	Donaroma's Nursery, 143
Rehoboth	Tranquil Lake Nursery, 54
Southampton	Tripple Brook Farm, 122
Truro	Rock Spray Nursery, 73

MICHIGAN

Chesaning	Country View Gardens, 94
Fennville	Wavecrest Nursery & Landscaping Company, 212
Fowlerville	Perennial Plantation, 176–77
Galesburg	Ensata Gardens, 108–9
Grand Junction	Hartmann's Plantation, 212–13
Hopkins	Englerth Gardens, 59
Kalamazoo	Oikos Tree Crops, 211–12
Vulcan	Reath's Nursery, 137

MINNESOTA

Albert Lea	Wedge Nursery, 118–19
Andover	Orchid Gardens, 133
Blaine	Rice Creek Gardens, 176–77
Cokato	Busse Gardens, 153–54
Edina	Savory's Gardens, Inc., 90
Faribault	Borbeleta Gardens, 109–10

OKLAHOMA

Oklahoma City	Mid-America Iris Gardens, 98

OREGON

Albany	Nichols Garden Nursery, Inc., 84–85
Aurora	Coenosium Gardens, 203–4
Bend	Joyce's Garden, 157
Brooks	Iris Country, 105
Canby	Swan Island Dahlias, 50
Corbett	Bonnie Brae Gardens, 46
	Oregon Trail Daffodils, 46–47
Drain	Kelleygreen Rhododendron Nursery, 168
Estacada	Squaw Mountain Gardens, 197–98
Eugene	Greer Gardens, 168–69
Hubbard	Grant Mitsch Novelty Daffodils, 47–48
McMinnville	Trans Pacific Nursery, 228–29
Medford	Siskiyou Rare Plant Nursery, 177–78
Newberg	Chehalem Gardens, 113
Portland	The Bovees Nursery, 170–71
Roseburg	Garden Valley Dahlias, 49–50
Salem	Schreiner's Gardens, 104
	Whitman Farms, 221
Sandy	Porterhowse Farms, 204
Scio	Nature's Garden, 178–79
Scotts Mills	Dr. Joseph C. Halinar, 34
Sherwood	Caprice Farm, 138–39
	Red's Rhodies, 169–70
Silverton	Cooley's Gardens, 104–5
Springfield	Gossler Farms Nursery, 220–21
	Laurie's Garden, 112
St. Paul	Heirloom Old Garden Roses, 190
West Linn	Stubbs Shrubs, 170
Williams	Forestfarm, 219–20
	Goodwin Creek Gardens, 84
Wilsonville	Edmunds Roses, 192–93
	Justice Miniature Roses, 195

PENNSYLVANIA

Aspers	Bull Valley Rhododendron Nursery, 163–64
Coopersburg	Tilley's Nursery/The WaterWorks, 16
Indiana	Carino Nurseries, 205–6
	Musser Forests, Inc., 205
Kintnersville	Rarifolia, 200–201
Loretto	Hickory Hill Gardens, 55

Titles available in the Taylor's Guide series:

At your bookstore or by calling 1-800-225-3362

Prices subject to change without notice